Incidents from an Elephant Hunter's Diary

Incidents from an Elephant Hunter's Diary

BY

W. D. M. Bell

Safari Press

An imprint of The Globe Pequot Publishing Group, Inc.
64 South Main Street
Essex, CT 06426
www.globepequot.com

Library of Congress Catalog Card Number: 2016946170

ISBN 978-1-57157-498-5

Printed in India

TABLE OF CONTENTS

FOREWORD

Walter Dalrymple Maitland Bell was a fascinating character. For generations, hunters and armchair safari enthusiasts have thrilled to Bell's descriptions of his elephant-hunting adventures in East Africa during the golden age of hunting. Less well known are his exploits in other parts of Africa—West Africa where he hunted with the Pygmies and Central Africa where he confronted leopards, cannibals, and elephants on the islands of the Ubangi River. All these and many other stories are in the volume you now hold in your hands.

Before this title was even published, we received a number of inquiries from various corners around the world about the "new Walter Bell book." The first question always was, "Are these stories just repeats, or do they represent new material?" The second question everyone asked was, "Where did this material come from?"

Since the first question demands an involved answer, let's begin by talking about where we found this rich cache of Bell writings. First of all, we had access to a great number of letters Bell had written over the years. These provide wonderful insight into who Bell, the man, was. We also discovered in the United Kingdom a large collection of short stories—very much like *The Wanderings of an Elephant Hunter*—that Bell had not published in any of his books.

Finally, we knew a private collector who had many years ago acquired a treasure trove of Bell's personal writings. A big Bell fan, obviously, this person contacted us to see if a book might be published from this bonanza. His collection was vast: ten school-type, bound notebooks in which we found either handwritten or typed manuscripts; three huge ring binders containing about twenty plastic sleeves of typed essays, and stories; and folders full of handwritten notes, photos, and original drawings by Bell.

Once we had amassed all the materials from our various sources, we then spent several weeks making an inventory and reading . . . and reading. It is impossible to say with accuracy what the word count of all the materials is, but we estimate it to be over 300,000 words. This huge body of writings will be made into two volumes. *Incidents from an Elephant Hunter's Diary* is the first volume. The second volume of new materials, which will be released next year, will include not only the rest of the cache not used in *Incidents.*

So, now let's get back to the first question: "Are these stories just repeats, or do they represent new material?" The simple answer is that the stories in *Incidents* and the volume to be released next year are all new. That, however, does not completely reflect the true nature of what we found and how we made our decision to include what we did in each volume.

After several days of reading, a few things became obvious. One was that Bell wrote many versions of the same story. For instance we found three versions of the same hunt for a lone, crop-raiding elephant with huge tusks that was hiding in a forest during a rainstorm. Each version was of the same event, but the details given varied considerably. As a matter of curiosity, when we found instances like this, we tried to reconstruct how these various versions came to be. From the sparse, few times that Bell indicated a date as to when he had written a story, it evolved that often these variations of an event were written over a period of decades. We can only surmise that Bell wrote one of his favorite "incidents" in a detailed story, put it away in his archive, and then, possibly a decade later, put to paper the same event once again. Memory being what it is, different details would surface during the writing of the second or third versions.

What we did in a case like this was to take the best of these stories and then add the details from the other two stories. The result was a complete and beautifully descriptive—as only Bell could write—tale. Much of this Sisyphean task fell on Dr. Jacque Neufeld, who also happens to be my wife, and even though I am surely biased, she did a great job.

Because of Bell's predilection for rewriting certain events, clearly some of the stories we found had fragments (or more) of both *Wanderings of an Elephant Hunter* and *Karamojo Safari* in them. When confronted with this, we had a difficult task. If the material was too similar, it landed up on the cutting floor. If it added significant new details, we kept it in. A great many of the loose sleeves in the ring binders mentioned earlier paralleled *Karamojo Safari* to such an extent that although the details were different, we decided to leave them out.

A few other things also became obvious as we read through our cache of materials. One was that Bell was a man with a keen technical eye and mind. For instance, we read that he ran his own miniature steamer up the Ubangi River. We also discovered that he guided primitive cars across Africa from west to east when virtually no roads existed and that he fixed technical problems in the field with apparent ease—we came to these conclusions from small snippets in his descriptions of the actual events.

Second, he was a keen sailor and loved anything to do with boats, whether wind or machine driven. This will become clear when reading about his Ubangi River trip.

Readers will note one final very obvious fact: Bell must have gotten along with the locals very well. Yes, it was true that he had a few unpleasant encounters, but this is true for all of us if we meet enough people. What stands out is that again and again he comes up to complete strangers in the bush—whether they be entire villages or a lone Pygmy—and he manages to make these people into his allies within the shortest of time. Many of these people had never seen a white face. Mind you, his alliances were based on the promise of great quantities of elephant meat, which Bell always delivered. Bell's descriptions of African village life, his trackers, the women, the bearers, and all the other comings and goings of Africa in the days before World War I clearly indicate he took an interest in the humans around him. This is so true that by the end of this volume, you will come to know Bell's main trackers and cohorts by name, and, just as Bell did, you will revel in their sometimes eccentric and flamboyant personalities.

The original *Wanderings of an Elephant Hunter* probably contains 60,000 to 65,000 words. This book is considerably longer and, as before, it contains many stories about shooting elephants. Unlike *Wanderings,* however, it also contains stories of happenings in Africa only peripherally related to hunting, and sometimes not at all. This volume, after all, is meant to be filled with "incidents" from Bell's diary.

Bell's own often sparse but ever-so-descriptive, words paint an evocative picture of an Africa that once was; it is a vivid portrait of the people and wildlife Bell encountered, brought to life for twenty-first-century readers. From these stories a vivid picture of who Bell was will emerge, leaving you with a clear understanding of not just Bell the elephant hunter but also of Bell the man.

I feel very privileged to have written an introduction for this book, and now, like that proverbial monkey at the head of a circus parade, I shall quickly get out of the way so that you can get to the real show, Bell's own writings in *Incidents from an Elephant Hunter's Diary.*

Ludo J. Wurfbain, publisher Safari Press
Huntington Beach, California
July 7, 2016

Note from the editor:

In reading the nearly 1,800 handwritten and typed pages that Bell left, we found a treasure trove of stories and autobiographical notes that had not been previously published. We also discovered more than a few discrepancies with his previously published books. Another revelation to us was the sheer number of redundancies in Bell's unpublished and published works. While we did our best to eliminate redundancies wherever we could, we decided to include some stories in this volume that, while they may seem to be familiar to the reader, actually contain new material or a different slant on the same episode.

Finally, we made certain decisions concerning the editing of this manuscript that may be of interest to the reader. The most important was to try to keep the orthography—as much as possible—the way Bell wrote it. We made this decision so that this work would reflect the time in which he wrote. You will, therefore, see "Sudan" spelled "Soudan"; "river bank" spelled as two words rather than the current fused spelling "riverbank"; and "antheap" spelled "ant-heap." We felt that maintaining the orthography (norms of spelling, hyphenation, capitalization, word breaks, etc.) of the period would make the book "feel" more authentic for the reader.

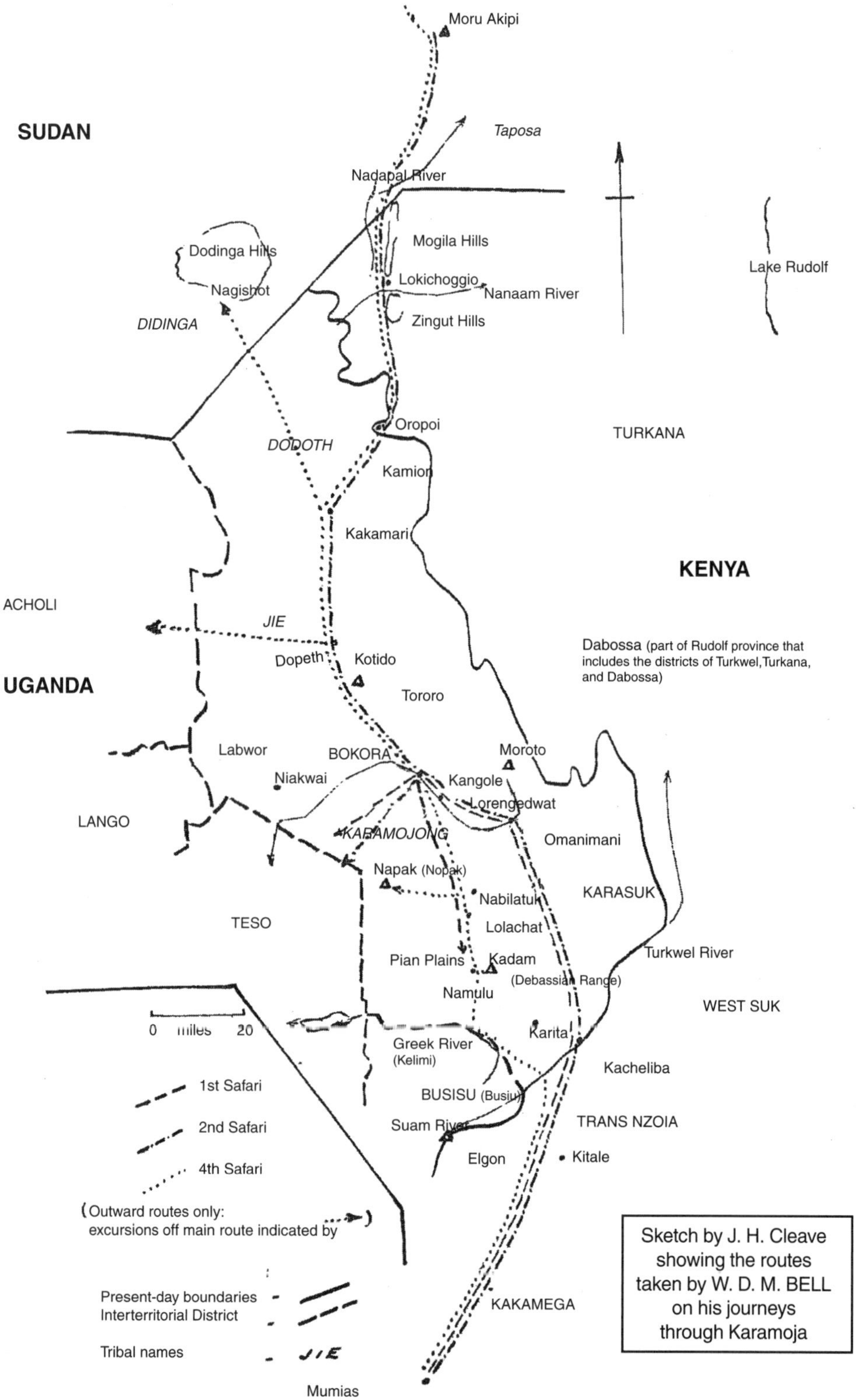

Sketch by J. H. Cleave showing the routes taken by W. D. M. BELL on his journeys through Karamoja

Bell in Karamoja

Introduction

By J. H. Cleave[1]

W D. M. BELL, one of the most successful elephant hunters of all time, sought his quarry across the length and breadth of Africa—from Abyssinia to the Congo and from Liberia to Kenya. But it is with Karamoja that Bell's name will always be associated, and it was there that he had his best hunting and found what, in his opinion, was the best-quality ivory in the heaviest-average tusks to be found in Africa.

Bell made four visits to Karamoja.[2] The first as a young man who was little over twenty years of age. This was in 1902 and 1903, and the last was probably about 1909. Bell describes three of these journeys in his books *Wanderings of an Elephant Hunter* (1923) and *Karamoja Safari* (1949). It is upon these writings that this attempt to trace his travels in Karamoja is principally based.

The first book was written shortly after World War I—in which its author served as a pilot in the R.F.C.—and we may suppose the incidents described would have been reasonably fresh in Bell's mind and faithfully recorded. *Karamoja Safari* appeared twenty-six years later, and in the story of the fourth safari there appear occasional events recognizable as happenings already described in the earlier book. From this, one can only suppose that time has been playing tricks upon the writer's memory.

Such slight confusions in no way detract from the interest of Bell's keen observations on the game and people of Karamoja fifty years ago. Comparing his comments with the position today, it becomes apparent that there have been great changes in the distribution of game in the area, not least of the great beasts

[1]*Wild Life and Sport,* Volume 2, Number 1, Kampala, Uganda, 1961. In this introduction, J. H. Cleave traces the routes that Bell, one of the most famous elephant hunters of all time, took on his forays into Uganda. In doing so, Cleave gives a clear overview of Bell's intrepid adventures.

[2]At the time, Karamoja was still undemarcated and included territory that has since been included in the Equatoria province of Sudan and in the Turkana district of Kenya.

he hunted, and that, as elsewhere, the stock of wild life has diminished greatly before the expanding population of humans and their land-destructive cattle.

Occasionally the remark is heard that naturally the wild life has diminished with such as Bell inflicting systematic slaughter upon the game. Such comments miss the crux of the matter. Even the four to five hundred elephants that Bell shot in the course of his years in Karamoja represented a minor proportion of the total elephant population, and his victims were all bulls. No such discrimination was made by the indigenous hunters using fire and traps.

Killing for meat has probably not been the main factor in reducing the vast herds of game that Bell found in Karamoja. There, as elsewhere, it may be assumed the disturbance of the animals by the ever-expanding tribes has reduced their breeding and, thus, drastically cut their numbers. Fortunately, the considerable variety of game survives even if its distribution is more limited than in Bell's day, and it is to be hoped that the present measures to preserve it as a valuable natural resource will be continued.

All Bell's ventures into Karamoja began at Mumias, then a small government post south of Elgon within the ill-defined area of the Uganda Protectorate. Today it is a small town with a handful of Indian *duka*s [shops] lying in the Kakamega district of Kenya; it is a town of little importance as the railway and main Kenya-Uganda road have passed it by.

His first journey to Karamoja took the intrepid young Scot round the east of Elgon through the Trans-Nzoia and West Suk districts (as they now are) to the Turkwel—a six-day march to "the northern boundary of European rule." Exactly where Bell crossed the Turkwel River it is hard to say, but from his description it seems probable that it was the Suam (which lower becomes the great Turkwel) and that the crossing was made in the region of Kacheliba. Almost immediately the presence of elephant was reported to him. Today they are remembered only by the broad paths they used to tread.

It was in this area that Bell met his first Karamojans—probably from the village of Karita. At the turn of the century Karita was an important Karamojong settlement, and almost the entire area of Karasuk and the plain and bush south-east of Kadam (Debassian Range) to the Suam River was seasonally grazed by Karamojong herds. The expansion of the Suk people across the Suam and Turkwel had barely started, and at this stage they occupied no more than a small enclave north of the Turkwel about thirty miles from Kacheliba. Today

Bell would not find a Karamojong within twenty-five miles of his camp, for they have retreated before the land-hungry Suk, who in fifty years have occupied some two thousand square miles of former Karamojong territory.

From the Turkwel, Bell and his followers moved north to Mani-Mani using the Swahili caravan route and passing east of Kadam. Mani-Mani he describes as the nearest cultivated settlement of Karamojo natives, some 150 miles to the north of the Turkwel. It is, in fact, rather less than 100 miles from the river boundary. The mention of cultivation has led many to believe that the camp was sited near one of the many water holes in the River Omanimani in the Kangole-Lorengedwat area, where the major area of cultivation is now to be found.

Whereas the European has given the name Omanimani to the whole of a sixty-mile-long river with its source on Mount Moroto, the Karamojong applies this name only to a small but important water-bearing stretch of the river about fifteen miles from its source. Today there is no permanent settlement, but there are signs—in the form of abandoned grindstones scattered among the shady acacias that flank the river—that formerly Karamojong homesteads were to be found in plenty in this area. Significantly, too, in a country where memories are short and history nonexistent, there is local tradition of this being the site of an important village and traders' camp. Further evidence that this is, indeed, the Omanimani of Bell's day is to be found in a report by W. Grant, sub-commissioner of Usoga, who also visited it in 1903 and places it "hours" east of Kwakwa, which he suggested as the site for an administrative centre for Karamoja. The Kwakwa site is identifiable about three miles downstream of Omanimani, though it is no longer a centre of population.

At Omanimani, Bell was close to considerable numbers of elephants then living on Moroto Mountain, but these he appears to have ignored both on this and subsequent trips. On his first expedition he paused at Omanimani for only a few days and then moved westward into Bukora—or Bokora as we call it now. There he made camp in the thickly populated Lokopo-Kangole area that, then as now, is the centre of the Karamojong tribe. Conditions appear to have changed all too little in the half century, for Bell found that the warriors were out fighting with the Kumam (Ngikummama)—the Karamojong term for their relatives, the Iteso (Teso).

It was in Bokora that Bell first met Pyjalé, who was to become his firm friend and faithful guide. Pyjalé died about five years ago, but his family still lives a few miles from Kangole at Kautaku, rich and respected, their fortune founded on the calves Bell gave Pyjalé as a reward.

From his central Bokora camp, Pyjalé led Bell southward again toward the long-grass area west of Kadam. It was the wet season and the westward-flowing rivers—presumably the Nabilatuk and Lolachat—were in full spate. Here, in an area that today is completely devoid of elephants, Bell found "the whole country black with them" and slaughtered seven before night closed in. Ostrich, giraffe, kongoni, and topi are still to be found on these plains in large—if reduced—numbers as when Bell was there . . . but the elephant has gone forever.

On his first expedition, Bell had no cause to move his camp from central Bokora. From here short expeditions into the long-grass area between Napak[3] and Niakwai—the village that was the site of the murder of Captain Kirkpatrick in 1898[4]—brought him all the ivory with which his train could cope. (C. W. Hobley in a government report dated August 1903 records Bell's visit to the area.) This success sufficiently whetted Bell's appetite to send him back to Mumias to fit up a much larger expedition with which to return to Karamoja.

In his narrative Bell accurately describes Karamojong customs and people—except that the skins worn by unmarried women are usually goat. These customs include the tattooing the body when a warrior has killed an enemy—man, woman, or child—the peace token of a bunch of grass, and the cruel snares with which these people trap anything from elephant to dik-dik. These same customs can all be seen today.

The form of the fortified village is changing, however. Attacks on villages (as opposed to attacks on cattle while being herded on the grazing grounds) are now fairly rare, and so the importance of the defensive stockade has lessened. For the same reason, the necessity for the Karamojong to band together in large villages embracing several extended families has also gone, and now, instead of villages three hundred or more strong, the traveler will find the average homestead occupied by only twenty or so people, with the former close grouping of homesteads now replaced by a wide scatter along the red-soil ridges.

Bell's own drawings show the head-dress of the Karamojong men as a flat "periwig" extending to the wearer's shoulders. This is now a rare sight, found only on a few old men. The predominant head-dresses today are a sausage-shaped periwig or, more often, a brightly coloured clay affair covering the entire hair.

[3]Bell called this area Nopak. See chapter 13.

[4]Bell recounted this story in chapter 3.

After his first safari, Bell submitted an interesting report to the government on the state of the country he had visited. "The country," he wrote "is very fertile and carries short, sweet grass during the rainy season. Its most grave physical fault is the want of any large perennial river." He said of the Karamojong, "Now, through their talent for killing the elephant and their thrift, [they are] a people rich in the finest cattle in Africa I have ever seen." Commissioner Grant, writing in the same year, also said, "The cattle in Karamoja are the finest I have ever seen in Africa and would compare favourably with home cattle."

Such comments on the cattle would hardly be made today! There can be no doubt that the rapid increase in stock numbers combined with reductions in the area of grazing available has rapidly and drastically reduced the quality of the herds and, at the same time, has ruined and is ruining still further once relatively fertile lands and has caused many water sources—which at the turn of the century were permanent—to dry up or at least to become less reliable.

About 1905, Bell set forth with a hundred-strong safari for the north of Karamoja. His route was again via the Turkwel and Omanimani into Bokora where again he met up with Pyjalé. After hunting on the Teso border, the safari then moved north into Jie country where a few elephants were taken; the party then moved on to the base-camp in Dodoth, described as "high-lying country among steep little granite hills."

The evidence suggests that the base camp was at Kakamari, about four miles south of the present county headquarters at Kaabong and lying on the old trade and slave route following the Dopeth River. I have heard from more than one source that until quite recently there were remains of elephants reputed to have been killed by Bell near the site of the present rest camp at Kaabong, but Bell does not mention killing elephants so close to his base, and the stories may not be accurate.

From the base in Dodoth, the huge safari moved generally north, across the north-west corner of Turkana, and headed for the legendary Moru Akipi (Mountain of Water) in Taposa country, which is now in the Equatoria province of Sudan. Bell reports finding buffaloes, elands, zebras, topis, oryxes, and the largest number of old bull elephants he had ever seen in one place in this area.

Although numbers are depleted, all these beasts are still to be found in northern Karamoja, along with lesser and greater kudu, rhino, lion, leopard, and roan. So successful were Bell's endeavours at Moru Akipi that he turned back from this point, the safari being too heavily laden with ivory for him to continue along the Pibor River to the north. And so he returned to Mumias with 14,000 pounds of ivory—worth in those days about £8,000.

In neither book—nor, so far as I know, elsewhere—does Bell reveal where he traveled on his third journey into Karamoja. What is described in detail in *Karamojo Safari* is represented as his fourth and last visit. Starting, as previously from Mumias, the long train moved slowly through Kakamega, round the eastern slopes of Elgon, and on toward the Turkwel, where it paused for a week while Bell wandered down the thorn-covered banks of the Suam/ Turkwel River and started his toll of elephants by taking eight bulls.

Thence the trail swung west over the stony slopes between Elgon and Kadam, across the inconspicuous watershed that divides the Mediterranean-bound waters from those due to end in Lake Rudolf, and from there down to a camp on the Greek River. This river they followed probably to about the present site of Nabiswa and then swung north. Bell had no difficulty keeping the camp fed with meat from the vast herds that then dotted the plain, and even today in spite of the depredations of the Sebei people, numbers of elands, roans, zebras, kongonis, topis, giraffes, and Grant's gazelles are still to be found on these plains, protected north of the river by the Debassian Game Sanctuary.

The Greek River was used for watering by large herds of elephants that in the early days of the century roamed the western Pian Plains. Through these, Bell's safari moved northward toward the foothills of Kadam and then on to "a stream issuing from the old crater." There is no certain indication to where this refers, but it is probable that it is to the valley above Namalu, the "crater"—I doubt whether a geologist would agree with this description—now partly flooded by a vast new dam. This lovely country fits Bell's description well. All that is lacking are the great herds of elephants that he so successfully hunted there on this trip and apparently also on his third. Buffaloes are still to be found in small numbers, but elephants have vanished from Kadam as they have from Moroto and Napak.

Bell comments upon the Tepeth who live on Kadam: "The mountain dwellers on these hills are related to those on Elgon. They are terrified of the Karamojans living around them on the plains, and the Karamojans have an equal dread of penetrating the forest. . . . The Tepeth are said to own a few goats and sheep but no cattle. It is probably owing to this that they can continue to exist so close to the cattle-raiding plainsmen."

The Tepeth are a fascinating people. Whether or not they are related to the cave-dwellers on Elgon I cannot say, but it is not unlikely, for they are found on all three of the major massifs in south Karamoja: Moroto, Napak, and Kadam. They have a language of their own, today rarely heard outside the domestic hearth, and which, I am reliably informed, bears no apparent relationship to any other known tongue. It is possible they were early occupiers of the south-central Karamoja plains, cultivators and collectors who retreated to the hills before the invading Karamojong, and lived there unmolested, as Bell shrewdly observes because, having no cattle, they were of no interest to the plainsmen.

Tepeth tradition agrees with this. About the turn of the century, the Tepeth began to acquire a few cattle, and with the establishment of Pax Britannica, the process accelerated. The Tepeth actively began pursuing a policy of inter-marriage with the Karamojong for the sake of the "bride-price," cattle that they could thus obtain. Both sides benefited: The Karamojong obtained good wives cheaply, while the Tepeth acquired the cattle they sought. The newly related people began to live side by side, and in spite of the Tepeth holding cattle, there was little serious trouble between them . . . until the Suk appeared on the scene.

The westward-moving Suk found the Tepeth as ready to welcome them as they had been to live peaceably with the Karamojong. Minority tribes cannot afford to argue. But to the Karamojong, the Suk were the enemy, and any friend of theirs promptly acquired the same label. So it is today that the Tepeth on Kadam and in the south-east of Moroto Mountain are the objective for cattle-raiding Karamojong youths. It is significant that those on the northern slopes of Moroto and on Napak continue to live side by side with the plainsmen without trouble or rancor between the tribes.

From Kadam, Bell again moved generally north through the parkland in which Nabilatuk now stands, camping beside the south-west-flowing rivers, in the sandy beds of which water is plentiful. From one of these camps news of elephants on Napak sent Bell striding westward, covering about twenty-five miles in seven hours. The effort was well rewarded, for between dawn and dusk the next day the hunter obtained twenty-six tusks. In the course of the following three weeks a further twenty-eight were added to this number—all from the area of Napak.

Continuing north, the safari passed through Bokora and then on past Tororo "much frequented by lions and great numbers of hyenas," and into the settlements of the Jie—"a small but very compact, rich, and independent tribe speaking the Karamojo dialect but the deadly enemy of all its neighbours." The main concentration of the Jie was then, as now, on the open ridges about the present site of Kotido. In this region, Bell pitched his camp. Bell made a profitable trip from Kotido into east Acholi, through tsetse-infested country, and then, after returning to Jie to collect his ivory, moved north again.

At this point some parts of the account appear to contradict others; consequently, it is not easy to follow the sequence of events; indeed, some confusion becomes apparent from here on between the accounts of the second and fourth safaris, for at least two incidents that are described in the account of the earlier visit are repeated, with slight variations in detail, in Karamojo Safari as occurring during the final expedition. Thus, in both his books Bell mentions the record day's bag in terms of weight of ivory—1,493 pounds (1,463 pounds in the later book) from nine beasts, and details of an encounter with Abyssinian slave raiders given in each narrative are so alike as to make it certain that the same incident is being described

It seems probable, however, although the evidence is not clear, that Bell moved on from Jie through Dodoth and into the Didinga lands, "A country of grotesque and savage-looking rock formations, their summits generally occupied by swarms of gigantic baboons and jutting abruptly and nakedly from rugged vegetation as scarred and worn as the hills themselves. . . . Everywhere were great elephant roads worn deep into rock on clay." The Didinga excursion completed—the bag including two tusks of 148 pounds and 145 pounds taken from one great bull—the safari appears to have retreated to Dodosi Rock (probably Kakamari) to set up base camp. There they left all the women and children and "any footsore, weary, and sick there might be" while the main party pushed out again north-east to return to the fabulous Moru Akipi.

Bell's description of his journey forward enables us to follow his route fairly confidently. One day's march from the base at Kakamari brought him via Kamion to Oropoi, "the last water hole on the trail to Dabossa." The day's march must have been about twenty-five miles. The fine view from the top of the scarp near Kamion is graphically described by Bell as "a checkerboard of bush and open glade with abrupt volcanic massifs breaking the valley bed. Very far away to the east could be dimly seen hills that must neighbour Lake Rudolf. . . ." From Oropoi the trail took them north, in two days' march to "Camp Kilassa," where a rear camp was left.

Camp Kilassa was almost certainly at a water hole at the western foot of the Zingut Hills, possibly Lokiriama. From there the hunting party followed the slopes of the Mogila Range northward. There is some evidence that they crossed to the east of the range through the pass south of Lokichoggio. (Bell says, "while traversing the pass that divides this range . . .") The more direct route, however, lies to the west of Mogila, and the fact that the party later followed a sand river northward suggests that the western track was taken. Probably, therefore, by "traversing the pass," Bell simply means crossing the western end of the broad gap etched out by the Nanaam River.

The end of his first day from Camp Kilassa brought Bell to the neighbourhood in which Lokichoggio now stands. The good water at Lokichoggio he appears to have missed, however, and he found only some small holes, similarly situated high up the mountainside, but very salty. (It is arguable that the party did, in fact, cross to the east and that the water he found was from the large salt-water springs on that slope of Mogila. On balance, the account suggests strongly that Bell followed the west side.)

It was probably along the Nadapal River that Bell continued his journey toward Moru Akipi where he made an abortive attempt at shooting elephants by moonlight. Elephants still water in the shallow holes of this river. From the end of the Mogila Range, Bell's route took him across black-soil plains due north to the western shoulder of Moru Akipi, thence on to a commanding hill north-west of the mountain from where a clear view of the Pibor Plains dotted with elephants could be obtained.

What a rewarding view to the hunter! Bell counted no fewer than 87 big bulls in a sweep of the telescope! On the next day Bell collected 10 tails. One elephant, however, decided not to stay to have his tusks removed, and one left only the stumps of what must have been monster tusks—the stumps together scaled 148 pounds—consequently, only 15 whole tusks could be entered in the record that night. The ivory shot that day weighed 1,463 pounds, and that total became the daily record in Bell's entire career as a hunter.

The rains were now imminent, and so, reluctantly, Bell started his final retreat from "Karamojo." He went back via Mogila, Zingut, and Oropoi. His goal was Dodoth and a return to the base camp at Kakamari. There ivory was uncached, the donkeys saddled, and the last march south began. From Bokora news of elephants on Napak diverted the hunter's attention westward—five good bulls killed there brought his total from within ten miles of Napak to ninety elephants in four years of hunting. At last he returned to Mumias via the caravan route east of Kadam, thus putting an end to over twelve months' continuous marching. It was the close of a chapter in the history of Karamoja.

Of the great herds that Bell hunted so successfully, few descendants remain in Karamoja today. From the southern Turkwel, Kadam, Moroto, and Napak, and from the long-grass plains of Pian and Bokora, they have disappeared completely. Probably four hundred beasts remain in Dodoth. In recent years they have appeared as far south as Napak and have, more frequently, raided *shambas* in Labwor, but these are chance incursions by small foraging parties that have strayed from their regular haunts in the north or in Acholi.

With the exception of rhino, the occurrence of which is now very much more localized than it was fifty years ago, the distribution of other game described by Bell has shown, overall, less change. Kudu, oryx, lion, leopard, zebra, Grant's gazelle, buffalo, topi, kongoni, hyena, wild dog, warthog, eland, oribi are still to be found in Karamoja—some even yet in large numbers. But, in general, numbers have decreased greatly as the cattle and human population has increased and spread out, and the protecting tsetse fly has been pushed farther and farther north.

Bell's observations on the Karamojong were keen and showed considerable knowledge and understanding of their way of life. Much of what he has to say, speaking of pre-1910, is as true today as it was then. Forty years of British rule have brought about remarkably little change on the customs of these fine, proud people.

It was for long Bell's intention to return to Karamoja, but in the years following his visits here, he turned his attention to Abyssinia, the Lado Enclave, and Liberia. He returned to Africa during his war service and for at least one hunting trip thereafter, but he never reached again the country he knew and loved so well. "Karamojo" Bell died at his Ross-shire home in 1954 at the age of 74.[5]

[5] These notes were based principally on Bell's own writings in the *Wanderings of an Elephant Hunter* and *Karamoja Safari*. Recourse was also had to reports held in the Secretariat Archives in Entebbe by Bell, W. Grant, and C. W. Hobley, all dated about 1903, and to an article entitled "W. D. M. Bell" by Charles R. Podmore in *African Wild Life*, vol. 10 No. 3 (September, 1956). The author is also indebted to Game Warden John Blower and lately Game Ranger Karamoja; P. A. G. Field, Acting Provincial Commissioner and lately District Commissioner, Karamoja; and L. E. Whitehouse, formerly District Commissioner, Turkana.

On the Nature of Natives and Elephants

Chapter 1

So now started my real penetration of Karamoja. This safari was to last on and off for four and a half years. At first we were greeted with latent hostility by everyone—trader, raider, and native alike. It never came to open hostilities although once or twice it came nearly to blows. Two of my porters were missing. So, eager to establish our presence in the land as a force to be reckoned with, we rushed out upon the native cattle herds with the intention of seizing them and holding them until such time as our lads were restored to camp. We soon found our mistake. The cattle, unused to clothed people, would not be held, and stampeded all over the place. But there is something in us all that delights in seizing other people's goods by force, and so the efforts of my otherwise rather lazy gang of boys reached prodigious heights as they tried long-range control of the great prosperous-looking herds of sleek kine.[1] The two delinquents were soon forthcoming—they had been swilling beer with the Karamojans and had lost their way.

The hunt prospered right along although it was easy to go for a whole month without a sight of elephant. This was in the dry season. Raiding by the Swahili, Arab, and Baluchi gangs was checked by the mere presence in the country of a white man, but whenever I came down with a lot of ivory and they thought I was leaving, out would go the gangs of two or three hundred guns and five or six hundred spear men to raid a neighbour. Centuries of equalizing tribal warfare having stabilized affairs between them meant that the intervention of the guns on either side spelt certain victory.

Great were the goings-on in these raids. Cattle, donkeys, sheep, goats, and young girls were the spoils . . . and in about that order of merit if you were a native of the country. But if you were a rich trader, young women had priority over all other stock, especially if they were virgin. These pleasant-looking, sturdy, independent, upright, virile girls would disappear into the harems only

[1]Scots for cattle.

to emerge as one more of the quashed, characterless creatures swathed in cotton from head to heel that formed the entourage of the big traders.

Only occasionally were the tables turned and the raiders were the ones who scored. My tracker and friend Pyjalé was once a part of a neat and well-tuned affair concerning a safari of three hundred and fifty guns. Pyjalé and his mates were briefed by whom heaven alone knows, and to each of the traders two spear men were allotted. Pyjalé was to give the signal by remarking loudly, "Look at this man's pants. They're the colour of dung." At the word dung, every spear was to be buried in a trader. It was, and not a shot was fired. Then Pyjalé and his merry men started running down and spearing the innumerable women and children. Pyjalé told me he would have kept some of them for me, but he did not think I would like them as they stank so. So much for our perfumes and scented soaps, and our clothes.

While on the subject of raided women, I was continuously returning such to their homes and presumably loving parents. Not a bit of it. Always the first questions were for the cows, and the natives would roar at me in their dozens: "Have you got my dun-coloured cow with the cock-eyed horns?" or "Yongellynung, Yongellynung, where is my brown cow with two white feet?" and so on. Never was it, "Is my daughter so-and-so safe?

The daughters, too, were extremely cool about returning to their homes. They had tasted the intoxicating power a well-shaped body and youth bestows when among high-living incontinents[2] like the traders, anyhow. Then, too, they loved cloth. They would bind a piece of Manchester cotton tightly round those lovely, firm, up-standing breasts nature had rewarded them with, and which our women go to such pains to imitate. Thus, would they deform those priceless contours.

I could not help roaring with laughter at some of these girls once. There were fourteen had-been maidens to be returned to their tribe. At the same time they were to act as emissaries, to tell the tribe we had some eight hundred head of cattle of theirs and to come out and meet us. You have to be fairly cautious about these first contacts lest it be of the nature of a spear thrust.

Well, the girls were got ready and appeared all in their execrable pieces of cloth much to my horror. "But you'll all be speared if you go like that" I said. "Your people will take you for traders; take off those rags at once."

You will hardly believe it, but they were highly indignant.

[2]Archaic, meaning those lacking moral or sexual restraints.

"What? Undress?" they shrieked, outraged at the very thought.

The same types had worn those rags certainly not more than twenty days, all the rest of their brief existence had been spent stark-oh. Was it perchance as an outward and visible sign of that power over the masculine head and heart that made them bear those dingy rags so proudly? I would venture to bet that at first they would high-hat the natives of their own villages as being merely naked savages, but I would also venture to bet that this attitude would not last long. I have seen how the native lads deal with a high-hat girl. They will beat her up with keen cutting switches, up-end her, spread-eagle her, stand her on her head, and generally knock sense into her by knocking nonsense out of her.

******

In the dry season many elephants retired to the lower Nile country west of Karamojo, but the rare and widely scattered permanent waters would be frequented by old cows and sick bulls, many carrying good ivory. About 10 percent of them would have one broken tusk while one in a hundred would have no tusks at all outside the lip. Generally heavy stumps would be extracted from their heads showing that the original tusks had been broken in fighting or digging. Many of these bulls were of great age, but there is no knowing how old. Many, too, were afflicted with diseased livers.

The boys would bring me round hard balls of compacted dry bile, in size ranging from a golf ball to that of a man's head. Often the livers were riddled with pockets of dry bile. In killing them, I dare say I was but anticipating nature by a few years.

The idea that in some remote part of the bush there must exist "elephant cemeteries" has had a great appeal to man for ages. Let us examine the question. To begin with there is no such thing as a part of the bush in Africa that is not visited by the native African. In the dry season the people of the villages penetrate to the remotest parts in search of honey, to hunt for meat, in fighting, and in surprising other parties similarly occupied. Certainly there are areas that for some mystical reason are taboo to some tribes but not to all. Since the value of ivory became known to the African, it is safe to say that no accumulation of tusks could now remain undiscovered.

Another thing is how short-lived the remains of an elephant are, with the exception of the ivory and the teeth. All the rest of the massive bones that look so indestructible simply melt away. Hyaenas with their powerful jaws and teeth gnaw them and drag them off, with the jackal's assistance, and what they fail to accomplish termites, rodents, bush fires, and sun soon put paid to any sign that an elephant has died. It can happen in an incredibly short time as I know from repeatedly looking for traces of former kills.

There was one particular spot lying between two hills where we had killed twelve elephants all close together. We could not mistake the spot. Yet on re-visiting it one year after, there was not a trace to be found of anything except the remnant of a skull, gnawed down, weathered away to the size of a football. As we seem to be on a de-bunking lay, let us have a look at that hoary tale of elephant carrying off their wounded.

I can never understand why man should wish upon the elephant such an unnatural desire. Anything better calculated to impede the herd's flight to safety than a helpless six-ton elephant cannot be imagined.

"What," I ask, "would be the idea behind such an action?"

They cannot, as humans would, hand the patient into the nearest hospital. No, I cannot see that elephants differ in this respect from any other animal. Wounded are an embarrassment and an incumbrance to the herd. As far as I have observed, what has evidently passed with other witnesses as attempts to prop up and even to carry off the wounded beast are merely the excited gestures of fright-induced rage, in no way different from that the sight and smell of blood induces in buffaloes and in other bovines as well.

They told me to see the film *King Solomon's Mines,* that there I would see the veritable act. I saw what I had often seen before, two enraged and frightened cows prodding at a dead bull, nothing more, nothing less. Those two cows had in their minds as they fled after the bull when a fatal shot or shots were fired: "You great blundering ass, what on earth are you doing making that beastly noise and falling down?"

Whereupon they set about to completely demolish what had frightened them. That bit of the film struck me as being genuine and unfaked. Personally, I lean toward the attitude of the new Scots elephant-attendant who, on being involved in his charges' ablutions, exclaimed indignantly. "You muckle bum-faced bugger, if I kent which end was y're heid, I'de kick your airse." This anecdote had a mild success in grandfather's time; it may be old enough to pass for new.

Karamojo

Chapter 2

This country of Karamojo, where I was to spend five happy years without the sight of a white face, was a high, dry, sandy ridge of country, interspersed with rock outcrops and some quite high isolated mountains. It runs parallel with the White Nile, distant some two hundred miles to the west, while Lake Rudolph lay simmering in the heat of its depression about two hundred and fifty miles to the east. It was very healthy country, and mosquitoes were not at all bothersome. Every other sort of pestiferous fly was well represented, however.

The country was thorn bush interspersed with open glades. Toward Rudolph the bush became denser with fewer open parts, and it was higher. Toward the Nile there were large stretches of country covered with high grass, and these plains became inundated during the big rains. The rivers on the high ridge where all the Karamojo permanent villages were congregated consisted of seemingly dry, sandy river beds; they only ran water in the big rains. During the rest of the time, water was obtained by digging in the sand, both by humans and wild life.

Besides this source, the natives built large dams that filled up in the big rains and helped in the watering of the large native herds of cattle, donkeys, sheep, and goats. But these dams by no means sufficed for their needs all the year round, and when the grass had been burned, most of the stock and humans would trek off in search of pasture. That was the time when raiding each other's herds was the chief pastime.

After approaching by night, the raiders would make a sudden rush at dawn. There would be some rapid spear fighting, a few women would be killed, and if the raiders' luck was in, they might detach a small herd of cattle and rush them off into the no-man's land separating the two tribes. More frequently, perhaps, the opposition would be found too strong, and the raid petered out into a hot, long chase for twenty to thirty miles. There was less chance of bringing off a successful raid when everyone was at home in the permanent villages as these were heavy stockades with very high, hard-wood stakes set very close together and pushed deep into the ground.

Beyond designating the country as British on the maps, there was as yet no attempt to occupy or administer it. The Abyssinians raided it freely and frequently, but chiefly for slaves. The boundary had not been fixed, so it was a sort of free-for-all scramble in which the British-sponsored traders from British East Africa were only too willing to join.

Everyone had firearms except the owners of the land; they had only spears. The Habash[1] had fairly modern rifles, and the Swahili and Arab traders had a ramshackle lot of fire-tubes—from muzzle-loading percussion caps up to the heavy double-barrel products of all the famous London firearm makers. Ostensibly these arms were allowed for the protection of peaceful traders. Inevitably they were turned to other uses as there was not a single authority in the land. All the old slavers in Africa seemed to have found a last stronghold in this land. They had little to fear except from a large band of Habash, who were the better armed. But both sides were mighty scared of each other and would both retire smartly to the rear as soon as any contact was established.

The traders' settlements were a sight worth seeing. They were well and truly dug in. Well defended against any probable attack, they laid out their establishments on a permanent basis, comfort for themselves and for their innumerable women being the key-note. You would see representatives from almost every tribe in Africa kicking about these permanent camps, even the Persian types from Lamu. So enjoyable was life that some of the *tajirs*[2] never left Karamojo at all.

They still found "the good old days and ways" held sway. They would combine forces and join up with one tribe to knock the hell out of some other one, dividing the spoils—cattle, sheep, goats, donkeys, and girls—on the basis of a system known only to themselves. Old men, old women, and women *enceinte* [pregnant] were simply slaughtered. Young African men usually escaped because they are hard to catch or kill, even with firearms.

I had occasion to round-up just such a raiding party, to count their guns, and to take such evidence as I could get from the participants in the raid. A very strong

[1]Abyssinians.

[2]Rich men.

party had been assembled—some 500 guns and about 1,500 auxiliaries—to raid my good friends the Dabossa. They had fallen upon two large stockade villages just as the cattle were being liberated from their cramped quarters. With paraffin torches shot from lightly charged muzzle-loaders, they soon had the grass roofs of the closely packed huts ablaze. It was a case of come out or fry within.

Many of the miserable inmates were speared by the auxiliaries and many had their throats cut in the true orthodox Mohammedan fashion. Only some of the unmarried girls were secured by the traders, some being speared to death by the blood-mad spear men in spite of an agreement that they should all be spared for the harem-owners.

As far as I could gather, native women never offer resistance in such crises. And yet they are amazingly strong and active. See them at the dances: They will go on forever and appear rather fresher than the men. And yet when it comes to defending themselves, they do nothing. There was some evidence that the *enceinte* women were slashed across the abdomen with knives to the great merriment of all beholders. I checked up on this and came to the conclusion that it was a veritable fact.

As regards the young men and boys, they appeared to have mostly escaped. Primitive man presents a difficult target—he is long in the wrong direction—is extremely active, and instinctively does the right thing like dodges into smoke, jinks at the right moment, and finds cover where there is none.

The neighbouring villages appeared to have barricaded themselves in their strongholds and contented themselves with shouting defiance at their enemies. This was about the safest thing they could do. It would be useless to fire a village when closed up tight. As then everything within would perish including the cattle.

When it came to the question of returning the women captives, out of fifty or sixty only eighteen wanted to go back. Of course, they had been well-treated by their captors, and they had come under the fascination of clothes already, although they had not been with their now masters for more than four days. They had experienced a new way of life infinitely more leisurely than that of an African native wife with its yearly baby and its incessant toil.

The eighteen returnables then followed us about for some time on our hunting trails, and when we were within a reasonable distance of their homes, I proposed that they should beetle off to their people to tell them we had come to return their cattle.

All these merry doings were known to be taking place, but the government could not see its way to sending in an occupation force. But if a decent white man could be found to remotely represent those in power, they were willing that he should be there . . . provided he did so at his own risk and—above all—at his own expense. It was in the government's own best interest because a white man's presence in the country would serve as a check on the raiders. My good friends Partington and Ormsby both saw that I was that representative.

At the beginning of my sojourn in this delightful land, the native Karamojans looked upon me as just one more trader. They stole some of our sheep. It was essential to nip this sort of thing in the bud. We had just returned from a successful hunt, and I sent Pyjalé to his home with a handsome present. I knew he would establish with the locals what sort of people we were.

After a few similar incidents, the whole native population decided I was their friend and settled down in a very peaceful and pleasant manner. Our stock could roam unmolested where they listed, and our troubles were almost over. I say almost because there were always the native drunks to reckon with. As they were so fully armed—carrying stabbing spears and even rings on their fingers with cutting blades or large hooks mounted on them—they became a menace when in their cups. Fortunately, I never had occasion to shoot anyone because the people always backed me up in any punishment I had to dole out.

With the Swahili and Arab traders, too, it was the same thing. They never resisted my authority although I had none. I simply told them what to do and they did it.

With the Habash, too, I had a marked success. The very first time we saw any of these roving gentry we walked straight up to their encampment. Judging by their behavior, they evidently expected to be attacked. But not a shot was fired, and we were soon in amicable intercourse. I explained that they were well inside British territory, which I hoped was true, and that if they were caught by the military—who, I suggested, were just round the corner instead of being hundreds of miles away—they would get hell. They gave me a riding mule and a cute little French carbine while I gave them a tusk. We parted on good terms. They must have reported to their ras[3] that the country was occupied by the British, for as long as I remained in Karamojo there was no recurrent raids by them.

[3]"Ras" usually refers to the emperor of Abyssinia but it can also mean a local ruler in Abyssinia.

A small native boy was in the act of plinking an enormous elephant.

I often chuckle when thinking back over those days. How easy it was for a hunter of elephants to subdue the most truculent tribes without bloodshed, and yet how costly in lives and money the same operation became when it was carried out by the orthodox method of penetration by force. At the cost of a few elephants, buffaloes, giraffes, and antelopes, a whole country was brought into such a state of readiness to accept white rule that in the recent World War four thousand Karamojans accepted service to fight in Burma for us. And there were no smouldering resentments, as a forceful occupation with the resultant inevitable killings would have produced. I understand the whole country is now planting cotton and that there are railways operating and the chiefs are running about in motor cars.

I remember getting a very pleasant thrill from an officer in the Sudan service. Although unknown to me, he wrote to say that he had been on a mission to the Taposa tribe. The white men had asked the assembled notables if they wanted the whites to occupy their country and so afford them protection from the Habash. They still remembered me, and they said that if they, the whites, were brothers of mine, they would be welcome, but not otherwise.

******

Like all primitives, they were all tied up with theories that we lump together and for lack of a better word call "medicine." If a certain bird called on the left hand as you left for a hunt, it meant one thing; if it called on the right side, it meant an altogether different thing. They were at the mercy of all sorts of omens. Their medicine men could do almost anything with them so long as they enjoyed the people's confidence. But let them predict rain without rain coming in time to save the planted crops, and that medicine man's number was up. They would club and stone him to death unless he could find a convincing-enough excuse by "passing the buck" and blaming some unusual happening or the advent of some stranger for his failure. So long as he was lucky, he enjoyed good eating and drinking at the common expense.

At the beginning of a hunt, there would be much tossing of sandals, just as we toss a coin to see if it falls heads or tails up. But as they never announced beforehand what indicated what, it became merely a pastime. Wishful thinking governed the issue entirely, but anyone who could do it with a sufficiently grave and weighty manner would soon collect an intent audience.

On Loads, Meat Camps, and Hunting with Yongellynung

Chapter 3

Now that my hunting was prospering, I began to experiment with all kinds of rifles, ranging from the .256, .275, .280, and .303 I already had to the lovely double .400/.450 hammerless ejector propelling a 400-grain bullet by a charge of 60 grains of cordite. This weapon was a real masterpiece of the gun makers' art at its best. It was a joy just to handle, and while it weighed 10 pounds, it felt like 7. But what were the results in actual practice in the field?

In the rainy season, the action was liable to jam because of mud getting on the close-fitting action faces, which would happen when following mud-bathing elephants in high grass. You could not dry-shoot it for fear of breaking the strikers unless you had dummy cartridges, which were promptly ejected and a nuisance to find. The third and subsequent shots came slow, and, finally, it did not kill any deader than the smallest calibre in my armory when the placement was right, while it was considerably noisier than any of the others.

In order to see if there really was anything in the big-bore's theory of shock, I thought I would try pulling both triggers together. At my first test on a target, I found it difficult to get the two strikers to fall together because one was slightly in front of the other. I then tested tying the two triggers, first with twine and then with wire, and I was finally able to place the two bullet holes close together.

It was no fun projecting 800 grains of lead driven by 120 grains of cordite, but I took the infernal contraption to the bush with me. I was not going to chance any nonsense on really valuable stuff, so I chose as a trial the tracks of a breeding herd that had two or three herd bulls. We tracked them into some pretty dense thorn that lined a dry water-course, and I was lucky to get a fair shot at a bull across the fifteen-yard-wide river bed. The placement was correct and the animal fell, just as it would have done with any of the other bores.

The strip of bush was surrounded by immense open plains, and the herd did not leave the bush but continued along it. I was soon into them again, in spite of the fright they had got when that explosion had registered with their huge sound-collecting ears. This time I used a frontal brain shot, and I must have flinched for nothing happened except for their instant flight. There was no stunning, no delay, no staggering even.

I must have pulled down my barrels at the moment of firing and, thus, placed those two so-called "solids" three or four inches too low in the tusk-socket arch bone. Moreover, if I had been using my .303 or .275 and had missed with the first shot, I think I would have got a side shot into the brain as the bull turned away. *So much for the shock business,* I thought. I gave up the heavy doubles and never returned to them.

Fully convinced that shot placement was everything, provided that the bullet had sufficient penetration and held together, I redoubled my concentration on the study of the anatomy of the head shot. I found it an aid to cut short, straight sticks, slightly point them, stick them into a bullet hole where they could be induced to follow the wound channel enough to indicate the course taken. I peeled the top end of the stick so that white, fresh wood would show. Then, when viewed from about the firing distance, the peeled stick would show up well against the gray background and give a fair indication of the course the bullet had taken.

As it just happened, the military round-nose bullets then in use were well-nigh perfect for this job. The velocity being moderate, round about the 2,000 f.p.s. mark, the nickel jackets were not ruptured nor did the bullets deform; consequently, they kept a straight course. There were exceptions: The .256 was found to be too long for its calibre, and it bent. But the .303 and .275 appeared to be trouble free. I never had a chance to try the American .30-06, but I should think that this cartridge with its 220-grain, round-nose bullet would have been ideal for this work.

I had hitherto confined myself to the more-or-less straightforward frontal and broadside brain shot, with variations in angle, naturally, as the head was generally in movement. Now the area of least movement is centred in the huge universal ball-joint at the junction of spinal column to the skull. If you accustom yourself to look for this spot—ignoring all the external signs such as eyes and ear holes—and direct your bullet toward it, you will often be surprised on searching out the tiny dusted area denoting the bullet entry how very improbable its location would seem to promise a kill . . . and yet there he lay safely in the bag. Sometimes the puncture would be well out of centre, sometimes behind the eye, sometimes over it, and other times under it.

The same is true with the side shot at the brain. Sometimes the surface puncture would be found well in front of the ear hole, sometimes exactly in it, and other times behind it. It is the latter that led me to the discovery of a most important and rewarding shot—the brain shot from behind. It happened thus.

I had gone to the bush at the invitation of my blood brother Yongellynung, whose portrait I venture to enclose here.[1] We were well provided with all that makes for jolly living, if not perhaps for hard running and good shooting. The old boy—he was about three times my age—liked his comforts and being a very wealthy man was much married. He used only his younger wives and daughters on these forays and kept them busy seeing to his guests' comfort. Grass roofs found their place in all our camps so that the sun should not annoy our leisure hours while his sons searched the bush for elephants. A constant flow of fat sheep, chickens, eggs, fresh milk, and beer was kept up from his village to our camps, no matter the distance. According to native custom, all his possessions were mine and all mine his. Luckily, it never occurred to him to ask for a rifle.

With such efficient staff work, it was not long before a runner appeared on the scene to announce the discovery and locating of seven good bull elephants. Yongellynung asked who was left to watch them. On being told, he seemed to be re-assured and called for more beer. The sun was over the bump and I was for instant departure. But the old man would not hurry and said it was not far and that there was plenty of time for one more pot. So I left him and followed the guide.

Soon we came to where the guide had left his companions to watch the browsing herd. They were not there, so we took up the trail. I was soon full of misgivings for the spoor led due west toward some immense grass swamps still unburned, and the course never deviated. It looked to me like one of their flitting acts when they will lay behind them fifty or sixty miles non stop just for the hell of it. At last we saw the familiar white cow birds or false egrets appearing intermittently over the quite near horizon of grass, and presently along the lane of laid grass we saw the watchers.

They said the elephants had not stopped once to eat or even to bathe. *They're headed for the Nile,* I thought to myself, about two hundred miles away. Things were looking gloomy when along came the old man simmering with

[1]Unfortunately, we did not find a portrait of Yongellynung in any of the materials.

beer and high spirits. Instantly he laid on some ten or fifteen of his lads with instructions to get along and head off the elephants. Off they darted right and left into the sea of grass while the old boy and I lagged along the trail as fast as we could. Just before sunset we got into them. The boys had accomplished the miraculous feat of outstripping their eight miles per hour traveling gait by passing them well to the side—all in high untrodden grass—and had now halted and then turned the phalanx back in our own direction. They were hot on their heels and brought the tight bunch hurtling right on top of us.

You never saw such a mix-up. Spears were flying, shots whizzing, Long shouting and roaring, and elephants trumpeting and bellowing. Soon all were quiet, one of them too quiet. I was about to give him a finisher when he suddenly arose and began a rush almost straight away from me. I tried the brain shot from behind and it worked. Thus was added to my repertory this most useful shot. While jubilant at the discovery of this new shot, I was ashamed to find one of the tusks of the slain had been struck by one of my bullets and damaged.

I will spare my readers an account of the doings in that colossal meat camp that night. It might make my publishers curious, and it will make for cooler judgment of the merits—or otherwise—of this manuscript if I confine myself to recording that Long's whole harem came on that night carrying much beer and performing their duties to everyone's satisfaction.

I know this: Everyone was uproariously happy. Gone were the irksome restraints that man has devised for everybody's discomfort including his own. If an explorer had lit upon that camp and had said: "Behold here is a bunch of happy people. I will take them home and show my people what happy people look like." What would have happened? He'd have been locked up.

I liked hunting with brother Long. Unfortunately, his country held but a limited number of decent bulls who were regular frequenters of the few springs that held water throughout the dry season. After I had taken ninety heads off this landscape, the supply was perceptibly diminished. But I must record one more day with Long.

As it happened, his lads had located the tracks of a small bunch of bulls, and we were soon on their trail. It led us due west, and I began to despair of catching up with them in day light. That meant a night out among the mosquitoes. Toward sun down there was still no sign of our fugitives, and everyone began to think of water and firewood. I remarked that things were going to be tough when Long said "No! We'll go to the Kunama villages. See that hill! They are the people who killed the white man, and they still have his rifle. If you ask for it, they will give it to you."

This was a reference to one Fitzpatrick, an officer on MacDonald's treaty-making expedition made some years previously when the scramble for territory and spheres of influence was at its height. Large expeditions dispersed themselves in every direction carrying quantities of small Union Jack flags and parchment treaties signed by Queen Victoria that only awaited the signature of some quite illiterate savage to become operative. A flag was given to him as a sign to all and sundry that Britain claimed his country and people as part of her sphere.

It did not matter who the chap was—anyone who came forward received the six-by-nine-inch flag. No matter what his motive in doing so might be—cupidity, curiosity, or merely that he looked well-fed and affluent—he became for the strangers the king of the country. But the natives themselves cared not a hoop for his new status, and these uncrowned kings became a perfect pest to those who subsequently traveled through their countries, for they always had complaints to make and seemed to think it was every white man's duty to uphold the status conferred. They became quite peeved when nothing could be done about it.

I was wondering what our reception would be like among these hillmen. Apparently they had had no difficulty in disposing of Fitzpatrick and his men. Long seemed in no doubt whatever and led the way in the declining light toward the hill, which looked to me an uncommon long way off. Food, beer, shelter, and the fun of entering what might be hostile territory gripped us all, I think. Soon fires and smoke spoke of comfort and ease.

When he was within shouting distance, Long hailed the closely shut stockade village. All the stock was inside, both human and other. It was now dark. Again Long shouted something on the air. A strong murmur was heard from inside the villages and presently an answer came. Long, seizing his spears, said, "It's all right, come on!"

We all entered through the door in the hardwood palisade—a palisade that would turn or stop dead all leaden bullets as well as spears, arrows, etc. The only fault with them was the defenders could not do much to the attackers. Consequently, the latter had only to approach near enough to shoot a burning torch from a muzzle-loader into the closely packed grass-roofed huts, with the result that can be imagined.

The torch was made of any old rag impregnated with liquid gunpowder bound to the end of a stick. This shoved down the muzzle on top of a good wad of fibre over a small charge gave the projectile a nice, high trajectory and usually did the trick. If a wind was blowing, all would be in flames in a few moments. This method of subduing a village was seldom resorted to by the traders, of course, because a lot of the young girls would get blemished if not killed outright.

Soon we were seated in a good hut on a polished cow-dung floor as clean as any perfect floor at home. Cow dung and blood makes a wonderful cement, kind to the frame, warm at night, cool by day. Life for some is signalized by automobiles and spring mattresses; for others it is a smooth, flat, welcoming cow-dung floor.

Let us look closely at this so-called higher standard of living. We steam-heat our houses and feed ourselves to repletion with heat-raising foods of all descriptions; we guard ourselves from all rude contact with the elements, and we go to bed on the softest mattress we can find. There we cover our poor bodies with the warmest of blankets and then we go to work, with what result? It is all over in an instant. Now take the other fellow. He wears nothing; the elements blow hot, blow cold, and they reach every part of his body. He sleeps naked on a smooth, flat floor with possibly a wooden pillow. He has no covering of any sort by night or by day. What happens when he goes to work? A long, hard, time-consuming, worth-while job.

Beer was soon produced, and none of my companions seemed to want anything more, but I felt very hungry indeed. Great talk was going on meanwhile between Long and our hosts, presumably about Fitzpatrick's rifle. Long had an extremely gruff voice, and I dozed off on my mat to the drone of his authoritative voice booming on and on. Pot after pot of beer was brought by the women of the establishment, and about midnight food was set before us.

The outcome of it all was they brought the rifle and five cartridges to us, saying that was all that remained. It was a short Martini-Henry .303 calibre and must have been one of the very first of its kind, for on opening a cartridge, I found it contained hard, compressed black stuff that I subsequently learned was called "Rifleite," which is merely compressed black powder. What the ballistics were with this stuff, I could not say. Nothing great I should think.

Implied in the bargain was the killing of some elephants in return for the rifle. They thought I wanted the darn thing, but, of course, it was of no use to me. I was only interested in recovering a white man's property that possibly might appeal to his people. I sent it down to the government *boma* at first opportunity, but a year or two after I saw it kicking around, so evidently it was all trouble wasted.

I thought we ought to take up the trail that had brought us to this country, but Long counseled, "No," let them find some elephants."

So we remained in our village drinking milk and watching the girls going about their chores. They had not a stitch on except a three-inch fringe where Eve had put the fig leaf, so you saw all that sight could tell you about any of them. Some were very smart, indeed, and a joy to gaze upon in their well-fitting satiny skins. I never ceased to marvel at the beauty of their breasts, so firm that even the under contour did not show any sag even when the breasts were full and large. It is sad to think how all that beauty will be lost when clothing comes along, as it inevitably will.

While waiting the return of the game scouts, I got the big telescope high up on the hill before heat-haze spoilt the visibility. There were great sheets of water away to the westward, and I hoped we might not have to go there for our elephants as the country looked unburnt and uncommonly like high grass. And so it proved to be. But we smothered six of them in a mud bath and two as they fled, and this gave our newly acquired friends all they wanted by way of work and meat.

Of course, to keep meat from the flies, you have to get it pronto onto the smoking racks, and there was not a stick of firewood for miles. All twenty-four or twenty-five tons of meat had to be carried to the nearest grove where smoking operations could be done. That is when you see what the country contains. In their anxiety to get the job done, all hands are called out, and those who would otherwise be kept from the lecherous eyes of strangers appear unrestrainedly on the scene. Those lovely, almost boyish forms when quite young, in all stages of bloom up to maturity, show exquisite balance and grace under a staggering load of elephant beef.

Soon we were once more at base camp, and here we were greeted by news of a great raid on the Dabossa. Pyjalé and Long had feelings of jealousy where I was concerned, and they never both came with me at the same time. So now it was Pyjalé's turn for a spell of bushwhacking. We must try to cut off the returning raiders.

******

Many and varied were the amusements and relaxations in camp. There was our own brand of football subsequently adopted by the King's African Rifle regiment as part of their training and called "Karamoja." It was a simple game uncomplicated by rules of any sort. As many as wished could take part, in equal numbers on either side naturally. It was the only popular game where there were no male spectators as all were taking part in the game.

Often the ground would be murderous, littered with ant-hills, thorn bushes, boulders, and whatnot. Nothing mattered. If the boss took part, he had to take what came his way like everyone else. I, of course, had footgear of some sort while the others were barefoot. What fast, muscular, slippery beggars they were but always good tempered. They loved their game, but, like every game that develops, it began to become complicated when the colonel of the K.A.R. introduced a rule that biting was not allowed.

Then there was shooting. They went quite crazy on this. The practice weapon was a sports .22 and the target a fairly easy one at fifty yards. The prize was a fat-tailed sheep, and each competitor had to buy his cartridges. It was soon found necessary to limit the number of rounds to any single man; otherwise, some of them would have bankrupted themselves. Then, of course, there was the external age-long struggle to take each other's women. This, needless to say, afforded equal zest to both sexes.

With abundant meat and fat from elephant and giraffe, a sufficiency of grain food as this could always be exchanged for meat, it was a jolly, healthy, and happy safari, welcomed wherever we went by the natives. We were even pressed to visit parts considered hostile by all other travelers. Where others went armed to the teeth, if they went at all, we went without a thought and with our cows and our stock roaming the countryside.

What magic did we possess? Nothing more than a couple of decent small-bore rifles. The whole thing was based on the proper and efficient placing of tiny nickel-jacketed bullets in the vulnerable parts of large animals. This seemed like "magic" after a half century of mal-placing lead bullets in the non-vulnerable parts of large game animals.

Especially potent was the brain-shot! To the native mind, that was pure "magic." No weapon in their previous experience had been able to pierce the skull of an elephant; therefore, there must be some magic attached to those factory-produced .303s. It is no exaggeration to say that those two, 7-guinea rifles conquered and subdued an enormous region inhabited by hordes of undisciplined savages and infested by gangs of ex-slavers and raiders from every quarter of Africa and India. There were amongst these groups Baluchis and Persians, prominent if not numerous, given to trying to pass themselves off as white men.

But the native is not such a fool as he may appear to be. He is most observant, especially of strangers. So when our bold, light-coloured Baluchi would-be white man goes to the bush, his smallest doings are scrutinized by invisible but watchful eyes just as white men's are. It would surprise people if they heard and could understand the comment made on them and their habits by the so-called backward races when at home and at their ease.

As it was essential to stock up with native flour before entering the depopulated country lying below the Abyssinian escarpment, where those highly armed gentry had carried off or killed the tillers of the soil, we would have to get a lot of meat. The quickest and most profitable source of such a supply was bull elephants. But there were times when these wandering butcher's shops were unaccommodating enough to be absent from the scene; especially was this so in the dry season. Cow elephants I never did like killing. The kind of bulls I sought were past breeding and their tenure in life did not affect the future. Therefore, now we turned to the next most abundant providers of meat: giraffe and buffalo.

The hides of both were of great value in procuring flour. Pieces cut to sandal sizes and shield sizes went readily in exchange for flour. Whenever I had removed from the scene any of these large animals, I felt entitled to remove also any lion that I might meet up with. I called this "preserving the balance of nature" to myself, fraud that I was. So when I had laid out a sufficiency of meat for our requirements and while everyone was busy getting control of the situation, I sneaked off alone and did in a giraffe unbeknownst to anyone. This was to be bait for lion, to be visited next morning.

Sure enough they were on it. The smell from the meat camp had attracted quite a collection, and not being able to get near the meat camp because of the natives, they had found the untouched carcass and were busy on it. They must have been hungry as they had already made good headway. So much so that one, a leopard, was completely concealed inside the rib structure. It darted out at the first shot, looking like nothing on earth as he was all camouflaged with blood splotches.

These cats were so intent on their job that I got quite close to the party without their noticing the faded-khaki-clad figure, or if noticing, paid no heed to it. For this they paid dearly, for the same insignificant-looking creature carried the deadly 7mm fire-tube with which he proceeded to snuff out their vital sparks one after the other without more ado. They may have had nine lives each, but in that case all nine must have been in a row because one solid was enough to satisfy them. They asked for no more. Some took it in at one end, others at the other end.

Except the leopard. With one bound he cleared the carcass of a head-shot lion and a mass of entrails, and before the rifle could attend to him, he disappeared in the long grass. They are mighty quick, leopards. I have missed more leopards in movement than any other animal. I don't know why it is; they seem silky smooth in their movements, yet they just ain't where the bullet is.

Apart from the missing of the leopard, this little affair was as neat a demonstration of the deadliness of the "solid" bullet as could be seen. Five shots were fired and four tough felines were killed instantly, none crawling away wounded and bickering or protesting. The first shot was at a large bulky lion that was lying prone and chewing away at his chosen fodder. Of course, he was a certainty, or the hunter should have gone playing marbles; he was killed by a solid in the head through the neck from behind and, of course, from above. He never moved, a fact to be noted in neck shots, but not so pronounced in brain shots.

Learning the Brain Shot at African Elephants

Chapter 4

After much tackling buffaloes in the swamps of southern Uganda, I was fairly proficient and was longing to get at elephants. Apparently I had acquitted myself sufficiently well, for on returning to Entebbe, my friend furnished me with a letter to a man who was to mean a great deal to me later on and to whom I became greatly attached. Not only did he bring me through my first bout of malaria and dysentery, but he also opened his heart to me, embraced my cause with both arms, and furthered it in a way that is usually reserved only for those nearest and dearest. I was, indeed, in luck to have found two such staunch friends.

Almost on arrival at my destination I was greeted by my new friend with news of elephants. He said the country was crawling with them and that they were doing enormous damage in the native gardens. Since the government had taken away most of the native-owned fire-tubes, the elephants browsed at will, unmolested, wherever they liked.[1] The ivory, too, was enormous, being of the "soft" or most valuable kind as opposed to the "hard" or forest variety. M. warned me the grass was very high at that time and lousy. It was the rainy season, the most uncomfortable but the most profitable time to hunt elephants because the ubiquitous and all-pervading African is confined by the elements to his native village.

I shall never forget my first introduction to elephants. There were eight large bulls in a small mud bath. Now, attached to the station there was a soldier in command of the garrison, and he had killed one or two elephants with a brain shot, and he thought he knew all about it. He had very kindly drawn me diagrams showing the exact position of the brain from the side, and my head was filled with his instructions.

According to these, the brain itself was found very high up in the dome of the elephant's head, about where a man would place a bowler hat three sizes

[1] Now there is a government body called the Elephant Control; at the time of which I write, it did not exist.

too small for him. I regarded these instructions as infallible until six successive failures began to shake my faith in them. Either the elephant the soldier had killed had been afflicted with a brain that was worn on the top of its head, or the soldier had flinched and pulled down his shot and so had penetrated the brain in the proper place. I think the latter the more probable of the two.

But I knew nothing of this at that time. On I went lambasting shots into those massive domes without any effect whatsoever and, I think, with little or no damage to the dome carriers. At any rate, I caught up with several of my dome-punctured victims and found them—to my consternation—browsing peacefully along.

Herein lies an argument for the use of only small bores on elephants. Had I been using say a .577 or a .600, I still would not have killed my beast, but I would have damaged the dome perhaps enough to let the rain or flies or something into the cavity. Whereas a .303 or .275 or .256—all one-shot killers—would leave hardly a trace of their passage through the spongy structure, and the hide would close up tightly over the tiny puncture.

In a flurry of exasperation at seeing one of my dome-pricked friends calmly squirting water from a puddle over his sizzling hide, I gave him a .303 in the body just behind the point of the shoulder—not quite low enough for the heart itself. Here now was reaction at last. Hitherto my head shots had been received if not with contempt, at least in silence. Not so this body shot. The welkin—whatever that may be—split from top to bottom and the old fellow rushed off in an amazing way. Just as suddenly he stopped, swayed, and fell crashing to the ground. This was the body shot.

His mates were thoroughly alarmed by the splitting of the welkin and by the ghastly groans of the dying monarch. It would be safe to say that every elephant for a mile or two around would be alarmed. It was a lesson never forgotten, and I determined to master the brain shot or die in the attempt.

We were no distance from M.'s comfortable house, so leaving the boys to cut away all the hide and flesh from the head so that a thorough examination of the locality of the brain could be made, I must confess that I trudged off home somewhat crestfallen. Instead of six or eight thundering great bulls, one solitary specimen constituted the bag. So, damning that soldier and putting all the blame to his account, I confronted M. with my tale of woe and a demand for a saw capable of sawing down right through an elephant's head.

He had one, and on the morrow M., the station carpenter, his crew, I, and a lot of boys set about the task, only to find that we had to reduce the teeth of the saw. By this time the skull was clean and severed from the body, so with all hands on the job, it was set up on end and sawn in twain right down between the tusks to the enormous ball-joint housing on the skull.

That was the idea anyhow, but the saw went rather off plumb and finished up a bit to one side. As the two halves could now be laid down flat showing the whole intricate lay-out or stood up on edge so as to show a side elevation, it was a complete revealment of the secret recesses of the elephant's brain. I would say that no one should be allowed to have a license to kill elephants until he had seen and studied a lay-out such as we had out there in the bush . . . with swarms of buzzing flies around us. Every license-issuing station should have a mounted, stuffed, preserved elephant's head with the hide on one side and the other side cut out through the centre. It is unbelievably intricate, an elephant's head. Photos, diagrams, or drawings are not worth a tinker's cuss compared with a view of the actual works.

Having absorbed what I could of the entrancing problem into my mind, memory, and sketch book, I felt desperately eager to put my newly acquired knowledge to the test of actual experience. I don't think I slept a wink that night so fearful was I of forgetting the lessons learnt. Even before sun-up we were hot on the trail of some raiding bulls, my little .303 simply itching to be at them, my mind seeing perfect pictures of the road to the brain either from the front or from the side.

It was a normal rainy-season day, hot sun in the early morning, cloudy midday, and thunder, lightning, and downpours for the rest. We got into our game during a cloud burst with lightning fizzing about and crashes of thunder overhead. I doubt if the report of the .303 was heard at all. I was immensely relieved to find the medicine good and to see the first one drop with a side shot. With renewed confidence, I continued the good work and made the discovery that if an elephant is dropped stone dead where it stands, its companions are not much alarmed and continue to stand around, very greatly to the hunter's profit.

I hunted for some time under M.'s hospitality and got that brain shot thoroughly into my system. With experience came increased knowledge. I found that if a brain-shot elephant happened to touch a companion either by falling sideways against him or by prodding him with a tusk, it was calculated to alarm him. The solution was to kill first the farthest-away animal that seemed to have all four feet on the ground and was not swaying about from one foot to the other as they so often do.

When correctly executed, this first shot results in the farthest-away beast suddenly kneeling. The head is still borne by the elastic neck muscles, the ears still retain some motion, and the fellow seems alive although stone dead. The others regard him as if they wore specs low on their noses and had to raise their heads high to see through them. And that is when the hunter profits. Or should. Things can go wrong even then. One bungled shot may result in a stampede either toward or away from you. It was not until later in my career that I adopted and developed the shot at the brain through the neck muscles from behind.

******

Hoima [Uganda] and vicinity and the Masindi bush were all grand hunting grounds in those days, but, as with the Klondike, civilization was creeping in, and although its progress did not manifest itself in quite the same way, whores being thick upon the ground from time immemorial and virgins two-a-penny anyhow, yet game laws began to be operative. It was time to move on and out.

Slavery in Africa

Chapter 5

For many years past, the subject of slavery in Africa has ceased to agitate the mind of Europeans. The infrequent references to it in the public press have, seemingly, failed to arouse much interest. To all intents and purposes slavery has ceased—in the mind of the ordinary man, at any rate. Just lately there has been a reawakening in this country's press to the actuality of a very considerable traffic in slaves.

This traffic is largely an internal one because the holding of the seacoasts by European powers with their hostile attitude toward slavery has made it more and more difficult to smuggle cargoes of human freight through the cordon of patrolling gunboats. Occasionally a dhow—an Arab sailing boat—gets through by a judicious use of the flags of nationalities other than that of the threatening gunboat. Sometimes a clean pair of heels may even be shown to the more obsolete of the anti-slavers, for dhows have beautiful lines below water, and with a monsoon on the quarter, a steamer must travel hard to stay with her, let alone catch her.

These dhows are of all sizes: from twenty to two hundred tons and with one or two masts. The rig for all sizes is lateen, with the yard on the longest side of the triangle. This yard was a never-failing source of wonder to me, for it is made up of many short lengths all lashed together in an apparently precarious manner with coconut fibre rope. The mast is short and rakes forward at a peculiar angle. There is no boom to the foot of the sail, and as that part of the one and only sail, which is forward of the mast, acts as our jibs do, a rather complicated manoeuvre is involved when the ship tacks.

All the gear is of the most homely description and, in our view, utterly unreliable. Even compasses are often home-made affairs. A fruit tin sometimes forms the casing. A pivot of rough soft iron is fixed about the centre of the bottom of the tin. On this point a magnetized, but equally rough piece of iron is slung, and to this is fixed quite a neat copy of our compass cards.

The card was divided into segments and covered with what might have been Arabic characters but looked more like Chinese to me. What they all meant rolled glibly enough off the skipper's tongue, but I suspect he had learnt them by heart and that he could no more read them than I could. Then a roughly fitting lid of ordinary window glass completes the instrument, except for the usual "medicine." In one that I examined, this consisted of a handful of black peppercorns—to "keep out the cold," I was told.

The building of these dhows is a work of art. Throughout the process no molds are used, nor, I believe, are any measurements taken. None is required, as one can see by looking at any dhow that is high and dry. All is true and fair, and this is arrived at by eye alone.

When I first saw the under-water body of a dhow, I was immediately struck with the general resemblance it bore in its lines to that of one of our crack racing schooners of the very latest fashion. The design of the dhow never varies, and probably it has not varied for centuries. The design is impressed upon generation after generation of dhow builders. I may be wrong, but the lines seemed to me to be the natural sweep the boards would themselves take most readily.

No saw mill sees these planks—they are adzed all over. No nail even is used. Plank is lashed to plank along the edges with tough grass . . . and how they leak! Sometimes throughout a voyage of several thousands of miles, baling with kerosene tins never ceases. And do those jolly mariners mind? Not a bit of it. Far worse things than leaks occur. Yards carry away, masts go overboard, rudders come off with a big following sea—and the mariners go into the sea and bring them on again.

More perfect seamen do not exist, for the reason that really good seamanship is required all day and every day to keep those wonderful craft from utter disintegration. The crews, too, are unique. Of discipline there appears to be none. Anyone steers—sitting on a chair by the wheel and taking part in any meals or conversation that may happen to be going. When land is sighted everyone argues about it. Should sail be made or taken off? There is a general argument about it. Yet the right thing is most frequently done, such thorough seamen are they. Their knowledge of the local currents is almost uncanny.

The number of slaves landed and sold in Arabia in one year must, I think, be small. A dhow-master who, by a clever coup, shipped a hundred native labourers as passengers at one East African port for transfer to another some seventy-five miles distant, and put straight out into the Indian Ocean and was never caught in spite of cables and gunboats is the exception that proves the rule, let us hope. His cargo must have brought him in a very considerable sum since male slaves in the Persian Gulf fetch by repute £40 a head. But, judging by my own experience of East African dhows, more than half the cargo must have died of thirst before reaching land, as a more happy-go-lucky, improvident lot of sea rovers can nowhere be found.

I was once on a steamer that stopped to a signal of distress from a becalmed dhow. A small boat approached us and demanded water. We filled their barrels and kerosene tins and lowered them into the boat. The painter was cast off and we steamed away while the well-laden boat made toward the dhow. I watched this boat through glasses and presently the occupants stopped rowing while still some distance from their ship. They then proceeded to wash themselves with the precious water, splashing it generously about.

Meanwhile the crew aboard the dhow seemed frantic with rage, judging by their gesticulations. Presently splashes could be seen about the little boat that could only have been caused by bullets fired from the dhow. Our rapidly increasing distance unfortunately prevented my seeing what reception the bathers got when alongside.

Slavery in Africa is not now a sea-borne traffic of any great extent, as I have endeavoured to show. It exists, however, pretty generally throughout Africa, in one form or another, in all the country north of the Zambezi to the Mediterranean. The Mohammedan tribes of the northern half of Africa are the greatest and best purchasers of slaves.

They are also the best owners of slaves—from the slaves' point of view. They work their slaves hard, but they treat them well. Slaves are here treated as members of the family. They are clothed, fed, and housed and have certain rights. A slave of exceptional ability may rise in life and may finally free himself. In any case, slave men usually become mated to slave women, and in most cases lead fairly comfortable lives.

I have questioned many such, and they have had little to complain of, except that they seemed not to like the loss of their children. When asked why they resented this, their natural affection for their children was never brought up as carrying any weight; it was always the business point of view that they stressed. A girl child brings in so much when married off—besides she works in the garden, fetches water and firewood, and helps with the brewing of beer, etc. A boy brings respect and "standing," and supports his father in his old age.

In such parts as these, the coming of the white man has brought with it a great intensifying of labour for the slave. Besides doing all his ordinary routine work of cultivating his master's gardens, cutting ditches, chopping wood, and drawing water, etc., he has now to answer the never-ending demands of the white administrators for porters, road-makers, or builders. His Mohammedan master, of course, does no manual labour. Any money the slave earns from the white man is taken to the master, and in many cases an almost inexplicable devotion is shown in this connection.

I remember once paying off some boys after three months' work and finding from their master that every penny had been taken to him. He had returned to them each about 1s. 4d., which act had filled these boys with astonishment at his generosity. Again, slave men will travel hundreds of miles away from their homes, take service as workers in mines and whatnot, and carry every penny so earned to their masters. Against this the master is obliged to find homes for them; he must feed them between employments; and it would be derogatory to his dignity to have them naked, so he clothes them.

Such a slave master as I have described above has but little chance of acquiring slaves by the old direct method of raiding. This can only be carried out in such places as Abyssinia, as the greater part of Africa is now under European administration. But he can still purchase slaves surreptitiously and in great secrecy from the traders who penetrate every part under the guise of peddlers of beads, elephant and giraffe hair, cloth, charms, onions, and other articles too numerous to mention. These petty traders may be met with not only in every town and village, but also in the most unfrequented parts of the wildest bush, beating their way past or round some white man's post by paths only known to themselves.

They may have with them or not, as the case may be, one or more quite inconspicuous boys or girls dressed in clothes such as theirs. In either case the passing white man knows nothing and can see nothing wrong. Should they have such a captive, they are probably hurrying north by the most unfrequented paths to sell him or her to some wealthy Fulani or Arab landowner. If we could retrace their steps southward, we might find that this child had sustained the loss of both parents and had been sold by some distant relative, or that a famine-stricken family had parted with one of its members in order to buy food.

A small slaving dhow.

In this case Fate may be considered to be kind to the slave. At the worst, a life of unceasing toil awaits a male captive, while a girl may be given by some great landowner to his daughter as part of her dowry on marriage. A life of comparative ease may in this case be her lot, punctuated by outbursts, accompanied by thrashings of severity governed by her mistress's temper. In the cannibal regions of Africa, and in those immediately adjoining them, a much more gruesome fate awaits orphans and stolen captives. There is every indication of a very considerable traffic existing in human livestock for the table in certain parts of Africa.

Here it may be necessary to explain how it is that I am in a position to make such a statement. For many years my occupation was the hunting of elephants, and it naturally took me to the wildest and most unfrequented and least administered parts of Africa. Living as I often did in the villages of people still wild, I had many more opportunities of observing the inmost workings of the African mind than any mere passer-through, or even stationary official, could ever hope to have. The native African attitude toward a white man who followed hunting as a profession made intercourse more open and intimacy easier than that reserved for any other, not excepting even missionaries. I have, for instance, been offered slaves—and that in a country where the white man's antipathy to slavery was well known.

I now find myself appalled by the difficulty of describing adequately to Europeans a condition of mind that may have existed among us many centuries ago, but which certainly finds no parallel with us to-day. It is difficult for us to place ourselves in the position of an African about to sell his child, distant relative, war captive, or stolen person. It is equally difficult to imagine ourselves the buyer of such goods, destined, maybe, for our table.

But it is quite impossible for us to conceive the state of mind of the victim. Here we stand face to face with a dark and blank wall. For, knowing their fate as they do, none of the emotions one would expect to meet exists. Girls put to fattening, fatten rapidly, play joyously, sleep well. They appear not to think of the time when the knife and cooking pot will end their life, or, if they do, it is that they may do credit to their owner by cutting up well at the feast. This attitude seems incredible, but there are many incredible things in Africa.

I know one tribe where the custom is that when a feast is ordered, two plump young girls are told to go to a certain haunted pool, to stand knee-deep in the water, and to await thus their fate. They are invariably "taken" by the

Waiting to be "taken" in the Devil's Pool.

spirit of the pool. None returns or has ever been known to return. Yet, they go, without force or escort, and, dressed in their finery, apparently willing victims. To hear them spoken of afterward one would suppose that some great honour had been done them. I am as certain as one can be without actually having seen it that the victims "taken" were killed and eaten by the cronies of the village.

Under some such disguise as the above is slavery still rampant in parts of Africa. Sometimes it is put down to a well-known leopard, but more generally to spirits. With every man, woman, and child, including the prospective victim, backing up such a system whole-heartedly, how can the direct-thoughted races hope to arrive at the truth of the matter? What kind of evidence could be brought forward? I have but faintly outlined the difficulties to be met when any commission of enquiry into slavery attempts to bring to light the tortuous windings of the African mind.

A much more straightforward state of slavery is met with in Abyssinia. Here captives of raiding expeditions are simply sold into bondage, comparatively few of them reaching the shores of the Red Sea, thanks to the anti-slavery patrols, which are chiefly British.

Geographically speaking, the great inland waterways of Africa provide the easiest and safest territory for slave traffic, especially where they form international boundaries. The Upper Nile and the Ubangi River may be specially mentioned in this connection.

As to remedies to be adopted for the suppression of slavery, it would almost seem necessary to have some kind of control of births and deaths in the villages. To begin with, the various states should register all orphans. It is very hard for Africans to resist the temptation to sell their distant relatives at any time, but when that relative is also an orphan, it becomes almost impossible to resist. But if that orphan's name were written down in a government book, that orphan's life would be safe even were the name forgotten or the book destroyed.

Hitherto the official attitude of the various powers concerned has been too lenient toward slavery. Some, if not all, have countenanced it in some form or other. Probably, the proposed commission of enquiry should be international in character and its recommendations carried out by all. Penalties have been light in the past for those caught slaving. Capital punishment, carried out, would quickly stop it.

THE MAGIC HILL OF DODOSI

CHAPTER 6

The incident I am about to tell is not only one of the vivid kind of things that linger always in the memory, but it is also one of the kind of things that we call luck. It is something the Africans regard as a manifest sign of the possession of "medicine." When a reputation for "medicine" in hunting has been thoroughly established, smooth and easy is the path of its happy possessor.

It happened in Karamojo, at our base camp in Dodosi. The site of the camp in itself was weird and full of the suggestion of "medicine." It nestled under a huge, smooth, rounded stone the size of a little mountain about four hundred feet high. It was quite without soil, but was the sleeping place of hundreds of enormous baboons. The Karamojan men wear the skin of the big dog baboons at dances; consequently, it is in great demand. Whenever I wanted to reward a native, I shot him a dog baboon. This pleased him and cost me little.

There dashed away a large bull elephant.

There was some peculiarity about the shape of this hill, for when I fired my rifle at one part of it, the report would be magnified a score of times and the echoes would return and cross and crash into each other in a most extraordinary way. When I fired from another part, the report would be immediately swallowed up or damped down so that it would be hardly audible a couple of hundred yards away. Round the base, this rock might have measured seven or eight hundred yards, and on one side of it there was a grove of trees. The villages occupied the other parts.

This is the incident as it appeared to native eyes:

The bwana (myself) went out in the evening—carrying his rifle, certainly, but with no cartridges. (They were in my trouser pocket.) Those men who wished to go with him were turned back. (I liked to be alone on these evening strolls.) Almost immediately (in reality about an hour), the bwana returned with a huge elephant tusk with fresh blood on it, carrying it himself on his shoulder like a *mnyamwezi* (porter). (True.) No man heard a shot fired, and yet two dead elephants were there, and they were warm and freshly killed. One of them had been killed with such strong "medicine" that its tusks could be pulled out. *Inshallah! Dhawa!* (By the grace of God, medicine!)

This is my version:

I went out for my evening stroll taking along my .275 and a few cartridges in my trouser pocket. These solitary strolls were what I loved best—one cannot really enjoy hunting except when alone.

The camp was surrounded with villages. Sleek kine stood around the milking fires. Lazy streamers of smoke quartered the cooling but still burnished firmament. In short, it was evening. I entered the grove of trees, recently the scene of the usual activities inseparable from proximity to villages.

Now for the stroke of luck. I circled the rock, came to the grove of trees, and was immediately conscious of the necessity for extreme caution. I stopped and listened and peered about. Do not forget, reader, that we were surrounded by villages, and that this grove of trees was used constantly by the natives. There could be no thought of big game in it unless, perhaps, a leopard, yet, here I was all strung up, listening for I knew not what, but aware of the presence of something.

Hearing nothing, I moved on, but with the very greatest caution. Just because I had seen no sign of them nor heard anything meant nothing because when an elephant wants to be secretive, he can be completely silent. When warding off flies with their ears, the stroke is arrested just short of the wall-like

A huge, smooth, rounded stone the size of a little mountain.

side, so there is no slap. They control their internal rumblings, too. In fact, the only noise they cannot control is the soft *plop* of falling dung.

I had seen no sign of them and would have laughed if anyone had suggested there being any there, yet I felt exactly as I always do when close to elephants. And so it was on this occasion. The muffled *plop, plop* is what gave the game away. I realized an elephant was not ten yards away from where I stood.

With my eyes boring into the tangled bush, I began that thrilling approach inch by inch until he was partially revealed. Absolutely motionless, he stood like a petrified rock. He, too, was aware of danger. Suddenly, in full panic-stricken flight, the large bull elephant made a dash from the thick stuff right in front of me. Crossing an opening in the bush, he fell flat in answer to the report of my rifle, without my having consciously aimed it.

It is always safe to assume that there will be more than one elephant in these games of hide and seek, so when there was a terrific crash and a huge upheaval of the bush to the left, I was ready. Away raced a great gray body festooned with trailing bush. Off went my rifle without any apparent volition on my part, and down went that crashing hurricane simultaneously with the report. Dead silence reigned once more.

It was miraculous enough, just to find two bull elephants hiding in what might be called the village latrine, and I was now seized with a kind of trembling. "Well, I'm damned!" I said as I hurried toward them. Not finding them immediately in the thick stuff, the suggestion that it was a dream came forward, to retire again on the sight of an elephant on his belly with his legs stretched back underneath him and his chin flat on the ground, stone dead.

Hurrying on, I soon found the other one. I was curious to know where I had hit him. Search as I would, I could not find the small hole. This is not as surprising as it may seem. A small bore makes such a tiny hole and the spongy hide closes it up so effectually that it almost completely hides it—but when the hit is at any angle approaching a right angle, there is a patch round the hole about an inch and a half from which the dried mud and dirt flies off on the impact of the bullet, leaving it slightly lighter in colour than the surrounding skin. In the centre of the light patch careful search and probing will usually show the tiny hole.

Returning to the first elephant, I had no difficulty in finding the bullet; it had been correctly placed in the brain. In walking round the animal's head I gripped the end of one tusk. It was loose. More mystery! Seizing the other, it was loose, too! Shaking it from side to side, I gave a pull. It came out about three inches. I got excited and soon had it right out of its socket. The other one came, too.

I had never seen the likes of this—it was my first running brain shot. The elephant, traveling about twenty-five miles per hour, had fallen with such force on its tusks as to burst asunder the enormously strong bone sockets that envelop the tusks for about a third of their total length. Usually it requires a lot of hard ax-work in the ordinary way before the tusks can be freed from them. But here I had in two minutes drawn them out by myself and without a tool of any kind.

It is inaccurate to say that the tusk socket bursts on these occasions. What really happens is the torque on the tusk, resulting from the impact to the ground, severs the ligaments holding the tusk in the socket, leaving only the rubber-like lip attachment.

This gave rise to an idea in my mind that an outsize pipe wrench might save the time and labour of chopping out the ivory. My idea did not work. The steel teeth on the face of the tool produced creeping on the ivory before anything gave. It is not so easy to overcome nature's highly specialized jobs.

I thought, *By Jove, this will astonish them in camp!*

Here was "medicine," indeed. With all the noise going on in camp, ten to one no one had heard the little pings of the 7mm. Gathering the two tails and carefully omitting the customary reloading of the magazine, I shouldered

The bwana returns to camp.

the freed tusk jauntily enough, only to find it infernally heavy. Short as the distance was, it appeared quite long enough with this load up.

On nearing camp, I tried to assume as easy and indifferent an air as I could. I entered through a dense throng of natives and carriers, who poured from the camp to see the strange sight of the white man carrying a load. I was helped in this, no doubt, by the difference in my colour that makes it more difficult for the boys and natives to detect expression.

My entry was made in deep silence. No one had heard a shot. They did not even offer to take the tusk. Throwing off my burden as if it weighed seven pounds instead of seventy, I unloaded my magazine. You have to be a showman on these occasions, and I will not swear that I did not pretend to unload five rounds from that magazine. "Medicine" was about.

Only Pyjalé smiled his inscrutable smile.

If you want to really scare your following stiff with awe, go out by yourself, kill an elephant, and bring back a tusk all unbeknownst to and unaided by any assistance!

AFRICAN "MEDICINE" AND MARVELOUS SHOOTING

CHAPTER 7

In my time it was my chief aim to find new hunting grounds. The chance of doing so led me ever toward parts that had been avoided for some reason or other. Perhaps waterless desert made access difficult for carrier-borne safaris. Or maybe extensive swamps or pathless forest seemed to form the barrier. All these could be overcome by a little determination and organization.

The greatest barrier of all was a psychological one: The desired country lay in the possession of evil, bad people who killed every stranger appearing on their borders. These reputations became so firmly established in the minds of men and grew to such fantastic proportions that it became a major problem to get guides to enter these isolated countries. Then, too, your Africans had to have an unbounded faith in their leader before they would even contemplate placing themselves in the power of these wicked, savage tribes. There was always a lot of bad "medicine" mixed up in these palavers, and this element had to be countered by something that would induce confidence among one's following.

It is widely and astutely held by the wily African that the white man does not possess that magic quality loosely described as "medicine." There you are—we don't even have a name for it. We may split the atom, fly at 1,200 m.p.h., cure diseases, or do any of many other wonderful things, but we just do not have "medicine." That being the case, what can one do to repair this grave omission in the make-up of a would-be penetrator of myth-guarded territories?

The one thing that impresses your primitive more than anything else, and is at the same time easily available to the ordinary white man, is to cause instantaneous death. The trained and accurate use of firearms can almost be as great an ascendancy over the mind of primitives as that of the most potent magic monger. If such demonstrations could be carried out on humans, I have little doubt they would leave far behind anything the greatest of their fraternity could produce, especially so if the "medicine" man himself were made the victim.

Thus, at one fell swoop would his most effective bluff be called—that of being able to neutralize a bullet's lethal qualities.

Given how things are, the safari leader is in the first place, or was, compelled to seek other means of impressing himself on his own following. He had, in other words, to develop his own "medicine." Being an accurate shot was one way of doing this. The hits must be consistent for the shooter to seem infallible, and only hits in the right place in the brain or better still the neck of large seemingly dangerous game could do this. However good a shot you might be, leave nothing to chance. To do this, I would say to go in as close as you can before you shoot. A Mauser 10-shot machine pistol is a very telling show weapon.

The humble pocket pistol firing the .22 short can produce astonishment and dismay when properly used. So can a .22 LR. You can choose your own moment, and this fact ought to eliminate all chance of a flop. Try strolling out with a tiny .22 loaded with shorts—it will kill the biggest bull you are likely to have—and suddenly and quietly drop it dead at your feet and then stroll quietly on. The huge animal so full of power one instant, so inert the next, all done with so little show of force. One must have an audience, of course. Observe the result on primitives. You may not have "medicine," but you have a very good substitute.

In excuse I will only plead that nothing stands between as instant massacre at the hands of thousands of undisciplined savages but those little fire-tubes, the 7mm and the .303. I will admit willingly and warmly my admiration for these products of the human brain. Never in history were such efficient mechanisms placed at man's disposal as are those connected with killing.

So deadly and efficient are they that most people tend to think they will do the job alone, that training is unnecessary. This, of course, is the greatest fallacy. It is only hits that count, and that is why only an intelligent person can ever reach the ultimate in rifle fire. I will give an instance where a well-aimed, or rather accurately sighted rifle, brought a whole war to instant end. This is, indeed, "medicine."

My great friend M. had newly arrived to open up the administration of what had hitherto been a closed country with an evil reputation that was shunned by traders and travelers alike. Some murdering had been traced to this tribe and M. asked me to come with him. The natives were of that awkward type that shoot poisoned arrows at you from dense thickets where you have no chance at all. Fortunately, they were also ignorant of the range of a modern rifle.

The densely wooded heights, some of them wreathed in mist, frowned down on us from all sides as we followed a tiny path into the recesses of the jungle. I carried a rifle that had newly arrived from Dan Fraser. It was only a .303 military-type affair, but what a difference Fraser had made. His magic touch had transformed it into a light, snaky-feeling live thing. It was a pleasure to carry and a joy to shoot. I forget now why I had asked him to sight it in to eight hundred yards, but so it was. I think it was for ostrich.

Our way took us through the worst country imaginable. Presently in traversing the slope of a hill, a momentary view was afforded us across a deep ravine, a land-slide of the opposing densely forest-clad heights surrounding us. On one of these wooded bluffs there was a sheer, precipitous rock-face unadorned by vegetation. And on the top of the rock was a seated figure of a native, quite out in the open, while behind him on the edge of the forest could be seen a throng.

We paused to watch. As we did so the single figure rose and started some magic palaver. His gesticulations seemed to indicate his intense dislike of us and a strong desire to knock our heads off.

It is always difficult to judge the distance over steep hill-sides across mountainous gorges, and I had not the remotest idea how far that rampaging figure might be. I imagined, however, the curve that a 215-grain, 2,000 f.p.s. bullet would require in order to drop the target, and finding it coincided pretty well with the 800-yard sight, I sent a tiny envoy on its way, a message from civilization to barbarism. The little thing, so charged with energy yet so insignificant looking, had to traverse the purple-shadowed ravine, and I could

M'Sanya bow and poisoned arrow: The poisoned part is carried separately from the shank and carefully wrapped in buckskin.

distinctly see its loom as it sped on its way. Sure and true it landed on the dot, and down the rock face slithered the medicine man. "Magically," the screened throng vanished.

That night over the camp fire, M. asked me in a wondering kind of way, "Why did you fire that shot, Bell? You had nothing against that man."

"You'll see," I said.

He did. That shot finished the war. Although they had had a few minor successes in plugging arrows into our carriers—one man died in three minutes and yet was only scratched by an arrow—they came in to submit.

******

The real aim and object of all these accounts of marvelous shooting is this: I want to impress on all concerned the vital necessity of developing the soldier's rifle into what my hunting rifles were—a pleasure to carry and a joy to shoot—instead of remaining as they do, a burden to hump and a trial to shoot.

Just look at our .303 for example. What a lumbering piece of unimaginative junk. And its latest model is not even as good as some of its former ones. The only pleasure from carrying its unbalanced log-like carcass is the knowledge that in spite of its dead corpse-like feel, it will still shoot straight enough.

Much the same applies to the Garand, although here there has been some attempt to make it look like a gun, but still it feels like nothing on earth. A mule might suffer it, but to a trained rifleman it is an eyesore to look at and a canker to carry. These remarks apply even more so to the firearms of all the powers. If in doubt, take a look at any collection of the military arms of the world.

The cartridge, on the other hand, has become an artistic and beautiful creation. Here are signs of great thought and research. It is as if once the rifled barrel had been perfected, all endeavour then turned to perfecting the cartridge. No thought has been given to the miserable carrier of the piece. Everything—except the rifled barrel, the reloading mechanism, and the cartridge—has apparently been regarded much as the packing of a parcel might be regarded in a shop. Most shops, however, would be horrified by such an untidy job.

As far as my limited reading of history goes, no great war leader has devoted any thought to this problem. They have always been obsessed with new things like tanks, aeroplanes, gas, new tactical manoeuvres, surprise, and smart-alecky stuff of every conceivable sort. They have been quite oblivious of the opportunity that lay under their noses: the conversion of the humble infantryman from a disgruntled, tired, depressed carrier of a hated burden to a live, eager, confident killer. Even Frederick of Prussia, bouncing around Central Europe with his bottle of poison in his waistcoat pocket and with his urgent need, was only concerned with increasing the rate of fire of his infantry. This neglect of the rifle is all the more surprising when it is remembered that one-tenth of one percent increase in killing power of one rifle is automatically reproduced in all the others; thus, the effect would run to millions.

After a lifetime of making my way by rifle, I would say that the first requisite in a rifle is that it should be pleasant to handle. It must be light. No one goes out for a walk with a nine-pound walking stick. It must be pleasant to carry in one hand. It must be shapely. Having been built on these two attributes, the rifle will come alive. It will be a pleasure to point at everything that moves. It must be a joy to shoot.

When a man is at his lowest ebb, with his vital spark almost extinguished, it is ridiculous and stupid to say to him, "Fire that magnificent rifle of yours. It delivers so many foot pounds of energy and will surely flatten your enemy." In the estimation of the cowering figure in the fox hole, it is much more likely to extinguish the last flicker of his own feeble light. The fact is that those responsible for the present monstrous weapons never take any part in these doings, or, if they do, they are so full of corn as to be able to carry it off with a great air.

Once the weapon has become "a pleasure to handle and a joy to shoot," training should commence, but not until then. Much of the desired result will accrue from these two attributes. I have no experience in training others for war, but I can claim to have trained myself to be a first-class killer, not only of game but of armed equals on the few occasions it has been my lot to encounter them. I will, therefore, recount how I arrived at this result.

I was endowed with a very moderate, rather mediocre sort of physique, neither one thing nor the other. Easily upset by hard liquor if taken in quantity, I, in my self-adopted role of trained killer, early adopted a habit of abstemiousness when on the hunt. Between hunts was another matter. I was not endowed with outstandingly good eyesight; mine are merely good, average eyes. I was not even very enduring in spite of the fact that I have walked some seventy-thousand miles on foot after game pointing to the contrary. Excessive fatigue always prevented sleep, and that is a great handicap. I was of a rather nervous disposition, too, and that brought its awkward moments. I was never what is called "a good natural shot." I was rather a timid sort of person, and, lastly, I had poor digestion.

All that bundle of disabilities formed no mean barrier to my becoming a first-rate killer; it will hardly be denied. To take the last one—poor digestion—first: This I overcame by living much as the natives did—on milk and meat. My timidity I overcame by acquiring confidence in my capacity to kill whatever I wanted to, instantly. I acquired this confidence by constant and unremitting practice. The same practice made me willy-nilly what is called a "good shot."

To do this, I lived with a rifle in my hands—not slung round my body. At all times I was playing with it, dry shooting it at anything. Even at night after a terrific hunt I would sit relaxed by the camp fire, throwing my rifle from one hand to the other, doing arm exercises with it, aiming it with one hand—it was a never-ceasing exercise of some muscle or other. It may have appeared crazy, and probably did, but it gave me the necessary confidence to tackle anything, and the assurance that, should it be required, I had at my disposal a swift, sure, and deadly answer to any threat.

That is what I call training. It brings with it in time a sort of automatic centralization of fire that is extremely deadly, and that does not desert one even in moments of extreme terror. It is only when such tests have been successfully passed that the hunter feels that surge of "exultant joy" Selous speaks of that comes as a reward for ceaseless training.

If a very ordinary individual like myself can become a deadly machine-like killer through training, why should an army of a million men not become an army of a million killers? Think what that would mean. It would be physically impossible to live in opposition to it. Our only superiority over the barbarous hordes coming along is in intelligence; let us use it to become trained killers.

It can be done, I feel convinced, but not on present lines nor with present equipment. The rifle must be "a pleasure to handle." (It cannot be more than six pounds, better still five and a half.) It must be "snaky" and feel alive; it must be slim and good-looking. I had the thing once; it was a creation of Dan Fraser's. He worked over a .256 Mannlicher-Schöenauer and refined it down to five-and-a-quarter pounds empty. It was "a pleasure to handle" all right, and when I killed twelve large bull elephants with twelve consecutive shots, and shot a young guinea fowl's head off for supper, it certainly was "a joy to shoot." Just imagine what could be done now.

A rifled steel liner in a duralumin tube would take care of the barrel weight and parcel stiffness. There is no necessity to marry wood to metal. They will never pull together, but always contrariwise.

Finally make it a joy to shoot by using a cartridge that does not beat the last remaining flicker out of its firer but rather snuffs out that of his opponent. Look at and approach the problem from the user's point of view instead of from that of the armchair-seated, well-stuffed-bellied, high-up brass, as hitherto has been the case.

Thus only could a body of killers be created.

Hunting on the Islands of the Ubangi River

Chapter 8

Never in my long experience of African hunting was I so surrounded by elephants and yet so reluctant to hunt them as when I had a floating home on the Ubangi. This extraordinary reluctance or laziness I put down to the excessive luxuriousness of my travel and living arrangements. Steam spoiled me for hard work by enabling me to carry an abundance of good food and to sit in a long chair while traveling. How I came to acquire a steamboat I will now relate.

I was traveling by the regular river steamer from Brazzaville to Bangui when, at one of the wooding stations, we stopped to load up with wood for fuel. To pass the time I borrowed a canoe from the captain and paddled across with my boy and a rifle to a large island lying near the opposite bank. We landed on a delightful sand bank at the up-stream end of the island. At the edge of the sand, the forest stood like a green wall into which you plunged from brightest sunshine into cool twilight. I thought I might get a bush buck for the pot in the forest glades, so, tying up the canoe, we entered.

Almost immediately there was a commotion among the monkeys—rustlings and chattering with an occasional crash as some heavy monkey landed on a branch after a spring of twenty or thirty feet. The underbrush was intersected everywhere

Islands on the Ubangi River.

by game paths, most of which showed hippo tracks besides bush pig and small buck tracks. It was the dry season, and tracks were difficult to recognize.

After some miles of cautious prowling and peering without seeing anything in the way of meat for the pot, we turned to search another stretch of bush on the way back to the canoe. I redoubled my caution, for I felt pretty certain that there was game about. I have often had this feeling when near game, and have often been astonished that the natives with me don't have it. Now I stopped every few paces and gently put aside the screen of underbrush, expecting to see any moment some wily forest animal equally intent on listening. In this sort of still-hunting, ears are of greater value than eyes. It is intensely exciting for anyone with a vestige of imagination, for at any moment a leopard, bush pig, rare antelope, or even sleeping hippo may be met with.

Presently, what I took to be monkey rustling was heard ahead of us and low down. I crept silently toward the sounds, parted some evergreen underbrush, and stood face to face with a large bull elephant. His trunk was about eight paces distant from me and he was listening intently. With his head motionless and directly facing me, he presented an easy frontal brain shot, and my 7mm bullet brought him down instantaneously. He had nice tusks of sixty pounds apiece.

It now began to dawn on me that the maze of game paths we had seen were not hippo paths at all. They were elephant paths. But I did not yet realize that the bush was full of elephants. So, after cutting off the tail of our elephant, we started noisily to blaze our trail back to the canoe so that we should have no difficulty in finding our dead elephant when we came for him.

While busily blazing our way along, we must have startled another elephant, for the boys on the steamer saw a large one appear suddenly on the sand bank, step swiftly across it, and disappear again into the forest a few seconds before we emerged on to the bank. We soon reached the ship, where my elephant tail created great excitement among the passengers.

Although the wooding of the steamer was finished, I easily persuaded the captain to delay his departure. I promised him the meat of the elephant for his crew—provided they cut out the ivory. He agreed readily to this as meat of any sort in that country is difficult to come by. I soon had a steel boat full of boys to help me.

On revisiting the island, we again ran into hiding elephant in spite of the noise made by the gang of boys. I did not shoot as we only caught a fleeting glimpse of them disappearing, and besides, I knew that the captain would not wait while we handled another elephant. I determined to revisit these islands some day and to hunt them properly. The natives from the opposite bank who came to the dead elephant for meat confirmed what I had already in my head. They said that all the large islands were full of elephants at a certain season, and that only bulls visited them. It was this experience that determined me to purchase a small river steamer of my own.

Specially designed with a very powerful rudder, she was of shallow draught, drawing 1 foot, 3 inches loaded, and had her propeller running in a tunnel. The engine was a minute, triple-expansion set running in an oil bath. The boiler was a water tube of very light construction, and yet worked at a pressure of 250

Face to face with a large bull elephant.

pounds. She had a very efficient condenser, and was altogether the finest little power plant I had ever seen. For fuel she cost practically nothing. Stopping as we did to camp about 4 P.M., two or three boys were sufficient to collect enough firewood for the next day's steaming.

Green wood could be burned with the aid of forced draught supplied by a fan belt driven from the engine. The stoking, while under way, was done by any boy who was awake. He sat by the boiler and every now and then put in a stick or two. The little engine was practically noiseless and quite vibrationless. She ran at 1,000 r.p.m. when all out. The hull was of galvanized steel and built in sections. She was, of course, specially built for the job and cost a very pretty penny in the first place, but a prettier penny still before I got her to the hunting grounds.

In order that I might have a quite lavish accommodation afloat, I constructed a catamaran with two specially chosen and matched native dug-outs. They were twice the length of the little launch and were attached rigidly together right forward and again about amidships. They were the width of the launch apart, and the forward portion was completely decked in. Over this deck a sun-awning was built. The two native canoe hulls were decked in completely with canvas and was properly stayed.

At the after-end of the catamaran was a movable distance-piece of wood that came just abaft the stern of the launch when she was in between the two canoe hulls, ready to push the floating house wherever we might wish to go. On tying up anywhere, the launch could be cast off, the distance-piece raised, and the launch would then steam out astern, ready for any small hunting expedition up the side creeks.

Upon the house boat itself there was ample accommodation right forward for my camp bed, mosquito net, a table, and long chair, while further aft a clay bed for the kitchen fire was made. Here cooking was more or less continually in progress. Altogether, the thing was practical, economical, and comfortable to a degree I had never experienced before. I have forgotten to mention that when under way the current of air caused by our speed was sufficient not only to be comfortably cool, but also to keep down to a great extent those biting pests, the tsetse and other stinging flies.

On the Ubangi there are many bad rapids, especially above the town of Bangui. To pass these it was generally necessary to haul up the catamaran

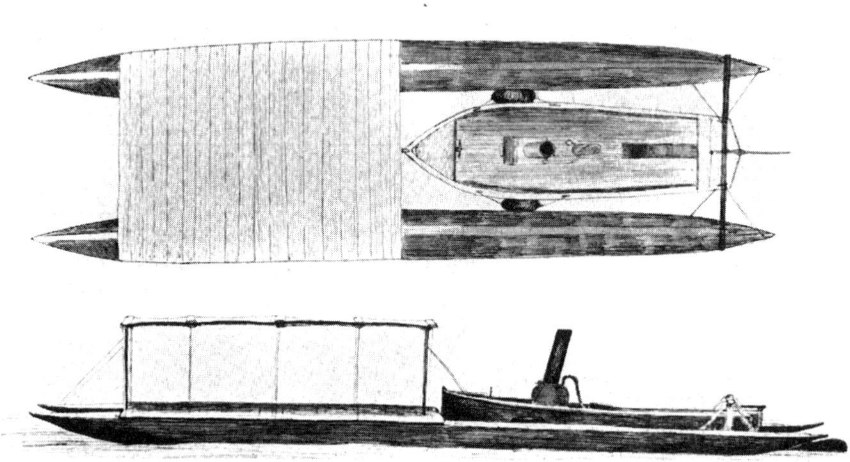

Bird's-eye and side views of the catamaran.

and launch separately by long chains. Native help could always be obtained, for which they were rewarded with smoked meat, of which we always carried a quantity. Descending rapids when the river was high was easy as the rocks would then be well covered, but it was also rather alarming owing to the whirlpools and breaking water at the tail of the races.

The whole contraption would come steaming down a steep shoot at a terrific speed and almost dive under on meeting the boiling mass of water at the end. Sometimes one could look right down into the centre of the whirling mass of brown water as the long canoes bridged the horrible thing. The boat heaved and lurched from side to side, and I was always thankful when we got through. There would be no chance for even the strongest swimmer. With the launch alone in such big, strong water and with her rather high weights in the boiler, the motions were sometimes positively alarming. When looking at such water from the bank above, the great swirling hollows and bulges are not apparent; it is only when in among them and with a great boiling mass rising feet above one's gunwale that they are properly realized.

Frequently we towed behind us an unladen Canadian canoe, and when passing through bad water I noticed that it was not at all disturbed by the under-tows and the upburstings of the agitated river. So I determined to try it alone through a really bad place. It was perfection. It glided smoothly along with a delightful easy motion. Its small immersion gave to the water-devils—as the natives call whirlpools and up-bursts—no hold at all.

When descending rapids in the dry season, I tried a new method. At this season, rocks stick up everywhere, and if the ordinary method of steaming down-stream faster than the current is employed, a frightful crash and corresponding damage to the hull is sooner or later bound to occur. My method was to turn the bow up-stream at the head of the rapid and to drift slowly down stern first while steaming against the current. This method allowed for splendid steering, and if contact with rocks could not be avoided, it was made so gently as to avoid all damage. By carefully governing the steam throttle, perfect marvels of navigation were performed. Sometimes the craft was brought straight across a rapid to another opening among the rocks and there gently lowered between them by slightly cutting off the steam. In this way quite dangerous water came to be passed successfully. I have often wondered why river steamers do not employ this method.

Ubangi rapids.

On one occasion we came to the foot of a bad rapid where we meant to camp before chaining the outfit upon the morrow. As we came in sight of our sand bank, we saw that a river steamer was tied up to it. On drawing near, we saw great activity, and it became evident that she was down by the stern. All hands were unloading the enormously valuable cargo of ivory and rubber to the sand bank. Tons of elephant tusks were already piled on the sand bank, and I was told that the vine rubber would go for eighteen francs a kilo—and there were baskets and baskets of this stuff.

The crew said that a rock had been struck during the mad descent and a plate knocked out. The sand bank had evidently been reached just in time to prevent the ship from foundering in the deep and boiling pools at the foot of the rapid. I noticed that the ship was powerfully stayed to trees and rocks with wire hawsers. I noticed all this before we passed on to a camping site higher up.

I naturally supposed that the steamer would be repaired, the cargo reshipped, and the voyage continued. I was, therefore, astonished in the morning to see the steamer had vanished. In answer to enquiries, the crew said that she had slipped off into deep water at the end of the rapid in the night. They said that both steamer and cargo were a complete loss. Looking around for broken hawsers, etc., I could see nothing. I thought it very funny indeed, but it was none of my business, and I passed on. Sometime later I happened on an announcement of the total loss of this steamer and its cargo. The statement declared that the whole had been underwritten by English insurance firms. I have often wondered how insurance companies investigate these types of claims when they happen in places like this and whether they pay out for such losses.

******

Some queer tribes inhabit the banks of the Ubangi. The Banziri live entirely by fishing and canoe transport. They are an immoral lot, too, for they make a practice of temporarily selling their girls to the highest bidder, after which the girl returns to her tribe and marries. The girls themselves seem rather to look forward to this temporary freedom. There is also a certain amount of traffic in slaves from one bank to the other.

As regards the sport on this river, this is not of a very high order as far as variety goes—that is, for an African river. Elephants are the chief game animals, inhabiting both the dense forest-clad banks and also the high elephant-grass country. On some of the larger islands, buffaloes are met with, as well as elephants, bongos, and bush pigs. Being otherwise deserted, they are delightful spots in the dry season.

As the islands are long and narrow, I conceived the idea of driving elephants, and I determined to try it. With this purpose in view, I visited a group of native villages, and, after the usual talking and palavering, I got together a fine lot of young men and boys. They tried hard to persuade me to let them have a rifle or two, as they said the elephants were very bad in the islands. I thought it better, at first, not to give them one, although eventually I was compelled to do so.

After loading up the catamaran with forty-odd beaters, we pushed off for one of the largest islands. Other natives followed in their dugouts. The island we proposed to try was about fifteen miles long, but only half a mile wide at the narrowest part. My plan was to land the beaters at the end nearest to us, steam down a few miles to a narrow part where the bush was less heavy, and then station myself in as clear a position as possible. I was not very hopeful of any elephant coming to the rifle at first, as natives new to driving are always too noisy, and the cunning old elephant almost always breaks back through them, sometimes with such suddenness and violence as to demoralize the natives completely. Leaving two of my boys to superintend the drive, I steamed off amid a burst of applause as our boiler blew off steam.

Having the stream with us, I soon reached the narrow part of the island and landed. It was barely four hundred yards across, but rather thicker bush than was desirable. Only in one place was there a break in the forest, and here there was a lot of rather high underbrush. This meant that only a very fleeting glimpse of passing elephants would be had, even if any came directly within one's view, which extended perhaps thirty yards on either hand. This meant that numbers of elephants might steal quietly by without the rifle being aware of more than a slight rustling.

Choosing as good a stance as the surroundings afforded after dropping the launch down-stream a bit and after banking the fire and threatening everyone if any noises were made, I took my position. I sent a boy up a tree that looked as if it gave a fairly extended view; he was to assist me by pointing out the direction of any approaching elephants he might "spot." That might give me time to get more directly in his path should the elephant happen to be off to one side of my position. One need never enter into long and complicated explanations with Africans on hunting matters; they seem to do the right thing instinctively. We then proceeded to wait and listen, although the beaters were still a long way off.

When elephants come at all, they seem bound to come unexpectedly, and one must be always prepared even at the most unlikely moments. It was this that taught me to carry my own rifle and cartridges—always. Now, while waiting, I was keenly alive to the slightest rustling, but the same could not be said for my boy. He was in the tree busily digging for a thorn or a jigger in his foot with a large knife as he sat on a bough forty feet up.

Almost at once a rustling could be heard in front and to one side. I watched the boy while listening hard. No one without previous experience of this game would have connected the slight gentle noises with so ponderous

Driven elephant.

an animal as an elephant. The boy looked toward the sound, craned forward, altered his position, turned, looked down at me, and silently pointed. No other sign was necessary. I stole as swiftly and silently as I could so as to intercept the approaching elephant. After going perhaps a hundred yards, I stopped to listen. Not a sound. The elephant was listening, too, maybe within twenty yards of me.

Here the bush was very thick, indeed. Was the elephant listening for me or for the sounds of the beaters that were probably caught by his huge sound-collecting ears, although quite inaudible to ours? If he were listening to me and I moved, he would be off. The hunter's god was directing me, for I never moved. The wait seemed interminable. I could not see my boy in the tree. At last I heard a sound and saw a movement in the bush, and there emerged the low-held forehead of a large bull elephant pushing his way straight toward me only a few paces distant, but so uncannily quiet.

I fired on the instant, keeping well above the eyes, eight or nine inches higher than would be correct if the head had been in a more usual position. With the echo of the shot, that huge animal lay motionless except for the leg-tremors, which indicated that the brain had been reached.

Hoping that the sound of the shot from my 7mm would have been swallowed up in the heavy forest and prevented by it from reaching any other approaching elephants, I took up my stance again. We waited and waited. The boy was now all attention. Every time a monkey moved, we felt certain it was another elephant. Nothing showed up except some bush pigs. They made more row than ten elephants.

After some time I began to wonder why no sounds from the beaters could be heard. *Could it be possible,* I thought, *that these people were ideal beaters and knew the game so well?*

Presently I heard a call from the direction of the steamer and went over to it, looking diligently for signs of any elephants having passed between us and the bank of the river. At one place I thought some tracks I saw were mighty fresh, and, sure enough, the people on the launch had actually seen an elephant glide by quite close to them.

At the launch I met the two boys I had left with the beaters. They explained that they had instructed the beaters to go as quietly as possible and that they had done so until someone had seen an elephant. This man had then started

His head and trunk came swirling violently through the branches just above.

to shout, and then everyone became excited, with the result that some part of the line had become entangled with elephants breaking back. Panic had seized the beaters, and they called off the beat and returned to the banks where their canoes were tied up. Elephants cannot be driven except by stealthily allowing them to think that they are undiscovered and escaping from people unaware of their presence. They had not heard my shot. We withdrew and camped on an island some way off so as not to disturb the elephant island.

On the following day I cast off the launch and tied up our floating home at a point only a few yards from the dead elephant of the previous day. Here I set the boys to cutting creeper ropes so that we could surround the dead elephant with a kind of rough fence. This was necessary in order to prevent the natives from rushing the pile of meat before they had carried out a drive on the other part of the island—a drive I hoped to induce them to do by the sight of and the promise of the dead elephant. I then steamed up to their villages with the launch alone.

After choosing about twenty of the stoutest-looking men, I explained what had happened yesterday. I described how some of their youngsters had spoiled the whole thing by getting frightened, and how I would send a couple of rifles along with them the next time. At first they were not a bit anxious to come. They did not yet know that I had already killed an elephant, for I wished, if possible, to bring off the drive before telling them. However, it was necessary to tell them after all. The news settled it, and I soon had some on board and others in canoes alongside.

Rapidly we got under way and headed down-stream for the lower end of the island. Soon we had to slow down as there was fear of filling the canoes with water from our bow wave. We had a good current with us, so we were not long in covering the length of the island.

At the starting point of the drive I impressed upon the beaters the urgent necessity for silence. I tried to explain that no more noise was necessary than they made on any ordinary traveling through the bush. They could keep in touch with each other in ordinary tones, and above all they were to go slowly and not shout when they saw anything move. I armed my two boys, one with a .22 rook rifle and the other with a spare 7mm. They had orders only to fire in the event the elephants began breaking back.

Leaving them, I boarded the launch, and with a full head of steam we flew along up-stream almost as fast as we had come down, for we hugged the backwaters in under the banks, which our shallow draught and lack of awnings allowed us to do. Only occasionally our smoke-stack fouled the over-hanging branches.

Reaching our objective—the narrow part of the island—I took up my position just as on the previous day, except that I put two boys in trees this time, but I had some difficulty in finding a position from which I could see both at the same time.

In a short time the boy on my right signaled an approaching elephant. I ran to intercept the elephant, but I was too late to get a shot. All I saw was

Standing brain shot: first position.

Standing brain shot: second position.

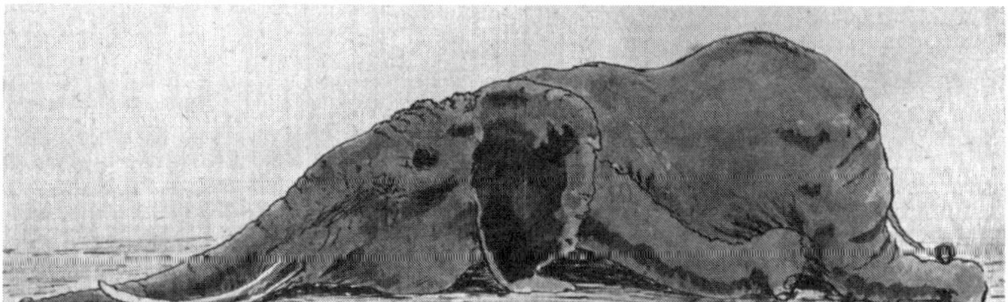

After the running brain shot.

a shadowy stern momentarily as the bush closed behind it. I was tempted to follow it, but luckily I did not, for as soon as I had reached my position again, I saw from the excited way in which the other boy was pointing that more elephants were about. I made my way where he indicated and ran almost into a huge bull standing motionless and listening. His head was very much obscured by branches, making a certain shot very doubtful. I began to step sideways while facing him and at the ready, for he was barely ten yards away. I grasped in these few seconds that I was face to face with a real monster.

His grizzly and mossy-looking head was so massive as to make his huge tusks look quite ordinary. Barely had I put foot to ground when he was upon me. I had been looking for this very move on his part and thought I was prepared for it, and yet, he was, as I say, almost upon me before my feeble little rifle went off in his face. I missed the brain—by a foot or so.

The monster trod down a fair-size tree, which pushed me violently aside as it fell. That tree moved me quicker out of the way than I could have moved myself. This was fortunate because when you trust to your rifle, as I did in those days, and for any reason the shot does not come off, you are very liable to find yourself in a mess. I came violently against something, still facing the elephant, and I saw that only the top of his back was visible over the branches of the prostrated tree.

He was listening again, and as I moved to get another shot, his head and trunk came swishing violently through the branches just above me. I let fly a very hurried shot, well below the eye. I found afterward this was at the correct angle, for down he came almost beside me.

I felt intense relief, for if this shot had not come off, I would have become quite demoralized. No one who has not experienced it can imagine the lightning speed and force of these old gentry of the forest. In open country, elephants are quite at the mercy of the rifle, but in the stuff I am describing, the chances are sometimes uncomfortably equal.

I was proud of my last shot, and I soon found excuses for my previous miss by explaining—to my own satisfaction, at least—that I had been obliged to poke my rifle at him through the intervening branches. I was also pleased with my success because it was a shot at the brain from an unusual angle—thank goodness! There had been no time to calculate where to hit him, and I had shot for the brain without regard to the position of the leading marks of the exterior—a thing I have always tried to do, but not always with success.

This little mêlée had, of course, rather disturbed the forest. But it did not last long, and I realized the beaters must still be a long way off. They did not, in fact, hear either of the shots—but the elephants must have heard them, for no more came our way. Some of the elephants probably passed us at some distance, for the island was about three-quarters of a mile broad at that point.

However, I was quite pleased with the tusks—they weighed 121 pounds and 116 pounds respectively, besides being of enormous girth. They were later classed by an expert as being wide enough for a good carving of the Crucifixion to be made from the solid section; this fact, according to trade circles, gives very thick tusks a peculiar value in Roman Catholic countries.

I turned the meat over to the natives, of course, and there were soon the usual lively scenes. All were delighted with our first drive and promised to assist again whenever I wanted them.

Later I intended to cut some sort of clearings through some of the islands, but the war broke out and prevented this scheme from maturing.

In the thick forest country I have been describing, the brain shot is the most satisfactory. Sometimes, when a motionless elephant is killed instantaneously, it drops its behind but remains erect in front for some seconds. It may then come to its front knees or topple over sideways. This is satisfactory enough to the hunter, but the shot that really elates is the brain shot on a fast-running elephant. Down he comes crash—sometimes with such force as to loosen his tusks in their sockets.

ABYSSINIA

CHAPTER 9

It was 1908, and Harry Rayne and I found ourselves in Addis Ababa. This was in the good, old days when the world thought Abyssinia was full of gold. After entering the port of Djibouti on the Red Sea, a ramshackle railway had conveyed us to the Abyssinian boundary. Thereafter, we had trekked by mule and camel to Addis Ababa, the capital, which stands at an elevation of about 10,000 feet above sea level. To penetrate farther west, we were told it would be necessary to get a permit from the emperor.

To acquire this important pass, one had to approach one's country's minister in due and humble form, for only thus could permission to traverse the hinterland be obtained for nothing. To get it in any other way would have meant the oiling of many palms and considerable delay. Apparently in these diplomatic matters one's financial standing is all important. Luckily we carried a letter to the local banker, so all was well.

At that time the negus, or emperor, was Menelik II, a very big man, indeed. After his success against the Italians at the Battle of Adowa, he was firmly established on his throne. He wielded absolute power and was greatly courted by all the powers then striving for trade with his kingdom. This rivalry led them to amusing and sometimes ludicrous lengths. The custom of the country demanded that any man with pretensions to social standing should surround himself with all the pomp he could possibly manage; consequently, you saw some of the funniest sights imaginable. Whenever any of these important personages issued forth from his legation, he did so with the most numerous and the most showily dressed escort he could possibly muster.

Most of the European powers contented themselves with military escorts dressed in their most showy and striking regimental regalia, including cocks' feathers for the Italians, skull and cross bones for the Germans, and so on. The French were very picturesque in their enormously baggy pants and tight upperworks, and the British were content with the khaki-clad Bengal Lancers, looking very well with their pennant-bedecked lances. Of course, all were mounted; only slaves or elephant hunters ever walked on foot in Abyssinia.

When it came to the representatives of large trading interests, it was a different matter. They had nothing cut and dried to fall back on, so something had to be invented. For example, an Englishman representing the London firm who had largely financed the Djibouti to Dire-Dawa railway blew into our camp one day for a drink and a chat. He was surrounded and followed by a body of Abyssinian horsemen dressed in gray bowler hats with curved swords sticking out behind. Riding with extremely short stirrups, through which only the big toe is put as is the national custom, they looked so like monkeys that Harry and I could not help roaring with laughter. Matthews, who was a grand fellow, laughed too and explained the necessity for all this show.

"But why the bowler hats?" we asked.

"Well," he said, "what would you have? Toppers? They would not stay on unless individually fitted. And besides you must look at it through native eyes. They see from papers and from visits to European towns that the bowler is a ceremonial headgear of the white man. Although not a strictly military hat, yet it carries an air of respectability, a standing of its own."

Having so ably defended the noble bowler, he relaxed and told us many amusing tales of the Ethiopian capital. Our nearest contacts were with the two bankers, great fellows both, and extremely friendly.

Before the advent of motor roads and automobiles, everyone lived and thought horses. Everyone rode the native pony everywhere. The horse-market offered you a selection from which to choose at will and at a low price. Only the big Abyssinians rode mules because they were more comfortable, but they would always have a horse all saddled and decked-up, and these were led around after them wherever they went. Whereas a good pony could be bought for twenty Maria Theresa dollars, a good riding mule would cost as much as one thousand. Consequently, everyone was racing mad.

While waiting for our permit, we took part in the doings of the town. As it happened, the annual race for the Macmillan Cup was about to take place. Macmillan, whilst on passage through Addis, had presented a cup, the Macmillan Cup, to be raced for and won by three straight wins. The British Legation had won the cup twice in successive years and required only one more win to retain the cup for keeps. There was terrific rivalry among all the legation people, but feelings ran fever-high as everyone in the town, including the emperor, strove to prevent this one further win by the British Legation. The bankers were determined to prevent this decisive win, so they decided to do something about it by importing a first-class, pure-bred Arab pony from Aden, Yemen.

After one of the marvelous lunches with Goldie of the Bank of Egypt and some other bankers, they took us into their confidence and told us of their fears and anxieties anent their importation of the Arab pony. Now Addis stands in a hollow, but this hollow stands ten thousand feet above sea level whereas the Arab had been born and bred at sea level. There was no doubt about his quality and breeding. Indeed, he made the Abyssinian country-bred ponies look like dirt. But in the trials that had been carried out, the Arab had invariably been beaten. They were certainly very worried bankers, indeed. Was it the altitude?

Now I had with me as partner a very potent little horseman, Harry Rayne, and I suggested Rayne should ride this Arab pony. Harry was the son of a New Zealand horse-breaker, and what he did not know about or could not do with a horse was not worth knowing. Harry had done a lot of racing and was of those men who completely dominate a horse the moment they contact them. He could transform any horse from a dull sluggard into a winner provided only that it had four legs. Heart, courage, and speed he seemed able to instill from his own ample store of those useful commodities. Although he weighed considerably more than a light native jockey, I had no hesitation in telling Goldie that he should offer Harry the mount.

He seemed filled with joy and hope at the prospect, but apprehensive that Harry would not accept. "Try him," I said.

He did and Harry said, "Let us have a look at him (the Arab).

He was a lovely gray stallion. One look at him was enough. Rayne accepted the offer to ride him. He was offered any trial he cared, but he seemed satisfied with what he had seen.

As soon as the news that Rayne was going to ride in the fast-approaching race, the legation got busy. Our permit to proceed arrived pronto, and we prepared to move. Indeed, the legation people now pressed us to go while the going was good. So we gave up the idea of waiting for the race, made our excuses to the bankers, explaining how the land lay and that we would have to push off or we might have our permit revoked. They laid their long heads together and bade us farewell. We rode off after our safari, which had left Addis that morning.

As is the way of all safaris, the first march was a short one. That allows things that have been forgotten to be retrieved, wives to take a last squeeze from husbands, and deserters or run-away mules to be captured. Hence, it was quite early in the afternoon that we rejoined the safari, all now comfortably camped in an ideal spot.

We were just having a refresher when who should ride into camp but H. Julian Humphreys, a hard-bitten Irishman who represented a large armaments firm. He, too, had a horse entered, not in the race for the Macmillan Cup, but in a steeplechase. He, too, was determined that Harry Rayne should steer his horse to victory. This was on the eve of the all-important opening day of the race.

"Now," he said, "you are coming back to Addis with me. They'll put you up at the bank. You can easily send on your safari and catch up with it after the races are over."

"But the legation will raise hell," we objected.

"Oh, tell them to go to it," said he. "Your safari is on its way, isn't it?"

So we galloped back to Addis and right royally were we done by the bank where we spent the night in the usual hard way.

Rayne had not yet had a ride on the Arab pony, and I wondered why he did not do so. No, he didn't seem at all anxious about it. Instead, we went to look at Humphreys's steeplechaser. What a shock we got when we saw it. A dark gray native pony, it was as fat and round as a pig. It certainly looked anything but the winner of a race, however good its chance of a prize in a Fat Stock Show.

Seeing we were not very enthusiastic about his chances, Humphreys assured us he could help, which was more than some of them can do, he said. He only wants waking up!

Rayne said nothing at all.

Passing along what was one day planned to be a wide street but was only a de-brushed area with a narrow track wandering native-fashion all over the place, we passed a large compound surrounding a large house. In the compound could be seen a horde of men and mules.

"What's on here?" we asked.

"Oh! That's so-and-so. He lives there and he wines up the natives and then tries to buy ivory from them. Come on in, he's always got champagne."

On entering we were introduced to himself. Sure enough, he gave us champagne. He represented some big United States piano makers, and was a very cheery bloke.

Soon we rode off to the race course. Here was our friend Goldie of the Bank of Egypt acting as Steward of the course, and he was in the smartest new market rig-out: brown top boots, bulging breeches, flyaway jacket, billycock hat [bowler], and hunting crop. He was galloping up and down clearing the course of the thousands of spectators who swarmed all over it. And he didn't half use that whip of his, either.

Conspicuous on the grand stand was our rival from the British Legation, all done up in frock coat and topper. When he saw us, he gave us a very hard look, indeed, but said nothing then. All awaited the coming of the emperor.

As is usual with these African potentates, we had to wait a long time. It seems as if it enhances their dignity to keep everyone waiting. However, at last a huge mob was seen to vomit forth from the palace on the hill, and centred in it was the great man himself. Our banker, no respecter of persons, assisted the rearmost elements of the throng with his hunting crop.

As soon as the great man had settled himself in the royal box, the first race was started. We had ample leisure to examine the competing horses. It was quite a field, too, because everyone hoped to prevent the third and outright winning of the cup by the British Legation. The emperor's entry was regarded as constituting the greatest menace as naturally he had the pick of the whole horse population of the country.

The Abyssinians rode their ponies in native saddles—rather like the Mexican article—and spade bits, but all the European-owned ones had the proper racing saddles and snaffle bits. Considering the locality, it was quite a show. The banker had warned Rayne to expect foul play should he find himself in position to pass the emperor's horse. This opposition was not to be lightly regarded either, for although they know little about training ponies for racing and had no proper flat saddles, their jockeys were simply told that if they lost the race, they would likewise lose some very precious elements of their physical make-up. So it is little wonder that foul riding of every description was expected of and resorted to by the Abyssinian riders. Goldie, of course, warned Rayne what he might look for should he be in a position to pass any of the emperor's horses.

At the drop of the flag, everyone went hell bent full out. Well, there was only one horse in that race, and that was Harry Rayne's mount. Rayne's pony had begun to draw ahead when a savage cut from a rhino-hide whip paused the momentum temporarily. One of the emperor's jockeys, at any rate, was not going to be a candidate for a boys' choir if he could help it. Without a sign of anything at all happening, Rayne got his shoe toe under this fellow's heel and tipped him over as neat as neat. No one saw a thing. That Arab left them standing, and Rayne took the lead to win by twenty lengths.

Protest? Yes, of course. A mob of a thousand excited, armed ruffians, supporters of their emperor, spilled over the course to lodge a protest. But it was in vain. Goldie was Steward of the course, and this gave him his chance for exercising his duties by clearing it—a chance that seemed much to his liking. In short order, all were made to clear off. Harry was the hero of one section and the deadly enemy of the other.

Mr. Frock-and-Topper tackled us with venom, real enduring hatred, as he accused us of dallying in the capital after he had taken so much trouble to get our permit. We explained as mildly as we could contrive that the safari was on its way, and we should catch up with it in no time at all. But I'm afraid we had got ourselves well into his black book and certain subsequent difficulties that we encountered were due to this unfortunate contretemps. On the whole, his was a remarkable exhibition of feeling.

Then there followed the steeple-chase. Humphreys's horse certainly looked the most unlikely animal in that bunch of starters. Again Rayne's horse won. Rayne seemed to electrify that sluggish pig-like character beyond measure. In the process of waking him up, R. lost his whip. He took off one of his stirrup leathers and so wound up his mount as to bring him in first, a feat that anyone would have laid any odds against.

So ended the race meeting, for us at any rate. Against all pleadings to stay the night, we insisted on riding off to overtake the safari. We thought we had probably sown ourselves quite enough trouble as it was.

******

Our safari had almost completed the crossing of a swollen river on a groundsheet raft when a chap arrived. He was from Ceylon, and he was making a survey of the wild rubber vine of the Abyssinian forest for some financiers who thought that this vine would prove valuable. The long forgotten, but to those who experienced it, the ever-memorable rubber boom was in full blast, and anyone with inside knowledge was making a fortune.

The chap asked if we would help by carrying his gear over.

"Of course," we said.

We then camped together. He was an interesting type who had helped to plant the Ceylon and Malay rubber estates. He told us to invest every penny we could scrape together in some estates he named. We did not do so, of course. Had we only followed his advice, our fortunes would have been made. Instead, we invested in land in Kenya, grew the wrong kind of rubber, and practically went bust.

******

After much difficulty and many frustrations caused by the greed and general hellishness of the Abyssinian chiefs, we finally reached our goal by way of a then-unknown tributary of the Pibor. The whole country was covered with twelve feet of grass and most of it awash under two and three feet of water in places. Mosquitoes were in their billions but apparently were not contaminated by contact with humans. At any rate we did not suffer much from fever.

The chief difficulty was to find enough dry ground for a camp, and when we found it, we had to battle every kind of ant, scorpion, and snake also seeking dry ground. There were no inhabitants of the human kind, and this added enormously to our labours as we had to turn to and do the dirty work ourselves. It was easy to get elephants, but what a labour it was getting their ivory. We saw no other animal but elephants in this ocean of grass, and we had, perforce, to live on elephant meat.

At first we chopped out the tusks in the orthodox way, but this was altogether too much work, so we left them to rot. We found that the upper tusk of a sideways-lying elephant could be drawn out of its socket on the third day and the lower one on the fourth. I shall never forget the effect on Harry Rayne when he drew out his first tusk. The stink is perfectly appalling and hits you with the blast of a large bomb. Poor Harry staggered back and vomited his soul out.

To get a sight above the grass, I tried shooting from a boy's shoulders, but I found it a very wobbly stance. So I fitted a small board to the top of the big telescope tripod. This brought my eye level with the topmost stems of the grass, and at that height I was able to reach an elephant's brain. Only a light-calibre rifle could be fired under these conditions, and even then the recoil was enough sometimes to knock me off balance. This was quite sufficiently exciting when a dozen of those animated tanks were careering about. What a time we had.

We were, of course, waterborne since we were always in three feet of water; consequently, no other means of locomotion except by canoe was possible. All our mules and camels had returned with their Abyssinian masters to their beloved highlands, and mighty glad we were to see the last of them.

In no time at all our native dug-out canoes were loaded right down so that the slightest breeze raised sufficient popple [rolling or rippling] on the water to come lapping over the sides. Once or twice the whole flotilla sank. Luckily this never happened in very deep water, and we always recovered our valuable cargo. So we went on with the current, endlessly it seemed. We had not the faintest idea where we were. Maps showed nothing but blanks in those days.

But we trusted in Providence and gravity to convey us finally into the waters of the Nile. But it was exasperating to have to leave good elephants standing on the banks because we could carry no more ivory. Latterly we shot elephants only to eat and always their tusks were fitted in somehow on the overloaded canoes. At first we thought a 3-inch free board was the limit it would be safe to go to. Finally this was reduced to 1½ inches with the steering platforms in the sterns just awash. No man born could have left those lovely tusks on the shore.

Strangely enough nothing happened until near the end of the voyage. Although we had seen and passed myriad crocs, it was not until the last few miles before entering the Nile that trouble overtook us. A huge old croc came up behind the leading canoe and grabbed the steersman. He was practically sitting in the water anyhow. Within a second or two and before the boy had totally disappeared, we fired at the croc and it let go. But the croc had caused terrible havoc, and the poor tyke died soon after.

As our swamp-hunting technique was highly developed by this time, it was determined to carry on to the big swamps bordering the banks of the White Nile. By the time these were reached—they lay 1,500 miles by river to the south—they would be full of elephants. There I parted company with Rayne who was hell bent on buying land in Kenya in order to plant rubber, about which we had heard so much. I continued the hunt alone and got 210 bull elephants in the country that was then known as the Lado Enclave.

Here was a peculiar state of affairs. The British, who claimed the land, had given King Leopold II of the Belgians a lease of it during his lifetime. On the king's death, it would revert to the British with their hampering game laws and restrictions. Luckily for me, a clause had been inserted in the lease to the effect that the Belgians should have six months after the king's demise in which to remove their installations. As these consisted mostly of native-built, mud-and-wattle huts, this was soon accomplished by setting fire to everything. They were out of it in a month.

Thereafter lay a country once more in the possession of its original owners, the natives. As well as being almost the last remaining haunt of the white rhino, the land teemed with game, but, above all, there were elephants. In the dry season, hundreds upon hundreds of them came to the big swamps. Great herds of three or four hundred were common. All the high bush land was burnt. Nothing would induce these herds to leave their sole refuge, the high swamp grass.

It was in this kind of hunting that the small bores came into their own. With their absence of recoil, the small bore could deliver a shot with sufficient accuracy from the most precarious stance, whereas a heavy recoil weapon would have sent its firer's arse up into the ditch.

One day I met a user of such weapons. He was full of moans about the height of grass. He didn't seem to like it at all. He seemed very dissatisfied with things in general, but what got his goat completely was his raft. He explained how he had built this beautiful raft from the surrounding trees on a convenient sand bank in order to cross the very considerable river confronting him. All was ready to commence his crossing when his boys flatly refused to venture on it.

The Bwana, thinking it was some hold-up strike for more pay or something, flew off the handle and started laying into them. With the help of his Nubian askaris, he forcibly tied down eight of the workers onto the beautiful raft and shoved it off the sand bank. It promptly sank. He did not know that nearly all African wood sinks when green. Had he used balsa wood, all would have been well. His boys must have tried to tell him, but he was the kind who never spoke or learnt "n---er" talk.

He was a burly bearded buck from Jericho or Jerusalem, always had a hippo-hide whip slung at his wrist, and seemed to think the only way to a black man's mind was to galvanize his body with a cut from a *kiboko* [whip]. To hear him, you would have gathered that the eight types had committed suicide expressly to annoy him. After telling him what I thought of him, which he took unexpectedly quietly, we showed him how to make a grass-filled groundsheet raft and left him.

In their new-found freedom, the natives of the Lado Enclave were at first somewhat self-assertive. They had little liking for their white overlords and were in no mind to welcome what for all they knew might be the forerunner of another wave of oppressors. But they soon came under the spell of free and abundant meat. In the course of our hunting operations, we came to the edge of the Ituri Forest. The country changed abruptly from rolling grasslands to a wall of forest—the Darkest Africa of the old explorers. Soon we had several thousand natives following us about—men, women, and children.

Presently we were overburdened with ivory. As we did not trust the natives of those parts so well, we decided to get rid of the ivory by ferrying it over to the British side of the Nile. There was a convenient post, and we landed the stuff about a mile from it. A runner was sent to the local chief asking for carriers to take the tusks up to the government *boma*. Hundreds arrived for what they regarded as a kind of show. As each man came up, he was given a tusk to shoulder. Headmen lined them out in single file on the wide, straight road leading to the post. As the last tusk was shouldered, word came back along the line that the leading files had arrived.

This purely accidental affair immediately aroused interest and, of course, gained much in the retelling. The news spread far and wide that Emin Pasha's long-lost hoard of ivory had been discovered. Emin was a German in Egypt's pay who had escaped from his mutinous troops and was supposed to have buried a huge quantity of ivory somewhere. He had the title of Governor of Equatoria. He became another victim of Stanley's rescuing operations and died in Tanga from an after-dinner fall from a veranda; whether he was pushed or not remains unverified.

Now the cat was out of the bag with ginger under her tail. Every Tom, Dick, and Harry threw down their tools and left their jobs from as far away as Nairobi. Engineers, masons, publicans, and bartenders rushed to the Lado. Borrowing, taking credit wherever they could get it, up they came to disturb and ruin a hitherto peaceful countryside. Big bores were in terrific demand, and one Italian merchant I knew made a fortune hiring out such guns on the basis of 50/50 in tusks. Most of these people had no experience whatever, and the havoc they wreaked on the herds of poor elephants can only faintly be imagined.

But worst of all they had no savvy where natives were concerned. As there was no law in the land, shootings and killing soon started. Everyone became nervous of strangers; everyone distrusted everyone else. The only remaining Belgian post was so on edge, thinking the British were invading their adjacent and recently discovered gold fields, that they opened fire on anyone they saw. I myself had a tit-up with some itchy-fingered black troops of theirs. It ended up honours pretty well even, as they had a machine gun of sorts.

After this devastating invasion, it was time to pack up. Once more the search for new hunting grounds began. Just before leaving and while saying farewell to the chiefs who had helped so well, one old man asked me to rid him of a marauding rhino that was upsetting his people. It had already killed one woman and gored several others. I had to do something about it, so taking a .350 Mauser, which I had not used much as it appeared to me to be neither a big nor a small bore, I left for his village.

Now I was about to learn a thing or two about rifles. It was a beautiful weapon with a Mauser Magnum action and a 5-shot magazine. The cartridge, a long rimless case, burned 60 grains of cordite behind a 300-grain, round-nose, steel-jacketed bullet, with the jacket heavily reinforced in the nose portion. Like all bullets with open bases, the lead filling was liable to squeeze out. I had been humping this gun around for a long time without using it much, and I thought it only fair I should blood it sometime. It was nearly my undoing.

We tracked the old rascal into some high grass quite near the village. As soon as he heard us, he came straight toward the sound. At five yards his head was dimly visible, and I fired but did not drop him; instead, the shot turned him slightly. What should have been the second and finishing shot occurred when the rifle was actually touching his neck. Instead, I heard a "*click*."

I had re-inserted the fired case when re-loading. The bolt-travel was too long, and I had failed to get it back far enough. But he had had an awful jar. Instead of some old lady gathering firewood, he had bumped into something quite new in his experience. What a chase he led us until he got a steel-coated 300-grain bullet up his stern. That curbed his style a bit, and he was finally laid low. But what a lesson.

From then on I went to practicing a shove forward with the left hand each time I worked the bolt of even the short-throw 7mm. I gave that beautiful .350

to an old prospector with plenty caution and told him of this episode. I made the old boy practice dry-shooting until he got the idea, and I heard later from him that he liked the gun and did well with it.

Before leaving this country, I thought my boys should all have a chance at elephant. They were eager to show what they could do, and especially the cook, Suliemani. He had often boasted of what he could do. So I gave him a .318 and thirty rounds, and off he went by himself amidst the jeers of his friends. Meanwhile I climbed a hill hoping to see the fun. The country was crawling with elephants, albeit the grass was high.

We watched Suliemani as he searched for fresh tracks in and out of the grass. Soon he was on to something and started off like a bloodhound on the trail. Presently, away ahead of him, we saw his elephant, a herd bull. Suliemani could not see him and presently he bumped right into his stern. Next thing we saw the bull launch into instant flight in one direction while Suliemani came back as rapidly in the other. We had a good laugh, and I thought, *so much for Suliemani and his boasting.*

We descended to the camp and everyone went about his ordinary ploys thinking that was the end of it. But Suliemani did not return. Presently we heard from far off shot after shot. There was no lack of friends to count them. Many reports had come across the still evening air when darkness enveloped the aching bush. Still no Suliemani. When we had all supped and were about to turn in, here comes Suliemani with no tail. He had failed to kill.

There was a roar of laughter and leg pulling. Suliemani said not a word, but got his grub, kept ready by his crestfallen wife. Satisfied, Suliemani got up, washed his hands and teeth, and finally strolled out of the camp amidst roars of laughter to return with a freshly killed elephant tail.

AFRICAN DISEASES AND GENERAL MENACES TO HEALTH

CHAPTER 10

There are many diseases in Africa, but few of them attack a bush-dweller. Because of this, every hunter ought to simulate that life style. Bush tracks are not infected. Perhaps I should qualify that statement to read "were not infected." During the olden times of tribal warfare, there existed large areas of no-man's-land, and these necessarily interposed themselves between settlements. The result was that disease carrying was greatly minimized.

They had other uses, too, these tribal wars. They amounted to intermittent massacres that kept the population numbers down through the habitual killing of the female sex. With all our ingenuity, we have found nothing to replace this necessary check on population growth, unless it be, perhaps, by way of long-range sterility brought about by rising standards of living.

I myself suffered a good deal from malaria, just as most Africans also did. For years I never carried a mosquito net. I noticed always that an attack, i. e., infection, came on after a visit to civilization. I hardly ever suffered an attack in the bush.

When the African's blood becomes too heavily charged with malaria, he has heavy discharges of blood from the anus. This I thought was dysentery until I had it too. It does not appear to be dysentery at all but seems to be Nature's way of cleansing the system. It soon clears off and one feels very much the better for it.

******

I am often asked if snakes were a menace. Generally speaking, a stranger depended largely on natives of the country to guide him about, for there were no detailed maps in those days. The African native born and bred among snakes from childhood up is very quick to spot a snake, which is only to be expected. So the blundering white man with his sun glasses and whatnot is not in danger of treading on the deadly mamba as he would undoubtedly be if on his own.

******

Some parts of the African continent are worse than others as to the number of snakes to be found. I know of a valley that might well be named Viper's Valley, for there at certain times you would find it hard to be ever out of sight of at least one snake of some kind. There are your moments of astonished fright when you see a greenish-gray, slender, whip-like object waving about in front of you. You take a swipe at it with a stick only to find it is farther away than you thought. It is hard to focus for some reason or other. Maybe it is the vibrating that distracts you.

In all the years I spent in the African bush, I lost one cattle-herder. He was bitten just before nightfall, and we could not find him in spite of his firing a rifle. I also lost a pony and three dogs. These were imported terriers. When they were not baling up rhinos, they were chasing snakes. Catching a snake by its tail is no way to longevity in Africa. So my total loss to snakes over the years I spent in Africa cannot be called a big haul for the serpents considering the mileage I covered on foot.

A good many hunters have been killed by game but very few by snakes. Yet when you find yourself exactly between a black mamba and his hole and he raises two-thirds of his seven-foot length into the air and rushes straight at you and you do nothing about it, you are apt to think afterward he must have mesmerized you. Snakes in Africa, as elsewhere, have a habit of appearing out of bottles, just as sunstroke does.[1] They need worry no one.

******

Water is Africa's shortest commodity, in the dry season at any rate. But one may safely drink it just so long as it is removed from human taint. Other animal taint seems not to matter, however foul it may look. I would advise no one to shun water because it rots your shoes. "Don't drink water! Look what it does to your boots!" may have been sound enough advice when we still had the capacity

[1] Bell believed that the common cause of sunstroke, and likewise seeing snakes where there were none, could often be attributed to an overindulgence in gin.

for liquor possessed in such abounding measure by our forefathers. Now a man would be well advised to boil or otherwise sterilize his drinking water unless he is well away in the bush far from contamination by human settlements.

******

I never think people make full use of the wonderful aids to eyesight we possess. We seem to wait until we have been puzzled to make out some unfamiliar object before we use the binoculars we have so faithfully carried for so long. It seems to be as if we pretended to ourselves that we did not really require any aid to sight but merely carried them as part of the proper outfit, just as you may see people toting enormous binoculars to race meetings. I often wonder if there is anything in those stupendous leather cases.

The constant and patient use of binoculars, however good your sight, is a revealing exercise when hunting in unfamiliar territory. It enables you to find and distinguish objects that would otherwise escape you because of your unfamiliarity with the outline or colour of the territory, all of which would need to be pointed out to you by your native guide. It is good for these gentry of the bush to find that their employers can sometimes beat them to it in this and in other ways, too.

I find the 7X50 is cumbrous but excellent, so I would personally plump for a 6X30 worn without a case and slung over the right shoulder, with the glass nestling under the left armpit. The sling should be a stout one and smooth so that it renders freely round the body as the left or right hand raises it to the eyes.

I always carried among my baggage a tripod-mounted telescope. In forest country there was little or no use for it, but whenever mountainous country was reached, this glass became a joy to have and use. It magnified forty-five times and had a four-inch-diameter lens. Usually the mornings were the best times for seeing things because at midday heated air distorts objects. That glass showed me many things that would otherwise have remained unseen, and it also led me into some fearful chases.

The glass made it look so easy to descend from your hill perch and walk straight to where you had seen some ponderous tusker dusting his hide. But when the bush was of a landscape that hide all landmarks, look out. It is incredible just how very easy it is to become lost. That is where a native of the country becomes invaluable.

He finds the game or its tracks for you chiefly by remembering salient features of the bush. It may be that once he took a bees' nest from that tree, or over there he robbed a lion of its kill, or that ant-hill "flew" when he passed hereby maybe years ago.

You will soon come to recognize the unpalatable fact that without your African, you are a pretty helpless individual in thick bush country—even the most experienced of us are. Just as helpless as a Pygmy hunter would be if set down in the middle of, say, London. Of course, now that the motor car has come, things are simpler. In the dry season, anyhow.

The Debassian Mountains

Chapter 11

In a huge open plain north of Mount Elgon there lies a remarkable-looking extinct volcano known to the natives of those parts as Dabasi and to our map-makers as the Debassian Range—in this case a much nearer approximation to the native name than very many map names bear. With the exception of a few foothills, the gaunt and precipitous walls of the old crater spring abruptly from the plain, forming a semicircle. The remaining crater walls were possibly blown away at the time of the great upheaval, or, perhaps, they have crumbled away since.

However that may be, it is only when the traveler, skirting the western bases, comes to a narrow opening in the hills that he realizes it is an old volcano. For now he looks into a huge arena "glowered" over by precipices on the far side and contained by densely wooded hills on either hand. The floor of the arena is level and grows extraordinarily luxuriant grass in the wet season, eight or ten feet high, but early in the dry season it is a gray, ash-strewn level plain. Down

The extinct volcano known as Dabasi.

through the middle of the plain wanders a clear-water stream, while the level is dotted with huge ant-heap mounds, some of them fifteen feet high.

When I first came suddenly on the opening and looked into the arena, I thought what a delightful bit of country. I longed to possess it, to build my home up on one of the dark green hills overlooking it, to irrigate it, and to have oranges and other fruit growing in abundance. With water available and the richest of soils, almost anything could be grown.

Its real use to me as a hunter did not strike me at the time of my first visit. It was the middle of the dry season, and all the tall grass had been burned off, not only there but in all the surrounding country. Whereas outside on the open plains all was black, baked, and panting for the first rains, already here, inside, the humidity of the soil was such that there was a thick carpet of short green grass. The whole level was densely crowded with hartebeest, topi, and eland, while everywhere were tracks of buffalo. Of elephant there were no signs.

Camping by the stream, our donkeys and cattle were soon stuffing themselves with the sweet grass, while I entered to have a look round and to shoot some meat for the boys. Before long I had a couple of fat elands down and left them to be cut up. As I carried on toward the forest-clad slopes across the crater floor, I saw some smoke high up on the mountain-side.

On enquiry, when in camp again, I was told that these fires were made by the Dabasi. These people were of the same tribe of mountaineers as that inhabiting Elgon. They never descended to the plains except to cross the intervening thirty miles to Elgon, and that only at night. They were bad people and killed one with poisoned arrows on sight, according to the Karamojans.

On approaching the forest-clad sides, buffalo tracks ran into buffalo runs, all entering the woods. In the woods themselves there were innumerable elephant paths. I was astounded at the elephant traffic and wondered where they all were now, for there were no fresh traces of them. I skirted round, perhaps a quarter of the circle, and found the sun dipping. But everywhere I went there was a maze of elephant paths running from the level floor up into the wooded hills. While hurrying home to camp I resolved to find out from Pyjalé at what season of the year elephants came to this place, for I could not doubt that when they came, they came in great numbers.

In the dusk I came quietly upon a few buffaloes just as they emerged from the now black forest, while others could be heard inside the woods.

Pyjalé pushed aside some greenery, disclosing the great bulk of the broadside elephant.

Not wishing to fire, I sheered off slightly to pass them. They saw me almost immediately, but as the direction of the wind prevented them from scenting me, they simply stood staring at what to them must have been some queer khaki-coloured animal. These buffaloes had, probably, never been fired at, and they never moved while I passed them from about forty yards.

That night, while sitting in my pyjamas by the camp-fire, Pyjalé asked me to kill a bull buffalo for him as he wanted the hide for a shield. I asked him how many shields could be cut from one hide. He said that only the thickest parts were good for shields, and that, consequently, only four full-size shields would be got. But the rest of the skin would make first-rate sandals.

I explained to Pyjalé that I had seen signs of great elephant traffic, but all old. I asked him, "Where were all the elephants now?"

Pointing to the east, he said they were all down in the swamps but that as soon as the grass grew two or three feet high, they would return to the old crater. Then, he said that no man could approach it, so densely packed would it be with elephants.

I asked him if they never came before that time, not even an old bull or so. He told me that the woods surrounding our little plain were never quite without elephant.

When I told him that I had seen no fresh tracks or signs, Pyjalé smiled and said he would show me in the morning. Although much older and wiser than I, he invariably called me Baba (father), which at first rather annoyed me. But never would he call me Bwana (mister) as the boys did.

After this conversation, silence fell on the little circle. The cool air, the brilliant sky, and the splendid moonlight of an African dry-season night surrounded us. Everyone stared into the fire.

Presently Pyjalé made preparations to go to bed. First he leveled the lumps on the piece of ground where he proposed to lie. That done, he laid his two spears beside the site and lay down, completely naked as he was. As he reclined more and more backward, his wooden pillow swung round on its string. Shifting the little hollowed-out top of it to its position under the ear, there he was, turned in. So high are the legs of these little pillows that when you first see a native asleep on his back you would swear that he was in the act of rising. The other boys built themselves elaborate grass mattresses to lie on and covered themselves with blankets. But nothing of that sort for Spartan Pyjalé.

After a little while, as I was about to go to my comfortable camp-bed, Pyjalé turned to me. I had heard nothing, but I knew that he had. I also knew that he had heard elephants. What cared we for anything else? Then he pointed in the direction my evening stroll had taken me. Then I, too, heard the deep low rumble of elephants, the sound that so delights the hunter's heart—his sweetest music.

In the bright, cool morning we were off, breakfastless, of course, across the level green of the crater bottom. First Pyjalé, then I with the little rifle, followed by a Karamojan boy carrying my food, a calabash of milk. As we approached the wooded sides with their rocky and precipitous tops, the western walls of the old crater looked simply grand. Away up high could be seen the tiny smoke columns of the mountain folk. All about us hartebeests and topis were playing, while the more sedate eland stood staring like cattle on a western ranch. Buffaloes had already taken to the shady woods.

First we skirted the woods, cutting diagonally through innumerable buffalo and elephant runs, every eye darting glances right and left for fresh elephant spoor. At this time of year, the ground is so hard that the soft-padded foot of an elephant leaves no trace except for some dust or sand. Here the corrugations of the sole imprint themselves, but when the wind rises, the loose shifting particles soon fill them up and all is level once more. Then, again, the passage of game is often so frequent on these paths as to obliterate completely, by hoof marks alone, the tracks of a single elephant. The height of the dry season is, of all times, the pleasantest in which to hunt but the most difficult in which to track.

By nine o'clock, sun-time, we were half way round the crater and to the place where the stream entered the plain after its rocky tumble from the heights. I had a pull at the calabash and, half emptying it, handed it to Pyjalé. He likewise took a good share and the dregs went to his satellite. We were now fed and watered for the day. Should hunger again press us before our return to camp, a small buck would soon relieve it.

Somewhere on the soft banks of the stream we would certainly find the tracks of the owner of the rumble we had heard last night. If we could only follow them and hold them sufficiently long in the maze of game runs, we would as certainly see or hear him. Up-stream we went then, and came almost instantly on a wart-hog rolling in mud, coating himself against flies in the midday siesta.

We were now in high bush (forest) with a lot of troublesome undergrowth making visibility drop to about ten or fifteen yards. Colobus monkeys were numerous, peering down at us through the leafy tops like so many old be-whiskered and rather cross-looking butlers. Entering a little swampy opening, there lay about the centre of it the mud-bespattered patch surrounding an elephant's bath.

To the inexperienced eye it appeared not to have been used recently, for almost all the mud was dry. But a mere glance at it brought a smile to Pyjalé's face. So dry is the air at this time that even in shade, quite bulky chunks of mud dry up in no time. Without a word we took up the trail.

For several monotonous hours now it was a matter of advancing step by step, with halts innumerable and castings-round frequent. Up and up we mounted into deeper, darker, and moister forest. The baffling maze of game runs eased off the farther we went until we would follow the same one for several hundred yards before meeting another either converging into or diverging from it. The sun was well up as it was noon now, but we hardly felt its rays. Flies were much less numerous. Our quarry was single and a big one, by his feet, who would be silently dosing somewhere about in the dense shade. We must go cautiously.

Buffaloes emerging from the black forest at dusk.

Usually, I liked to be ahead at this stage of the proceedings, but on this occasion Pyjalé was still leading when he halted easily, pushed gently aside some greenery, and disclosed to me over his left shoulder the great bulk of a broadside elephant with another immediately beyond him. There they stood, silent and absolutely motionless, like some long-dead and stuffed prehistoric monsters.

The mossy appearance of the near one's head denoted great age. Not a quiver of the gigantic ears nor a flick of a tail denoted life, only the little triangle of the white of the eye kept elongating or flattening as the comparatively tiny eye—it is a good deal bigger than an ox's—roamed over us. Just as motionless stood Pyjalé. Without a glance in my direction, he awaited with equal indifference the muzzle-blast from my rifle near his left ear-hole and the antics of the elephant a bare six paces in front of him.

This description may give the impression that we took our time, but, in reality, by the time Pyjalé's right arm had finished pushing aside the covering greenery, my rifle had already sent its bullet to the brain of the nearest elephant, and almost before it had reached the kneeling position, I was past Pyjalé, obtaining in that swift moment an oblique heart-shot at the now retreating second elephant. Not feeling quite certain of this latter shot, I barged clumsily, but fairly fast, along after him, and I was quite close to his stern when he halted before toppling over.

It was a day when all went well. The ivory was huge; the camp was near; shade, firewood, and water were plentiful; and the boys were well fed and happy. Above all, I had Pyjalé.

I had meant to tell of my elephant drive in the old crater bed, but so fast travels my pen when telling of those happy days that the space is already full. It must keep for another occasion.

NOPAK

CHAPTER 12

Looking north from the higher slopes of Mount Elgon,[1] one sees an isolated mountain standing high and abrupt on the immense plains. It goes by the name of Nopak[2] among the Bokoras, whose country lies to the east, while west of it live the Kumam, the hereditary enemies of the Bokoras. Away in the dim distance the faint glisten of water may be seen, some part of what is called on our maps Lake Salisbury.

In the days when I used to trek from Elgon to the far northern countries, I used to visit Nopak both on the way in—or "climbing" as the Swahilis called it—and on the way out, or "descending." It is a remarkable fact that I never once failed to find elephants on it, and very good elephants at that. There were springs of good water at its base, and there was an abundance of long spear grass. For some reason or other—probably connected with the drainage from the hill—the grass on the slopes at the base remained fairly green when all was burnt up or parched elsewhere. And then it held fine old bull elephants with exceedingly heavy ivory.

Situated as Nopak was right in the middle of the neutral zone between Bokora and Kumam, its springs were practically never visited by humans, except raiders from either side. These raiders would never molest the elephants, being bent on other business, so Nopak remained a kind of sanctuary for the old bulls. It held the further attraction for these sour old gentlemen that cow herds had never been known to visit it.

I will now try to describe the kind of affair a visit to Nopak became for me and for the natives of Bokora. In course of time our joint expedition to this

[1]Although a similar story appears in *Karamojo Safari,* Bell completely rewrote this incident about a year after *Karamojo Safari* was published.

[2]For those of you wishing to see where Bell hunted, use Cleave's map in the introduction to this book. Note that Cleave spells the name of this place "Napak," which is also the current spelling for this mountain.

mountain came to be regarded as a kind of tribal holiday and the excuse for much dancing and drinking.

As soon as it was known that my safari was approaching their country, either "climbing" or "descending," as the case might be, bands of fellows would leave the villages to spy out where the elephants were. For, although Nopak looks, from a distance, to be a single mass, it is in reality a little group of masses, and it would take two days' hard going to encircle the base completely. Generally, by the time we arrived in Bokora, someone would already be there prepared to guide us at once to the spot where he had left his companions to watch the elephants they had found.

Our camp in Bokora was in a delightful spot under the shade of two immense wild fig trees. Here the main safari would be left while I, with one boy and half-a-dozen Nyamwezi ivory choppers, would depart with the impatient guide. I should have mentioned, perhaps, that at this time I was rewarding anyone with the gift of a heifer for news that led to the death of a number of bull elephants; I would gift a young bull or bullock for a lesser number. Everyone was out for the heifer.

The distance in a straight line was not too great to cover in a day, but if one did this, one arrived tired among the elephants, so what I used to do was to leave Bokora in the afternoon and camp a few miles from Nopak, and then on, fresh and easy, to the hunt the next morning. This first camp was nothing at all, really. There would be my camp-bed and my solitary box containing everything I needed—cleaning outfit for my rifle, a change of shorts and shirt, cartridges, and food. No tents for anybody—the boys slept on the ground.

Camp scenes.

An hour or two after my arrival and when, perhaps, I would be stretched out on my bed staring up at the great African moon, people would begin to arrive. It might be noticed that they were mostly women, mostly young and mostly attractive. In an hour or two, great numbers had arrived. At first their little fires would be made far enough away from the white man's—or Red Man, as they called me—but soon the little groups came nearer and nearer, as the heaving grunts of hunting lion or hyaena howls were heard above the chatter.

What a fascinating scene! Imagine it who can. It seems to me that imagination must fail, but let us try. The atmosphere must be right to begin with. Wonderful African night—still, cool, clear, brilliant, and yet misty. Stars by the billion—trillion, I would say. Here, there, and everywhere, by groups and singles, some upright, some bending, some prostrate, the shining ebony figures of nude African maidenhood could be seen.

Note how they move. What poise, what perfect rhythm. Place a hundredweight on the top of that small head and no bend will occur in the tall, slim figure. Place a crushing load on it and it would collapse at the knees, maybe, nowhere else. Look at the beautifully formed breasts. One had not imagined until now that the human breast could be so completely and simply beautiful. The ancient Greek sculptors knew it. Then the skin—soft, smooth, and with a bloom on it of perfect circulation, of fresh young life. The waist has no queer, unnatural, and inefficient slimness. They are splendid, these young women. And they surround one on all sides.

The bolder characters crowd close to Red Man's fire without being pressed, while the more attractive and shyer ones are pulled and pushed forward into the circle of flickering light in the hope that his eye will note them and remember them on the morrow when the dividing up of meat begins.

All these girls, with a few young men, are here to seize, cut up into strips, smoke, and carry home just as much elephant meat as hard fighting and harder shouting can procure for them. Meanwhile, a little flirting comes by no means amiss; dancing in a mild way and without much noise starts up; and smoke from the little fires all around me almost suffocate me sometimes. Finally we sleep.

Three hours before daylight everyone is sitting up by the little fires. The chilliest hour is at hand. Every one of the natives is nude, and the fires have almost died out. I doze off again while my boy makes coffee. I drink it and make to go to sleep again, but there is such a suppressed excitement about, such an air of impatient expectation, that finally I roll out and the bed is promptly rolled up. Everyone wants to be off, and long before daylight we move.

When the sun rushes over the horizon, we find ourselves close to the foot of Nopak. Leaving the open cotton-soil plains behind us, we are soon on the red sandy soil of the mountain itself. Hardly have we gone fifty yards when we strike at a right angle to a well-worn elephant path, some three feet wide and as clean and smooth as a city sidewalk. Now it is necessary to deal with the huge following that it can be seen straggling away into the plains slightly below us.

Choosing out some great beefy fellows, I give them a sort of temporary authority by merely the fact that I, Red Man, tell them to thrash soundly anyone who disobeys them. This is enough. Clubs are swung about in aggressive fashion, and soon the whole following of 1,500 to 2,000 natives is bunched up together and held in some semblance of silence among the thorn trees. This allows the hunters to follow the elephant road along the base of towering Nopak.

Presently we see ahead of us a native standing motionless by the side of the path, leaning on his spear. When we are within ten yards of him, he turns without a word and speeds rapidly away ahead of us. We follow as hard as we can. The path dips into a hollow, branches off up a gully—where there is a spring—but rejoins the main path again on the other side of the gully. We cut across. Now the path

Five enormous bull elephants coming toward us in single file.

begins to rise over a shoulder. We top it, and there, a hundred yards ahead of us, are five immense bull elephants coming gravely toward us in single file.

There is no vestige of cover for the blacks with me—no tree, no ant-heap, no stone, and not sufficient grass to hide a goat. Therefore, they must retreat the way they came. When they are gone, the scene becomes extraordinarily peaceful. How quiet those huge elephants are as they stride with padded soles along the worn path. There is hardly a sound in the still morning air. There are as yet no flies to worry them, so the great ears hang almost motionless. Trunks droop straightly. They have no suspicion that man is about, or, if they are aware, they seem to treat his presence with complete indifference. Possibly these old fellows have haunted the springs and slopes of Nopak for a century or so.

Confident in their spear-proof hides and with their brains tucked away in the middle of their huge and massive skulls, they have no thought other than to stride placidly on. But their day is over. Painlessly and instantaneously they die, one after the other, shot through their poor old brains. It is a one-sided affair, for they are all down before they have time to realize what is happening. Never have I seen such grand tusks, except for the one that was broken.

Soon the boys arrive, and, presently, the main body of meat collectors. Guards are quickly put on the different elephants. No one is allowed to cut meat except from the heads until these are clean and severed from the bodies. The ivory chopping-out gang then takes charge of them; after that the fight and scramble for meat begins. I retire to the shade of an evergreen in a gully after seeing that all the favourites have been suitably rewarded with meat. Here I stretch myself on the camp-bed and sleep.

Presently I am awakened to find a native man has come with news. He has seen an elephant and not far. We go with him at a great pace, and after a few miles we see a solitary bull roaming quietly along, feeding as he goes. It is an absurdly easy shot. I sit down at a comfortable distance of forty to fifty yards, wait until his head is motionless, and send the little .275 projectile into and through his brain—it can be heard whining away on the other side of his head. The ivory of this old fellow is very heavy also.

The lightest tusk—barring the broken one—in to-day's bag weighs seventy-six pounds. When in camp again, it occurs to me that this getting of a single bull will be the first occasion of the sort. Up till now I had never killed a single bull to one man's information. According to my scale of rewards, he would be given a bullock, while the other native man who had led us to the five elephant would receive a heifer.

Next day was given to drying and smoking the meat. I could not leave the natives, as they were out in the neutral zone and might be raided by the Kumams if I left them. Even as it was, they were rather nervous, and I was uncomfortably crowded at night by their meat-smoking fires. However, I placed all the spear men well on the outside of the huge camp and had most of the younger and more tender of the girls in the centre near my own little establishment. I do not mind confessing that it gave me exquisite pleasure to lie there and watch these merry children half-dancing, half-working throughout the night.

On our return to Bokora, all heavily laden, we found a great welcome prepared for us. Everyone came hoping for a bit of the share-out. Dusky beauties appeared who had hitherto been strictly kept away from our camps. Beer flowed in a torrent.

In the evening the boys came for their rewards. No. 1 was given his heifer, and he and his friends cut her out of the cattle herd and went off at a great speed. Then No. 2 was shown his bullock. Not a move on his part. Thinking that he did not understand, it was again explained to him that, as his effort had brought me one elephant, he therefore should receive a bullock and not a heifer. He was told to take it off.

Still not a move or a word. I now looked carefully at him. I could see by his sullen expression that he was not satisfied. He was also simply swimming with beer, full as a tick. I therefore turned away and went to my tent, appearing to take no further notice of him. He followed and squatted outside by the tent door. I pretended to ignore him, and after half an hour or so, I took a .22 pistol to try for a guinea-fowl in the bush about the camp.

That frightful pagan approached our unsuspecting boy at a prodigious speed.

As I left camp, I was aware that the truculent one had risen and was also moving. I thought that now he would go quietly home. Not at all. Presently I heard a shout from camp and looked round. Here, a few yards from me, was our friend in the very act of unsheathing his spears. I should explain that among these people the spears are kept very sharp and leather guards are worn to protect the edges. He remained motionless, looking at my leveled pistol, while I shouted for the boys, who came tearing along out of camp—eager, as always, to find a pagan in trouble with their bwana.

I told them to unspear the truculent fellow, which they very quickly and roughly did. Then we laid him out flat in front of a good gathering of his fellows, and the headman administered a sound thrashing in the quiet and ceremonial style for which he was famous. Our friend took it without a quiver or a sound. We might as well have beaten up a rubber tyre.

When it was over I told the boys to give him back his spears. They begged me not to do so, saying that he would surely murder someone, but I insisted that we were not afraid of anyone and that they might all have as many spears as they liked. Taking his spears, he strode off, his face sullen, his eyes mottled and bloodshot.

After going about fifty yards in an ordinary fashion, he suddenly let go a hoarse yell and like a streak of black lightning, he hurtled himself over and through thorn scrub, straight at one of our unsuspecting boys who was gathering firewood. When it dawned upon me that he probably meant to do the boy in, I yelled for my rifle. Then the whole camp realized the imminent tragedy and let off with one accord such a volume of sound that the distant boy heard, glanced up, and saw almost upon him a great flying black devil with spear up and ready.

Like a flash he put himself going at a right angle to the pagan's course, but, move as he would, he was caught almost at once in a masterly swerve by the flying Bokora, who leapt clean over the fleeing porter and pursued his way at undiminished speed until he disappeared over the horizon. I sighed in relief and then burst out in uncontrollable laughter. What a superb wag that pagan Bokora was. He became one of my personal friends, and I have no doubt that he is now a prosperous cattle owner. He called me "father" because I beat him.

ELEPHANT SWAMP

CHAPTER 13

Between Mount Mogila and Moru Akipi there lies about eighty miles of dry and arid plain without a drop of water in the dry season except at one point. Here there is a large shallow pan or slough in which water collects in the rains in sufficient quantities to saturate the ground completely, and when it overflows, it forms a stream. This water induces a luxuriant growth of tall swamp grass in the pan and a few trees grow by the side of the stream, which is bone dry in summer. Where the stream leaves the pan, in most years water may be got by digging. The slough with its grass attracts elephants and other game in great numbers. It is this area that forms the objective of our safari.

We had, of course, donkey transport to cover the forty or forty-five miles of "dry" plains. With our slow outfit, it would require about twenty hours' marching. Obviously it could not be done in one day without great hardship to the animals because the sun is quite merciless in this season. How we managed was thus:

Moving camp to the best and, at this time, the only water hole on Mogila, we grazed and watered our animals all the next day. Then, filling all water

The tall grass of the swamp abounded with game.

The pursuit along the banks of a dry river bed.

carriers, the donkeys were saddled up and started off about 3 P.M., marching on into the night by moonlight till midnight. Then camp would be formed, donkeys off-loaded, and a ration of water given out.

A hole was dug in the ground and a canvas sheet thrown over it. Into this the water bags were emptied. Then every mess boy would bring his large cooking pot and the water ration for his mess would be measured into it. This ration was ample for drinking and cooking purposes and left a little for the next day. After the humans, the donkeys and my two milk cows were served.

These, of course, could not fill themselves, but they all got enough to quench their thirst sufficiently to enable them to eat. Then, after a lie down on the ground and a short but sweet sleep, the safari would move off again about 4 A.M. and arrive in fair condition in camp at 3 P.M. in the afternoon.

On the evening previous to our departure, I climbed Mogila with my glasses and my large telescope, hoping to get sufficiently good visibility to examine the pan for elephant. After a lot of very rough climbing, I reached a rocky point overlooking the immense plains. I might have been fifteen hundred feet up, and the view was simply superb. There was not a sign of human occupation except for the smoke of a grass fire away in the blue haze of the Dodinga Hills. All belonged to the great game animals.

From this height, the pan was plainly visible to the naked eye. The pan appeared as a dark patch, and a line of trees, which appeared as dots, marked the course of the wet-season overflow. With 12X glasses it was hardly more visible than with the naked eye, and through the big tripod telescope, definition was so poor owing to haze in the quivering air that nothing could be made of it. Whether it was occupied by elephants, I could not tell. Turning my glasses on the plains immediately below me, I instantly saw, without searching, that the field was filled with game of various kinds. In the open parts great herds of oryx were interspersed with Grant's gazelles while giraffes seemed to be everywhere. But, search as I would, no elephants showed up.

Away down to my left front there appeared a long, light-yellow patch in the middle of dark bush. This was the dry sand of a river where I had, on a previous occasion, found and killed some bull elephants. This had happened in the wet season, and I did not expect to see any elephants there now. I thought, however, that I would turn my tripod glass on the river bed, just to make sure that there were no open water holes being used by elephants or other animals.

No sooner had I got the correct focus than I saw that there were undoubtedly open holes in the sandy river bed and that they had the appearance of being used. As I stared steadily at the numerous spoors lying about the holes, trying with the focusing screw to distinguish whether they were fresh or not, I became aware with a thrill that in the deep shade of the bank stood an elephant. Once "spotted," he was quite clear and plainly visible. Quite motionless, he stood with one of his tusks showing—quite a decent one of seventy or eighty pounds.

Now what to do? There was obviously water where the elephant was . . . and probably sufficient for the safari. Pyjalé and I would rush off there now and the safari must follow in its own time. I thought there would be time to reach the sand river before it became too dark to shoot. In any event, if we slept there, we would be so many miles nearer to Elephant Swamp.

After I squeezed up the tripod and gave the boy his instructions about the safari, Pyjalé and I began our rapid descent in a straight line to the sand river. Had the going been good, we might just have got there by sundown, but the sun dipped as we reached the flat. We crossed some horribly thick stuff at the bottom of Mogila where we not only got badly jabbed by the rapier-pointed sansevieria, but we also had a nasty dust-up with two drowsy rhinos.

I did not wish to shoot for fear of scaring our main quarry, so I had to content myself with cursing. They pushed both of us into some awful cactus and sansevieria, where we had to skip about in much too lively a fashion to escape all of the millions of sansevieria points just waiting to jab us. I wonder how many votes would be registered for their protection if the voters knew the rhino as intimately as we did?

The moon being up at the time, we had no difficulty in keeping our course, but it was late when we finally reached the river bed. Any elephants in the neighbourhood were pretty certain to be at the water holes now.

We crossed to the opposite bank so as to have the moon behind us, and we rapidly followed the dry course. The sand was very loose and powdery and Pyjalé with his broad giraffe sandals had a distinct advantage over me with my light but narrow-soled boots. We made quite a *crunch-crunch* as we strode along toward the water holes. The moonlight glared so from the white sand that one imagined one felt reflected heat.

Turning a bend, we came in sight of our elephant. He was drinking, and standing a few yards away was another, and sounds from the banks showed us that there were more in the vicinity. Unfortunately, these latter seemed to occupy the bank from which I intended to shoot.

I was not aware at the time of which I write that one can walk about among elephants at night as one might among flower pots in a conservatory and with as little notice being taken of one. I therefore paused and wondered how best to proceed. I wished, of course, to kill the two elephants out in the

A nasty "dust-up" with two rhinos.

open as I thought the light would be too bad for decent shooting in the bush on the bank. At the same time, in order to have the moonlight behind me, it was necessary to get between the two at the water holes and the others on the bank. Although the nearest was not more than fifteen yards from it, Pyjalé and I walked rapidly forward until we stood between him and the bank.

To my astonishment neither elephant took any notice of us. The nearest was not more than twelve paces from me. Pyjalé was all right against the deep shade of the bank, but I must have stood out quite clearly to the elephants' vision. Yet not a sign of suspicion did they make.

The drinking elephant was now standing up, and both appeared of a colossal size, almost terrifying in bulk and massiveness. And when they breathed, it seemed like the escape of steam from some huge, high-pressure locomotive boiler simmering with power. Was it with this puny .275 that I proposed killing these impressive looking bulks? It felt so small!

From these remarks, the reader will deduce that my confidence was just a little bit shaky. And the reader will be right. I was in a mortal funk. Behind us was a high, steep bank, so there was no escape that way. In front of us stood those overpowering bulks, almost within one of their lengths from us.

What of Pyjalé? There he was beside me with his futile spear, outwardly a cool and undisturbed man. How I wished I could know what he felt inside!

Taking a spare cartridge between my fingers restored my confidence, and I tried an experimental alignment of the rifle at the brain. I decided I dare not risk it. I could see the sights quite sufficiently well, but I don't believe I could have placed the bullet accurately enough. So it must be a heart shot.

Now, for this shot—as some of my readers may have also found—ten yards is too near. One cannot properly gauge the location of the heart at this distance. The broadside of an elephant is so extensive as not to be in proper perspective. It is much easier at fifty yards to see exactly where to place one's bullet. But there was nothing for it, and I fired.

The elephant moved straight forward along the river bed after making a sudden cringe toward us, caused by the entry of the bullet. His companion moved with him. We followed as hard as we could. There was silence from the others on the bank.

Presently the wounded animal came to a slow walk; he was ours. His mate was now ahead and slowed down also. When the wounded one came to a standstill, we

We came upon a drinking elephant of a colossal size.

were close up and I shot the second elephant when he stopped and turned. Then the first toppled over and let out a mighty bellow of pain and despair. I always hated that beastly heart shot; it not only seemed to give them such pain, but their dying bellows scared off everything in the vicinity, in the daytime at any rate.

Now a strange thing happened. As Pyjalé and I were moving off after the second wounded elephant, there suddenly appeared against the moon and sky above the bank the heads of several agitated elephants. They appeared to wish to come down into the river bed. Finding it too steep, they started along the bank. Thinking to get a shot at one against the moon or sky, I and Pyjalé ran along the stream bed parallel with them. I got no chance, however, and very soon we passed the second elephant toiling slowly up the opposite bank evidently mortally stricken. We continued this queer kind of affair for some distance—the herd trying to descend into the river bed and we two running along parallel with them trying to get a chance to kill.

Then they came to a break in the bank. Down they came straight to where we stood—three of them—sliding and slipping down at a fearful angle. I hated to shoot at those bobbing, slithering foreheads in the jumpy moonlight—it would have been bad enough in daylight. But I could not resist a shot at the last. Just as he lowered his front half over the top of the bank, he gave me what I thought a fair chance, and it came off. Shot in the brain—I found afterward through the top of the head—he slid and turned and landed at the bottom.

The other two were now almost on top of us. I simply could not see to shoot. They were in shade against shade, so I ran. Pyjalé came with me. I suppose the elephants thought we were a buck of some sort, for they took not the slightest notice until they strode into our scent. Then they knew, and one let out an alarm cry, while both raced across the river bed and climbed the other bank. For some reason best known to themselves, they had wished to get to the other bank all the time.

Pulling ourselves together, Pyjalé and I came back and climbed after them. We soon found ourselves in fairly thick bush and we could see nothing. Shooting here by moonlight would have been a very different thing from the river bed. Shadows were everywhere. We soon gave it up and returned to the river bed. First we examined the bull we had pulled down off the bank, and then we cut off his tail. He had tusks of about fifty pounds each. Then we went to look for the second elephant. He had managed to climb the bank but only just, and we found him under a large tree, dead. He had a broken tusk and a sound one of about 80 pounds. The first elephant had two grand tusks of 97 pounds and 104 pounds.

Now we went to one of the holes for a drink. Although the nights are cool, they are only comparatively so, and I, at any rate, had sweated quarts and was very dry. It was no easy matter getting the water. The hole was deep and the sand poured in whenever one trod near the edge. Pyjalé drank almost upside down, but I could not. It always ran into my nose. So finding a few large leaves, I made a scoop of them and I soon got my drink.

We now waited, lying on the warm sand, for the safari to turn up. It ought to have been near us by this time. I dozed off. Presently a very gentle pressure woke me; it was Pyjalé. He spoke no word, but I instantly became aware of a lion lapping water at the hole. We watched him finish his drink and slouch silently but busily away.

By the moon it was about midnight, so the safari must have lost itself. Pyjalé was for going off to fetch them, but I said I would go, too. We followed what should have been their line of country, but without result. I now determined to fire a shot or two to attract their attention in case they might be wandering about.

We were in an open plain, and there was a small ant-heap about a hundred yards away, and I thought I would try a shot at it by moonlight. At the shot I was astounded to see sparks fly up where my bullet had hit some stones, at least fifteen yards to one side of the ant-heap. So much for moonlight shooting. Firing a shot or two into the air, we soon had an answering shot from the direction of the dead elephants. The safari had passed the water holes too much to the west, had realized the mistake, and had come back.

Everyone was greatly elated at our success. Probably no people in the world are so genuinely pleased at their bwana's good luck as an elephant hunter's followers. They love the meat and the fat, not only to eat, but to trade with. Smoked elephant meat procures for them what money does for us. For a fortnight previous to that day we had not seen an elephant, and now the meat was handy to camp and to water and to firewood. There was lovely clean, soft sand to sleep on, and there were no mosquitoes and no rain. All was perfect.

Next day, while the ivory was being chopped out, I tried along the river to see if there were any more water holes. There were none. Everywhere Pyjalé shoved his spear far into the sand, but there was no water. He told me he could

A lion drinks.

tell from the sound made by jumping the spear up and down whether there was water below or not. Now, why was there water in one place only? I could only conclude that there must be some kind of watertight depression or bowl that held the water while the sand prevented it from evaporating.

On returning to camp we found the ivory already chopped out, scrubbed clean with sand and ready to be weighed and packed. The donkey headman had already soaked the necessary buckskins to make saddles to receive them. The hundred-pounder was too long for the donkeys and had to go to the boys. There was some difficulty in finding among the ivory carriers anyone to take it, as it was considered to be too small! However, by promising the boy who took it now that a larger one should be provided before we went back, it was finally disposed of. Soon all was ready for the forward march to Elephant Swamp.

By setting off in the evening, traveling half the night through great herds of game, sleeping briefly, and continuing half the next day, we arrived in good condition at the water holes in the overflow of Elephant Swamp. We made our camp some way back from the water and in some thickish bush. All that night, elephants, lions, rhinos, and giraffes could be heard about the camp, to say nothing of bucks and zebras snorting and charging around. I felt sure we would see elephants on the morrow.

Shortly after dawn I was up, and by the time the light was good, Pyjalé and I were ready. As we passed on our way to the slough, a fine lion on one side stared at us while a large bull giraffe stared at us from the other. We were soon among the long grass of the slough, and mostly it was trampled, but there were still patches of fairly upright stuff, high and thick enough to hide buffaloes. Everywhere were elephant tracks, which thrilled me from head to foot.

Pyjalé presently climbed a tree to look around. Anxiously I watched his face as he looked about. He gave that funny little grin of his, glanced down at me, and up I went beside him. Almost the whole green expanse of the swamp was visible. It might be a dish eight hundred yards in diameter, and everywhere there were elephants. They were mostly single and isolated, but all were bulls. Not a cow in sight. Indeed, I have never seen cows there or even any sign of them. It was one of those wonderful bull patches, the favoured of the gods. They were good bulls, too, for the most part.

Elated by the wonderful sight, and with heart swelling with resolve to do well and faithfully by my luck, we slipped to the ground. First it was necessary to get to the leeward side of the slough. Here we ran into a very old elephant with a single tooth of great size. His hoary head received the bullet, and he sank dead without a sound. No notice was taken by the other elephants of this first shot. With centuries of immunity to man-made weapons behind them, how should they be able to grasp at once that a new order of things had arrived?

Shot after shot vibrated in those great sound-collecting ears and were transmitted to those sagacious brains. And still the impulse to flee was denied those ponderous leg muscles. There they continued to stand awaiting their doom. Painlessly they died, one after the

A giraffe stared at us.

other. Only toward the end did a few of the smaller fry begin to become uneasy, and chiefly, I think, because they no longer saw their companions standing about. Most of the worthy ones were now down. It was time to quit. We returned to camp. I was satiated—for that day.

It will seem to most people a crime to have killed so many of these grand animals. I do not deny it. All I will put forward is this: These old elephants were really past the breeding age. They could not tolerate the presence of cows and would travel a hundred miles to avoid their obnoxious presence. They were of vast age, mostly, and apparently of no further use in the scheme of things.

Many had strange growths inside them. My boys were continually finding round balls of a dark olive colour of a size varying from that of a marble to that of a football. When cut, these balls showed the texture and colour of compressed curry powder. They originated in the liver. Often their livers were full of huge cysts. Many of them had extremely bad tempers. To have preserved these elephants much longer, it would have been necessary to have treated them in some way—obviously a great difficulty.

No, their day was up, and I consider that all those I killed were lucky. At any rate they were killed painlessly and were saved from inexperienced sportsmen probing their anatomy in strange places with bullets; from futile but painful spear jabs; from native pitfalls, snares, burnings; and last, but not least, from their own diseased livers.

A Day with the Pygmies

Chapter 14

For many years I had wished to meet those strange little hunting people called Pygmies. Their mode of life appealed enormously to me, and I thought that if I could come to be friends with them that they would certainly be able to put me on to good elephant haunts. The pursuit of my calling took me into the huge forest belt lying between the Ubangi and Sangha Rivers. I enquired diligently about the small forest folk in each riverine village, but without much success. All the information I got was that no man knew where they lived and that they had no villages or plantations; in fact, I was told that they had none of the customs and habits of normal people.

My informants, quite normal people, said that they came only at night to barter. They would leave whatever they had such as honey or meat a short way out of the village and then depart. On the morrow whoever wanted the goods would leave in their place such grain or other equivalent as custom had established. Then on the following night the shy little trader would remove it.

So timid were they supposed to be that the villagers said it would be quite useless to try to find them. It was out of the question for a white man to get in touch with them. They warned me that if I tried to do so, it would result in the Pygmies clearing out altogether. As there were hundreds of miles of unknown forest at their backs, this would not have been very difficult. I thought that if I could only manage to kill some big meat, they might come to it. With this in my mind I took to the forest with a modest little tent and gear.

It was toward camping time in the afternoon and we were traveling through the gloomy cool and damp forest when we halted beside a large calabash on the ground. The thought immediately was that the owner must be a Pygmy. Where was he? I and my boys began to look about for him on the ground, but our guide, a riverine native, looked up in the trees. Soon he spotted the owner of the calabash high up in the branches of a tree, from which descended a large creeper stem.

The calabash.

Our guide began to talk to him in the riverine language, a little of which was known to the bush-man. Our object in coming was explained and the little man invited to come down. This he flatly refused to do.

Knowing that if we failed to come to a friendly understanding with this, our first Pygmy, and that if we left him without coming to such an understanding, we should probably never see one again, so we decided to wait until he came down. Water was, fortunately, handy, so we made our camp under the little man's tree, which was luckily so isolated that he could not reach any of the other trees in the vicinity. A monkey might have, but certainly no man, not even a Pygmy.

Night soon fell, and our prospective friend saw that he must either come down or continue to sit up there all night. Rain finally persuaded him that it would be much more comfortable by a fireside, and he descended.

Seeing no soldiers and no arms other than my rifle, he soon became friendly. His calabash, full of honey, was restored to him intact, and he was given a share of some native beer we had with us from the river village. This, I think, completed our conquest, although it was with anxiety I regarded the coming night. I thought he would clear as soon as we were all asleep, and yet I did not wish to guard him in any way. Trusting to luck we slept.

Waking just before dawn—a habit one soon acquires in the bush—the first thing I asked was whether the Pygmy was still with us. The answer came that he had gone. But on looking round I saw the calabash still there. And as I was pointing this out, we saw him coming back to camp. I was relieved.

It was explained to him that we wished to be taken to his camp and that then we would hunt together. He was a very silent little man and had the most expressionless face I have ever seen in Africa, a land of expressionless faces. But he gave a sort of grunt that might have meant anything. We chose to interpret it as assent.

After packing our gear, we followed him. He led straight on through the forest. When I say he went straight, I mean that I suppose he went straight, for I had no way of telling this. The sun cast no shadows, and was, indeed, invisible through the heavy foliage overhead. I noticed that he took a fleeting interest in certain holes in the ground, but why and for what he was searching I could not learn. Here was a being living in another world. Although I knew a fair bit about the open bush country, I was quite at sea in this primeval forest.

All that was obvious to me was that I would need to fit a large-headed foresight to my rifle on account of the poor light. For forest shooting I came to find that wart-hog ivory was much more brilliant than elephant ivory, besides which it does not go yellow so quickly. A wart-hog tush that has been lying bleaching for some time in open country is most excellent for foresights. A set of small files of different shapes is all that is required to work up the material.

How I wished I could have talked to that fellow. What things he could have told me about the game animals of these forests. Things impossible for a white man ever to learn. And about his people: Why they are as black as any other natives without ever running much risk of getting sun-tanned as far as I could see.

Presently we were halted by our guide. He explained that we must wait here. He went on by himself. In a short time he returned and we followed him to his camp, consisting of three or four very shabby, poorly made, and extremely small huts or shelters, composed of branches and large leaves. There were a couple of women and some children about it. They had evidently been efficiently warned by our new friend, for they showed hardly any surprise at seeing a white man in their midst. Our modest little camp was prepared close to theirs and life went on much as usual. While waiting for the men of the village to come, I fixed up a larger ivory bead foresight to my rifle.

A white man's hunting kit in the tropics is a scanty enough affair, comprising felt hat, neutral-coloured shirt, shorts, socks, and boots. One would think that there was little room for anything to go wrong, but there is. With all our ingenuity, experience, and command of different materials, we cannot yet produce a boot that is always satisfactory.

The English shooting boot of stout leather will kill you in a fortnight. It is too heavy by several pounds when wet. When dry it is still too heavy and also too stiff. It will produce galls and rubs when filled with sand. It is noisy and makes you feel clumsy-footed. Football boots are light, do not slip, but do not last any time; they also give you the most dreadful rubs not only on the heel and ankle but on the sole also. Crêpe rubber soles with light leather uppers are silent but heavy, easily become too large, and squelch when filled with water—unless they are pierced along just above the sole, which allow, of course, sand and grit to enter. Canvas tops with rope soles do not last, but are

The Pygmy village.

light to carry, silent, let out water as easily as they let it in, keep out grit, do not slip often, and are, I think, on the whole the best of a bad lot.

Of these latter I found that I required two pairs per month. The fact of the matter is, bare feet are the solution to the boot problem. Properly hardened by constant use and wear, what can equal them? And consider the toe grip we lose when wearing boots. It is pretty safe to say that the average civilized man has lost almost all the power of his toes as a means of propulsion. Examine any African's track in sand, and you will notice how wide apart and deep are the impressions made by his toes. You will also notice that his foot is not pointed as ours are through generations of trying to look genteel. His feet are almost square in front. From this he derives enormous power and grip in shifty going.

Meanwhile, the men of the village had come in by ones and twos. I had our friend called and told him I wanted to speak with them all. They quickly came, and I had it explained to them that our reason in coming into their country was to hunt with them in order to kill elephant.

As a matter of fact, the co-operation of these people was essential in this forest country. No other natives, and certainly no white man, could do it without them, for they would surely lose themselves the first day. There are no paths, no sun, no moon, no stars, no landmarks; there is nothing to guide an ordinary mortal. His one chance of retracing his steps is to "blaze" the trees, and that entails the making of such a noise as would most effectively prevent his ever seeing any animal except a monkey. Therefore, our future hunting depended entirely on the good-will of these people.

Fortunately for us, Africans who live by the chase are naturally of a quiet, kindly, and peaceful disposition. Were it otherwise they would be the most formidable obstruction to any penetration of their country it is possible to imagine. With their cunning bush-craft added to the natural difficulties of the county they inhabit; with their total lack of seizable property, towns or villages, huts, or valuables; and with their independence of supplies of food, they would be almost impossible for an organized force to overcome.

As soon as our object in coming had been interpreted to the men of the village, a discussion arose among them. I had no means of telling what it was about, as my interpreter knew a mere handful of words of the Pygmy language. And, of course, nothing could be gathered from the expressionless faces before me. Of one thing I felt pretty certain, and that was that they could not very well flatly refuse to go with me into the bush. What I was most afraid of was that they would go with me and carefully keep me from game in the hope that I would soon leave their country.

The argument soon ended by everyone rising to their feet and going off to their little leaf bivouacs. There they simply picked up their bows and arrows. Our friend of the tree episode announced that they were ready to go hunting.

Here already was a marked difference. Ordinary natives living in villages need to make preparations before going into the bush. Food has to be prepared, and axes and knives have to be borrowed, found, or sharpened. The going off hunting is regarded as an outing, but here with true hunters, it was part of the normal day's routine. My little tent was soon rolled up, and we also were ready for the trail.

Off we went steadily through the damp and rather gloomy forest, in what direction I had not the vaguest idea, having no compass with me. Our first halt was caused by the leading Pygmy just stopping. There he stood, looking straight ahead at a thickish clump of underbrush with no gesture to indicate that he saw anything. He made no attempt to conceal himself or to caution his followers. Neither did he try to point out anything to me.

As I was trying to follow his glance and discover what he was looking at, there was a movement in the underbush and I caught a glimpse of a low form disappearing. When we came to the spot I saw pig tracks. I thought to myself I would have to keep a very much sharper look-out if I was to get any of these forest animals.

The next halt was at a clump of large wild palms. One of the Pygmies climbed the branchless stem of one of them, took from out of the very top a dirty wooden bowl, and descended with it to the ground. It contained some perfectly clear and sparkling liquid under a coating of white froth. It was fresh palm wine, sweetish and delightfully cool. Out of this liquid they make by fermentation a most potent toddy.

Later in the day our guides provided themselves with food by taking out of the centre of the tops of similar, but younger, palms the heart or cabbage. This, when cooked, is tender and good and nourishing. It destroys the palm, but what does that matter when there might be half a million palms for each human mouth? Elephants also feed largely on the tender hearts of the palms,

The little man seemed ready to take a hand.

destroying hundreds in a day's grazing. Nature provides abundantly for all her children in these regions.

We passed numerous tracks of herds of elephants but without paying any attention to them. It looked as if we were making for some particular place. Toward evening I saw a forest antelope, with which I was quite unacquainted, through a clearing in the forest. I hissed to the man in front because I wished to shoot it. He glanced back at me and then pointed ahead and went on. I surmised from this that he did not wish me to fire. He had probably seen the buck long before I did.

As we went along, it became apparent to me at last that they had heard something. I have noticed that all Africans have an extraordinary gift of listening to faint noises through other louder and nearer noises without the latter interfering with the former. One never hears an African ask another to stop making a noise so that he can the better listen-in, as it were. They must have a better selective ear mechanism than we have because they can certainly listen to and follow sounds amid other distracting sounds that we can faintly hear only when deep silence pervades. So now, these primitive men were hearing sounds, that were quite inaudible to me. They heard these above the noise we made crunching over stick-strewn and leafy ground with boggy stretches where feet sank in and sucked when lifted. And all this while not even halting themselves.

It was all intensely interesting and rather weird. It was tantalizing, too, that they could not tell me what they heard. But the matter was not long in doubt, for I was astonished to find myself suddenly in proximity to a herd of elephants. There they were, almost invisible only a few yards in front of us, their dull hides showing no contrast with the surrounding bush and deep shade. They seemed so silent; it was difficult to believe that we had tracked them by hearing alone instead of by their spoor. This was a revelation to me; I had never seen it before.

Now one of the Pygmy men began to approach the herd without further preliminaries, fitting an arrow to his bow as he went. He evidently intended to take a hand in the business. I got close up to him and took him by the arm. We were now only a few paces from the nearest animals. They were all resting and quite unsuspicious of our presence.

The light was very bad, indeed, I realized, when it came to aligning a rifle. The usual guiding marks on an elephant's head stood out hardly at all. Shadows and high lights were not here; all was soft shadow. Nothing was anything like as distinct as in the accompanying sketch. I was thankful for my large wart-hog ivory foresight. Finally I fired without conviction at the head of what I judged by his size to be a bull.

As I fired, the man beside me darted toward the elephants and fired his arrow at extremely close range. There was the usual stampede. Crashing everything before them, off the elephants went. In these moist surroundings, there was no dust. Following the Pygmy, I was relieved to see my beast on the ground; I thought he had gone with the others.

Racing on after my little friend, who was going two yards to my one, I was soon passed by the other Pygmies. The way in which they covered ground was astonishing. They seemed to pass over tangled roots with deep boggy holes between them as if they were on a tennis lawn, whereas I floundered along, slipping about, tripping, and with my feet shooting from under me and often falling. While walking through the forest, I would have said that it was quite cool, but now sweat simply poured off me in streams. I got completely left behind and never saw these elephants again except the one the Pygmies killed. They held on to the wounded one, a cow, and killed her miles away that evening.

They had filled her stern with poisoned arrows, as I discovered next day when they were setting apart the poisoned parts not to be eaten. I wished I had been able to be in at the death because I wished to see how the poison acted. It seems an extraordinary thing that they can eat the flesh of an animal that has had poison injected into its circulation. I have been told by doctors that the native poison has the effect of causing the blood to coagulate. If this is so, one could understand that the poison would not spread to every part.

We became very great friends with these people, and they showed me what a very poor thing a white man really is when tackling Nature in one of her rougher moods as here in real forest. It will be remembered what happened to Stanley when traversing the great Congo forest. His people starved while surrounded by meat, although armed with rifles. He was not friendly with the men of the country.

KANO TO KHARTOUM BY CAR

CHAPTER 15

I wish to disclaim at the outset any attempt at putting forward the accomplishment of this journey as a feat of exploration. It was nothing of the sort. The great main pilgrim route to Mecca used by thousands of devotees of Mohammed every year was followed for most of the way. The only novelty lay in our use of motor instead of the usual horse, camel, bullock, or donkey transport.

The first part of the journey was the uneventful passage from Southampton to Lagos. From Lagos we went by rail to Kano, the great trading centre of northern Nigeria, which was chosen as our starting place. Our motors arrived in their crates and were assembled there.

The town is in two parts: The one consists of the railway station, post office, and a few wide streets of modern commercial houses and shops, for the most part a perfectly hideous lay-out, with corrugated iron and imported wood the predominant features. The other part is the old native town, with native buildings of sun-baked mud surrounded by a mud wall. Kano, to my mind, is chiefly remarkable for the gaudily dressed police men of the native administration and the picturesque police station.

In both towns there is tremendous activity in the streets during trading hours. Picturesque camel caravans slouch leisurely along, and bullocks and

The boat trailer . . .

And the canoe trailer.

donkeys with natives from every part of Africa throng the wide streets of the commercial town. They are all dealing in that humble little commodity, the ground-nut, familiar to most people in their small paper bags. Here you see thousands of tons of it. Sacks of it piled mountain high in this dry climate waiting, maybe, for rolling stock to move it.

Once installed in our quarters, the work of assembling the motors began. There were four of them: a Fiat 30-C.W.T. lorry, a Citröen-Kegresse caterpillar, a one-ton Chevrolet and, of course, a Ford touring chassis. Besides these motors there were two Canadian freight canoes fitted with small detachable motors and a Saunders' folding utility boat, also with a motor. All these had to be fitted snugly onto trailers to be towed by the Fiat and the Chevrolet respectively. Meanwhile boys were engaged, and our stay at Kano gave us a chance to try them out, with the result that one or two were turned down.

At last all was ready for the road, and off we went. The going was astonishingly good for the first hundred miles until we came to our first sandy river. Luckily, the chief had *zana* mats down, and we crossed our wheeled cars on them, while the Citröen crossed on the sand with ease.

The first stage of our journey ended at Maidugari, a large native town. The Citröen had shown itself capable of crossing very loose, deep sand without assistance. But on good going it was intolerably slow and, mechanically, always very fussy. I doubt if its speed ever passed 15 m.p.h., and it boiled constantly. The Chevrolet one-tonner was a great success, except that it also boiled constantly, but it carried a great load and kept going in an almost uncanny way in sand.

Owing to its driver holding the peculiar opinion that when the radiator required refilling, it was better to drain off the boiling water and then to pour in cold water, it contracted a crack in one of its cylinders. I am bound to say that it made very little difference to its performance. The mileage was very good, indeed. With a ton and a quarter on, and the trailer with two canoes, it did 12 m.p.g.

In the flooded area.

The Ford also was astonishingly good. Of course, it carried next to nothing, but it went a long way on a gallon of petrol, hardly ever got stuck, and when it did, two or three people pushed it through. It boiled constantly, used a lot of oil, and was hard to start, but gave very little trouble otherwise. The Fiat carried about 2½ tons, trailed the motor boat, gave no mechanical trouble, but required quite a gang to get it through bad places. But, then, it could carry them. It never boiled its water, used very little oil and no water, and averaged, over the Nigerian roads, about 7 m.p.g., besides being as speedy as any of them on good going. On sandy roads it did about 4–5 m.p.g.

A road-making gang.

Bringing up material for a corduroy bridge.

The first bit of real trouble came when we were between Dikoa and Kousseri. Here, in the middle of the dry season, the boundary river separating French from Nigerian territory was very high. The reason for this curious state of affairs told to us by the natives was that Lake Chad banked up on the south shore when the strong north-east winds blew, and that this caused the river to rise. But we came to the conclusion that the reason for the river's

A calabash "canoe."

Mud architecture in Kano.

The native police station at Kano.

rise was the countless barrages erected right across the river by the natives for fish-trapping purposes.

The problem was how to get our four cars, one of them weighing a ton and a half when empty, across this deep river. Instead of fooling around building various combinations of canoes and motor launches, we handed the problem straight to the old chief, while we went off duck shooting. He proceeded to deal with it in a far more efficient way than we could have done.

They had ambatch, a wood so light that one man can hold a huge log out at arm's length, and what they did not know about the floating capacity of ambatch was certainly well worth ignoring. The chief ordered every ambatch canoe—which is simply a bundle of it tied together—to be brought to the scene. There the bundles were untied and made into a huge raft. Rope was passed round it, and there it was, ready for two or three cars. When the Fiat came to be driven onto it, twenty natives climbed up and held her in position, while fifty or sixty swam the whole thing over without a hitch.

While all this was going on, we had some wonderful duck shooting. Whistling duck in thousands, besides fast-flying teal and other ducks, flew in an almost constant flight up- and down-stream right over our camp. One of the party, who had a touch of fever, lay on his camp-bed and shot duck as they passed overhead. Our bag was only limited by the number that could be consumed by ourselves and our followers.

Once across the river, our troubles began. We were now on French mandated territory, and there was no made road. The administration of the country was in the hands of two military officers at Kousseri, and their efforts seemed to be confined to gathering taxes. Luckily for us the natives still had some of the respect for white men so well impressed upon them by the former German occupiers. Hence we were soon provided with large gangs of natives, who built corduroy bridges over the flooded arms of the rising river.

Every day more and more fish barrages were being built, and the river was constantly overflowing in new places. With the exception of these flooded parts, the going was remarkably good, our speed sometimes touching 25 m.p.h. Generally speaking, the native roads in Africa follow the best line of country, meaning the best way for a pack animal, which is also best for wheeled vehicles. It is only the necessity to have water that causes large deviations from the straight line.

Bird life on the boundary river.

Besides ambatch, the natives of these parts use two large calabashes with a stick between them to navigate on the rivers. They sit straddle-legged on this stick and paddle with their hands. From this custom it may be deduced that the crocodiles here have a wholesome respect for the human form, as most of it is submerged when actually afloat.

PART II

At Dikoa we were in Sultan Rabeh's capital. Rabeh, the Napoleon of the Lake Chad region, is known to every man, woman, and child in Central Africa. Like so many of Africa's great soldiers, he was the son of Negro parents, although he tried hard during his lifetime to have it accepted that his father was an Arab. His early life was spent in a good slave-hunting school with Liber in the Bahr-el-Ghazal, under whose command he soon became a leader.

Later he served Soliman when that chief surrendered to General Gordon's expedition, commanded by Gessi Pasha. Rabeh on this occasion warned Soliman against surrender and, when Soliman persisted, broke off his connection and left, together with some thousands of the best fighting spirits. From that time he became a most potent personage, fighting, and generally conquering, all over Central Africa. His empire became immense.

Then the French turned their attention to him. At their first contact with him in the Niellim Mountains, the French were beaten. But they numbered only fifty Senegalese and a handful of native allies under Administrator Bretonnet against Rabeh's thousands of well-armed men. The first trick was Rabeh's and also the second, although Rabeh himself was wounded in this battle. Then the third and last took place at Kousseri. Rabeh was killed on the field of battle as were the French commanders Lamy and Cointet.

We were shown a large burial pot in the compound of Rabeh's palace. These pots are used for the interment of dead notabilities. This one is a particularly fine specimen, and was awaiting transport to the British Museum. Had we been going to instead of away from Kano, we might have carried it on our lorry. The British district commissioner, whose quarters are in the palace, showed us where Rabeh's women lived. He told us he used to keep them in huts in a large walled enclosure on the palace grounds, and from his bedroom he could survey the whole compound. They numbered one thousand, and it is said that his bedroom was his favourite spot. I hope he had a pair of Zeiss glasses of large field.

As I said, immediately after we had left Nigeria our difficulties began. There was no longer any road, but, fortunately, the natural going was very good between the flooded parts. Bucks were numerous, and large numbers of roans were seen. There was never any difficulty in shooting sufficient meat for the

A burial pot for the British Museum.

False egrets on the marshes.

safari. Ducks, also, were plentiful, and flighted up and down the river both by day and by night. Spur-winged geese, black and white ibis, egrets, false egrets, and other birds were numerous and tame.

Some heavy corduroying had to be done at the innumerable overflows from the river. The natives were good at this work. First they cut down thorn bushes, stripped the branches off, and laid the trunks in the mud and water lengthwise. Then the branches were placed on these crosswise. After that came smaller branches and long grass, and over everything a few inches of earth.

At these operations, music—an essential feature of African labour—was provided by the native bands. Pots of native beer were sent by the chiefs. Hot-air merchants on horses, with swords and guns and large whips—which they dared not use—careered about. With plenty of noise and beer, the work was quickly finished, and we would be off for another mile or two until the next water held us up. Here the same performance would be gone through.

Our passage through the country had a curious effect on the native mind. At first they would take our appearance quite calmly; then they seemed to be seized with some idea that our cars were large wounded animals and ought to be chased; and, finally, the sight of ourselves seated in or on the large wounded animals seemed to tickle them immensely. The whole show became a kind of traveling circus to them. They would run for miles with us.

One day the Ford was ahead. The way lay through some thickish bush. A striped hyaena, hearing the car groaning along, and also maybe thinking of some wounded beast, came to the track and ran along toward the sound. As soon as the driver saw him, he pulled up and waited. The hyaena came padding along toward the car until the driver shot him at close range.

Our passage was really delightfully easy, thanks to the good will of the natives. If we got into any difficulty, the natives simply pulled us out of it. The driver of the Citröen one day thought he would show us all how to cross mud. He went about two yards and bogged down and stalled his engine. The natives pulled the Citröen out.

At Kousseri we were faced with the crossing of the Lagone and Shari Rivers, at the least a half mile of open water. It ought to have been difficult, but, as it turned out, it was comparatively easy, thanks to the kindness of the French governor and the agent of the l'Ouham et Nana Company. They very generously sent their steamer with two barges to ferry us over.

Natives would run with us for miles.

Struggling through the mud.

We found Fort Lamy[1] to be a beautiful little French town. Bricks were made on the spot as well as roofing tiles of native earth. Everything was home-made, including native wood doors, sashes, and native wood furniture. All in all, it was an astonishing show after the horrible imported wood and corrugated iron of Nigeria. The reason for it being that in Fort Lamy there is no transport and in Nigeria there is a railway.

We were most hospitably received by everyone. No nation can make you so welcome as the French. They put a house at our disposal, and we were given permits to shoot, maps, itineraries of the routes—all were forthcoming. Nothing was too much trouble; they were perfectly charming. We went to their races. One might have been in France, except that everyone was much more friendly. We drank "fizz" and watched the races and the pari-mutuel betting, and the ladies appeared to me to be dressed in the latest Paris creations.

After the races we visited one of our newly made friends' houses, and he showed us his menagerie—leopards, cheetahs, a lion, etc., all happy, familiar, well fed, and not in cages. Bits of very flimsy rope were tied to them, it is true, but the other ends were loose, as often as not. Their native women keepers had great command over them, treating them exactly as they would their own

[1]Present day N'Djamena, Chad.

children. If a leopard growled and looked vicious, one of the girls would seize it and drag it away, the leopard lying on its back and making itself heavy just like any other child. Altogether we thoroughly enjoyed our visit to Fort Lamy.

From Fort Lamy to Am Timam our road now lay through all kinds of going, some of it mountainous, some flat, but it was the latter that gave most trouble. In the wet season it was a sea of mud, churned up by the passage of animals and humans, and its surfaces when dry become of an indescribable roughness. All the cars were obliged to simply crawl on the lowest gear, and here the Ford showed to great disadvantage with its one low gear. The driver's leg became numbed with fatigue after a few miles of it. Everything groaned and creaked as the heavily laden cars lurched slowly along.

Several French posts were passed on the way, where we were charmingly received. As usual at French posts, we were supplied with abundance of European and tropical vegetables.

All the bush was thorn, and the Ford, fitted with Dunlop oversizes, began to have punctures because the walls of the tyres were not quite thick enough to prevent this. Luckily, the holes were small and easily patched. The stouter-walled, larger-size tyres seemed to keep them out, although they began to resemble pincushions with the innumerable thorn points sticking in them. The Michelin tyres began at this stage to develop a horrid habit of blowing out their valves.

What happened was this: In the process of blowing them up, by relays of lusty boys on the pump, the little rubber end of the non-return plunger simply melted, owing to the heat generated by the pumping when added to the heat already in the air. This fault caused us much delay and trouble because, as our stock of spare valves began to give out, we were obliged to pump slowly and pause to let things cool down.

Roan antelope were common wherever the bush was suitable, and dorcas gazelle, common hartebeest, bush partridge, and guinea-fowl often filled our pots. Lion tracks were seen on the trail, and two leopards approached to within ten yards, grunting and calling to each other in tall grass, only to spot me first and to fade away without being seen. A note in my diary says that the air was so dry here as to require a refill of ink in the fountain pen for each page.

The loss of petrol through unseen leaks in the tins was very serious. My diary notes that one four-gallon tin contained only one pint, and another tin one gallon instead of four. This loss could be reckoned around 30 percent.

An "original" jazz group.

About this stage the rubber tracks of the Citröen-Kegresse began to give us a lot of trouble. This, added to her almost continuous mechanical trouble, delayed us considerably. It seemed a poor thing except in deep, loose sand. There it certainly had a great advantage over the wheeled things.

At Abou Deïa we were shown some fine greater koodoo horns, an enormous set of wart-hog tushes, and some poor ivory. Leopards were very numerous in the hills and prey on large troops of baboons.

We were now approaching elephant country, and the going became worse. The Fiat stuck hopelessly in a dry sandy river bed, and we were obliged to unship the blocks and tackle and our large hemp hawser. These blocks had originally been a pair of four-fold, but the strain had been too great for the iron binding of one of them with four boys pulling, so the set had been reduced to a three and a four-fold. Even then, the strain of six boys when multiplied sevenfold was more than the very best hemp hawser could stand. It parted twice on this occasion, with six men on the fall, and yet it always withstood successfully the direct pull of forty-five or fifty men. By doubling the hawser, six men dragged out the Fiat, although it was down on the differential in loose sand and the get-out was up-hill and the car was heavily loaded.

We were attacked by bees during these operations. They came at us in vicious clouds. At first everyone was calm and cool and refrained from exciting them by trying to beat them off. Then someone was stung, and lost his nerve, and started flogging them off. That did it. Everyone was stung. Those who stood their ground had five or six each, but those who fled had dozens of stings left in them by the frenzied bees. It took some time to pick them out afterward.

Natives do not swell up after bee stings, but a French officer, who had kindly come to help us, was stung on the nose, which swelled up in a most painful way. He was our guest at the time, we having asked him to dine with us at camp that night. It was night when we got there, with the cook and his gear. Water had to be brought a long way, and was like green pea soup when it arrived. But the greatest misfortune was that our cook considered that it was up

Sheik Ahmet of Am Timam.

to him to produce what he thought was a fine dinner, but which turned out to be a procession of dishes of revolting appearance and indigestible consistency.

We passed three hours waiting for that awful meal, sitting in the moonlight trying to entertain our guest, who, I must mention, was in a delicate state of health. About 11 P.M. we sat down to dine. With fine heroism, our guest actually ate some of it, and when we produced some very bad "ink" we had bought at Lamy, he was polite enough to drink some of it. About 1 A.M. he departed on his thirty-mile ride to his post. He survived, for we subsequently heard that he had gone home on doctor's orders.

Bucks were fairly numerous, and we saw the tracks of a good-size herd of elephants. At Am Timam we were fairly in the home of Arab elephant hunters. We were introduced by the French administrator to the two big chiefs of the country, Ahmet and Fadel. Both of these men send hunting parties south each dry season.

PART III

Am Timam was the real starting point of our bush work. So far we had been simply following more or less well-beaten tracks. We had come from Kano in Nigeria to Am Timam in the French Chad territory in some fifteen actual traveling days. Motors had so far proved entirely successful. One may say that almost any type of modern car can cross the open, dry parts of Africa where there is any kind of cleared trail, during the dry season at any rate. The same journey by porters or animal transport would have occupied at least three months.

It was decided that two of the members of the expedition should proceed to the Bahr Aouk by car, there to attempt the ascent of that river by motor launch and canoes. These were being sent by native paddlers from Fort Lamy to Fort Archambault.[2] The other member decided to continue east, intending to enter and cross the Anglo-Egyptian Soudan to Khartoum.

Arrangements were made for the purchase of ponies for an elephant hunt in the rough country to the south of the Bahr Aouk, and Arabs were engaged to accompany them. Various dispositions of petrol supplies were also made from the stock laid down at Fort Archambault, for, of course, none could be obtained locally.

[2]Presently Sarh, Chad.

An Arab elephant hunter.

Saras bringing grass mats.

From the administrator we learned that something like five hundred licenses to hunt elephant had already been issued. These licenses are for one year and entitle the holder to kill an unlimited number of either male or female elephants, but with native weapons only. They cost the small sum of fifty francs. Because of this trifling figure every native and white man takes out as many as he can afford.

Each license forms the nucleus for a band of hunters numbering anything from ten to fifteen or twenty men. Each is provided with a pony, and all carry the prodigious elephant spear, with its head some two feet in length and up to nine inches in breadth. On the trek south these spears, as a rule, are carried without the shaft. This shaft is some twelve feet long and is of male bamboo. On reaching elephant country, fresh bamboo is cut and fitted to the heads, and these are again discarded on leaving elephant country. The heads are carefully covered with leather guards, and are always very keen, as much depends on this. Easy entry through the tough hide of elephant demands extreme keenness.

Sheik Fadel accompanied us in the Fiat. It was the first motor car he had ever seen, let alone ridden in. He came with seven or eight of his retinue, and seemed to enjoy it like a schoolboy in spite of the bad going.

After leaving Am Timam, we met with some extremely bad ground in the flat, open plains bordering the Bahr Keita. It was simply atrocious. The soil was hard, sun-baked mud in irregular hummocks.

On this hummocky ground, the rolling was terrific and the weaving of the chassis alarming. The heavy aluminum casting containing the gears suffered damage, one of the massive holding lugs being fractured. Only a crawl on first or second gear was possible. This speed for a hundred and fifty miles is no mean test of a car's ability to keep cool in a fierce sun. The Fiat never boiled and her radiator remained clear of grass seeds. In fact, we often wondered how it managed in cold climates. It ran so coolly in Africa that one would imagine it must almost freeze in a cold country.

These hummocky plains are bordered by light bush country where all game is fairly numerous. Sheik Fadel lent us ponies to try the bush one day. We saw a lot of hartebeests, roan antelopes, and kobs besides the old and recent tracks of elephants, buffaloes, giraffes, and lions. Our camp was distinguished by the great swarms of bees about it. Anything moist attracted myriad bees.

A Sara woman of the old brigade.

At last the pounding, bucking, rolling, and thumping ride came to an end on the banks of the Bahr Aouk. Permanent camp was made, and the cars blocked up. We had now to wait a few days until the ponies arrived from Am Timam and the canoes and launch from Fort Archambault.

The natives were Saras and quite friendly. All the tribal characteristics were evident. The women were quite nude, and they were hairy with silky skins, a wonderful condition, and in good shape. They formed a striking contrast to the Salamat Arabs through whose country we had so recently passed. There the women were prettier, but covered with filthy rags and afraid to come near the whites, due probably to their good looks attracting too much attention from the French passers-by.

While at permanent camp we went down-stream to a large pool where the natives said there were hippos. Thinking that they would be unwary and easy to film, we took our cameras. But we found them quite shy and none out of the water. There were about forty of them blowing and diving in the pool. We shot a few for meat, and while we were watching, we saw an old bull seize a dead cow by the neck in his mouth and raise the body some way out of the water. He appeared to be very excited. Some huge crocodiles came up and gave us some good shooting practice. Dotted about the pool were numerous turtle heads.

Another day when we were out in search of meat, three large, black, old bull buffaloes appeared directly in front of us from about 120 yards. I killed the first with a .275 in the neck and fired at another as the two survivors galloped across our front. My companion fired at the third with his .350, and they were all dead in a very few seconds, strung out in a straight line with about 50 yards between them. We both remarked that game has no earthly chance with modern rifles.

The Aouk was simply stuffed with fish of all sorts, so our large spinning rod was got out. A 2½-inch spoon was tried, trolling behind a canoe. The first fish was on for a few seconds, during which he took out a lot of line besides jumping several feet in the air, but he got off. Two others were also on for a similar time, and they too got off. Then natural bait was tried. Some half-pounders were shot and put on crocodile tackle. They were immediately taken, and the usual rushes and jumps in the air proceeded. One fish looked as if he was about 3½ feet long. He eventually broke the line on a snag. Several others were lost for no apparent reason. Possibly their mouths are too hard for the hooks to enter properly. But they are very game and sporting fish.

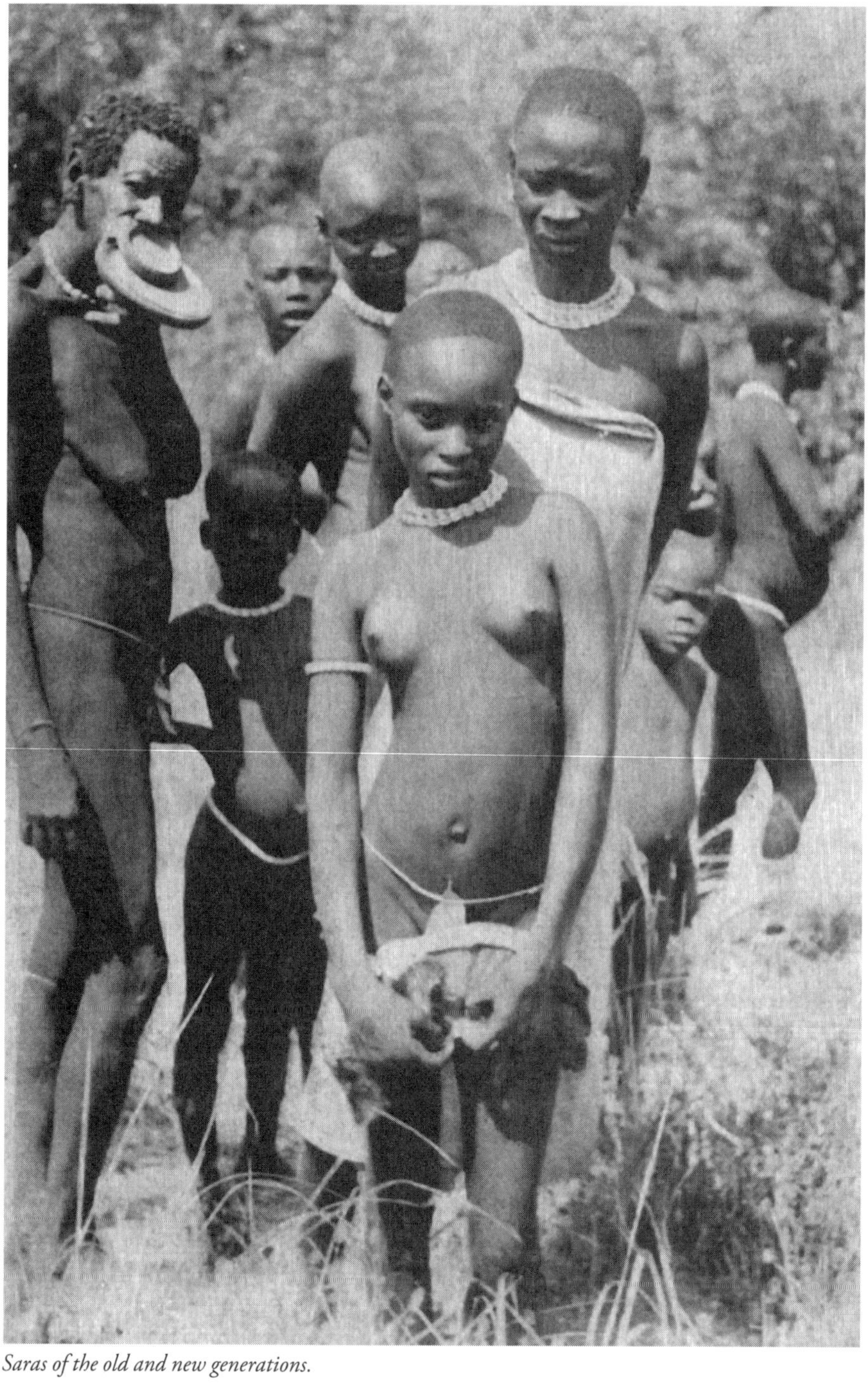

Saras of the old and new generations.

While waiting for the ponies and boats, we ran down in the Ford to Fort Archambault for our mail. It was 160 kilometers, and we were lucky to do it in one long day. The run included one river crossing where man-handling was required. This was the Bahr Keita. At Archambault we were much taken with a baby giraffe that had just been brought in by natives. It was quite tame, showing no fear of man. On the contrary, it would follow anyone and would suck a finger just like a calf. It seemed particularly fond of the French gentlemen shown in the photo.

And here I would like to remark upon the flair the French seem to have for rearing all kinds of wild animals. Lion, leopard, elephant, cheetah, giraffe, and many others may be met in their posts, roaming around as free as the air, and all extremely tame. The French will take infinite pains with their charges, and have a genuine and constant delight in them, which is altogether charming to see.

We saw a fair quantity of game from the car, and on the way back a herd of nine giraffes passed across the trail forty or fifty yards ahead of us. They looked magnificent. Of course, we had no photographic gear ready at the moment. A short way from our permanent camp we overtook our Arabs with the ponies. The latter looked fairly well, but tired, and we installed them at the native village where corn could be fed to them.

Next day the flotilla arrived from Fort Archambault. The launch, without engine, was poled along by two fine Saras, and each of the two freight canoes had two polers. Their engines, petrol, and other gear were in a steel thirty-foot boat belonging to the l'Ouham et Nana Company. These boats had come up-stream against the current all the way from Port Lamy, somewhere about seven hundred kilometres, and they were in quite fair condition.

My companion and I separated there, he going up-stream to Lake Mamoun and I south across the Aouk to the N'Délé hill country, famous for elephant. But first the ponies required a rest and corn, and the launch had to receive her engine.

This was quickly done, the engine and reversing propeller, silencer, and controls all being in one unit ready to drop into its place in the boat after removing the wooden plug that filled the hole in the skin for the propeller shaft. This done, the smaller of the two canoes was lashed alongside the launch, care being taken to have the two keels absolutely parallel, the whole forming a very stable catamaran of great carrying capacity. A sun awning was erected on the launch, and a successful trial carried out. The affair was not fast, but it was fast enough for the state of the river.

A young pet giraffe.

Fish really worth talking about.

In the heat and bustle of our preparations in our little harbour, time was found to weigh up the petrol brought by the steel boat. We found that loss by leakage amounting to 25 percent had been sustained. That it was not more was probably due to the fact that the cases had been in boats and, therefore, not so shaken about as on land.

In the evening we fished, and while procuring bait by shooting shallow-swimming fish with a revolver, a hawk swooped down and seized a dead fish floating down-stream. But that hawk had not reckoned with flukes, and a revolver bullet cut her down in the very act of robbing us of our bait.

Corn was meanwhile being shoved into the ponies. I added some salt to it, but this horrified the Arabs. They said salt was good for humans but fatal to ponies. However, they continued to get it, and certainly came to like it very much, indeed. It was a safe thing to say as we were going into "fly" country, and in the ordinary course of things, very few, if any, of the ponies would return.

When all was ready, I took the road with ten porters carrying very light loads, ten ponies, three Arabs, a native interpreter, a boy cook, and his mate. My companion took his departure with his flotilla on the same day. After all our rushing, organizing, fiddling with motors, repairing tyres, and calculating petrol, oil, and water consumption, etc., it was veritable peace and calm to get back to the native bush with nothing but natives and native affairs to worry about. It was delightful.

Native scarecrow.

Drawing near our first camp south of the Aouk, I shot a buck for meat. There were three standing together, and the survivors ran off. Immediately there was a thunderous cavalry charge past me. Off went all the ponies after the two bucks, the ponies appearing to enjoy the fun as much as the boys. Some of the latter were on corn-fed ponies with neither saddles nor bridles nor bits, and they simply went with the ponies. That was saying a lot, I thought, as they dashed along at full speed, swerving about the ant-heaps, thorn trees, and holes. They have wonderful balance and grip, these Arabs, and posteriors of cast iron.

The possession of a horse is to them the highest attainment of life, not excepting even women. Once acquired, the animal is cared for in the most lavish style. It is hardly ever allowed to roam about but is fed under some shady tree in the village and ridden to water, where it is often carefully bathed. The best of food is given it, and as they are never gelded, one can imagine the scene when perhaps two or three hundred young bloods come to the dance, each riding a gaudily caparisoned high-fed stallion. Of course, the ponies we had were not of this class. For going into "fly" country, only the bad or old horses are used.

We were a jolly little party as we headed south. The Arabs promised countless elephants ahead of us, and the porters had light loads and plenty of meat. At the first village we saw a girl who had had one eye taken out by a leopard. Then her father showed us the skin of the leopard that did it and finally the trap that had caught the leopard. This simple but effective affair of logs made a strong cage. It had a falling log door connected to a trigger mechanism of rope and sticks; it was baited with putrid fish.

PART IV

I wish to show how African big game really is being wiped out, not as is so commonly thought by white men with modern arms, but by the natives themselves with more or less obsolete arms, brought up to date by an ingenious combination of old and new methods. While all sorts of hysterical legislation is launched against the white hunter, such as the prohibition of the use of motors going to or from the hunting grounds, the compulsory use of large-bore rifles, and other futile and irritating restrictions, I will show how the game is disappearing at an incredible speed under the very noses of our law-makers.

The country we were entering is a land of hills and sloping plains covered with bamboo forests and fruit-bearing bushes. This bush forms the finest "bush grazing" for giraffe, rhino, and elephant, while it is sufficiently open to afford plenty of grass for roan, giant eland, hartebeest, kob, buffalo, and other game animals. Lions are plentiful. It is well watered by permanent streams and is, or rather was, a natural game country of the best description.

The population of this country is now small. It was greatest when the chief Senussi was at the height of his power. Senussi started life as a hunter of elephants. In the course of his wanderings he and his hunters found this well-watered game patch. They decided to form a settlement, and they called it N'Délé.

Surrounded by enormous herds of elephants and having plenty of guns and powder, they had but to kill in order to procure whatever they desired. So rich did Senussi become in guns through the exchange of ivory that he abandoned the simple and harmless role of elephant hunter and became a sultan. He adopted all the ways of sultans. He had many wives. He raided slaves and sold them. His name became known all over that part of Africa. People were terrified of Senussi. Then the French occupied the country, and Senussi was shot. Since then the population has been dwindling. It numbers now something like twelve thousand all told.

Toward N'Délé, then, we trekked about twenty-five miles per day. As a rule, we walked the ponies, but when we came to a "fly" patch, we galloped

Arabs about to attack.

through it. We were lucky to get corn for the ponies in most of the villages, generally by paying an extortionate price. The natives are great beer lovers and keep most of their grain for brewing, hence the high prices.

At one of the villages near N'Délé we saw in operation the new French scheme of rubber planting. The French recognize, I suppose, that when all the elephants are exterminated, the natives will have nothing with which to pay taxes; consequently, they compel each village to plant a certain area with rubber. Unfortunately, this species of rubber, Ceara, is practically worthless. The natives seemed very depressed, and many of them have run away to other parts.

During the trek I had many opportunities of admiring the horsemanship of the Arabs. To catch their horses, they would lay hold of the tail, and it would immediately stop. They would ride a pony all out through thick bush without saddle, bridle, or stirrups and "stick" pigs or antelopes with their unwieldy spears. I once saw the headman "stick" a jumping oribi right under his horse at full gallop.

Native traders were fairly numerous on the road, and I could not help admiring the native women. With their babies at their breasts and loads on their heads, they follow their men for hundreds of miles, attending to the male demands and keeping in the pink of condition, shown in their fine skins and cheery faces. They will eat a few ounces of flour and take a bees' nest on the way while their men may rob a lion of its kill, or club a mongoose, and there they are, their day provided for.

The country we were in had held almost countless elephants a few years ago. Now there is hardly a track. If there is, it is that of a fugitive.

My diary tells me that on 13 March [probably 1924] we entered the town of N'Délé. There is a French post with an administrator and a few ivory traders.

One of the latter, a Greek, passed as an Englishman, taking little pains to correct the mistake, I fancy.

My reception at the hands of the French members of this little community was mixed. They hospitably invited me to dine, and we dined long and well. As the night wore on, however, my hosts became really most abusive. They had reached the stage when men consider it necessary to shout. Later they arrived at the point where ordinary shouting and bawling do not suffice. It seems then to become necessary to shove your face close up to your opponent's, to screw your countenance into an expression of extreme ferocity, and, while breathing heavily into your opponent's face, to deliver a cannonade of expressions of opinion entirely contrary to what that person might reasonably be supposed to hold about his own country and countrymen.

As we dined in the open and the noise was terrific, the unsophisticated natives thought we were quarreling. When, finally, I retired, still accompanied by one of my hosts, my Nigerian boy rushed out with my revolver and an ax, thinking that I was being attacked. Luckily, my host took this to be a joke, and he seized the ax and pushed it facetiously edge-on into the face of his own lamp carrier, splitting his thick lips to the bone, and thereby completing this happy night's entertainment.

My friend, the administrator, kindly supplied me with a guide, ostensibly to show me the best game localities. In reality, I subsequently discovered, it was to steer me away from the haunts of his own native hunters. In other words, the Englishman was to be "done."

Ridden down and exhausted, elephants are an easy prey.

In spite of the laws of the land, which strictly prohibit the arming of natives with modern firearms for the purpose of killing game, every European at N'Délé had just as many native hunters as he could find rifles and cartridges for.

Arab sticking oribi.

The guide was a furtive-looking man with a head remarkable for its size—when set upon African shoulders, at any rate—and a sinister expression. He had been caught stealing women belonging to the Sultan Senussi and had been dealt with in Senussi's usual effective way, the result being that he now was quite proof against the most winning of female charmers. This peculiarity of his gave him a certain authority and influence with the porters and also with the native villagers, and it soon became apparent that he was very efficiently "muzzling" all my hunting efforts. We were coldly received in the villages, and any enquiries about elephants were at once turned down. No elephants had been seen or heard of, and this in spite of the fact that we had seen fairly recent tracks on the roads.

Then, one day, there came a side-light on the situation. We met an old man on the trail who had been a chief. He had been deposed mainly, I gathered, through the efforts of our guide. At any rate, the old man felt bitterly toward him, and our chancing on him when he was in liquor led to his laying bare the reason for our ill success. Among other things, he said that the villages ahead of us had been warned to chase away any elephants in their vicinity. This we found to be true. Muzzle-loading guns had been fired into herds that, in the ordinary course of events, we would have found.

It was necessary to deal with the situation. This was not easy as the porters were all completely under the thumb of our emasculated guide. Finally, I hit upon a pretty effective plan. This was simply to stop all meat supplies. Hitherto I had been supplying all hands with a liberal meat ration, every day shooting two or three bucks. Now I announced that I would shoot nothing but elephant.

For several days more we could find nothing in the way of game but antelope. The boys begged hard to have some shot, but I firmly refused.

Finally, a spokesman came from the safari to say that they had been working against me, but that now their bellies had conquered them and that they would lead me to better country. Now they wished me to get elephant. Meanwhile, perhaps I would not mind killing a few kob.

These were numerous, but I steadily refused. That afternoon while making a passage from the Tété River to the Bongol River, we found where a herd of elephants had passed in the night. With the hunger for meat upon them, all hands joined in the task of disentangling the tracks. Everyone was enthusiastic. Even our guide forgot his master's instructions. Although it was late in the day and the herd seemed to be leading away from water, we pushed steadily and rapidly along the trail, with the result that toward evening we heard but could not see them.

The Arab way of attacking elephants with ponies was new to me. All my previous work had been done on foot. I did not, therefore, know what to do, and finally I decided to dismount and approach them on foot. This I did, allowing my pony to be led behind me by one of my mounted Arabs.

The bush was thickish, and before we sighted our game, they heard the noise made by the ponies and stampeded. I mounted my pony and, together with the mounted Arabs, went at a hard gallop along the trail. In a few hundred yards we sighted the sterns of the rearmost elephants. They were not traveling fast. In a short while our particular lot joined another much larger group, the whole combined mass becoming more or less stationary.

They were excited, but were making so much noise themselves that they could not hear us approaching. Again I wondered what was the best thing to do. The old hunters of South Africa, like Roualeyn Gordon-Cumming and Cotton Oswell, sometimes used to ride up to their selected animals and shoot from horseback, but the result of some practice at trees I had done was so poor as to make me cautious of trying it on living animals. Therefore, I dismounted and approached the seething mass on foot.

The report of my rifle confirmed the most skeptical elephants that danger was about, and the whole herd stampeded. Luckily, they chose a route not occupied by the ponies. I mounted and chased the receding mob.

Now I began to appreciate the possession of a pony. It was a most exhilarating chase. I was thankful that my rifle—a .275 Rigby Mauser—was as light as it was, for there was no way of carrying it so well as in the hand. The ponies were extraordinarily clever and showed unmistakable signs of keenly

The thrust.

enjoying the gallop. If elephants became visible as we lumbered along to one side of the trail, they would prick up their ears and try to dart off after them. And yet I doubt if any of them had ever seen an elephant before.

About six hundred yards farther on we caught up with and passed some of the smaller elephant calves. They were still padding along at a pace that would have required a fast foot-running man to keep up with, but they were already showing signs of distress. What astonished me was that their mothers seemed to have abandoned them.

In foot hunting, cow elephants nearly always show signs of the instinct to defend their young. Sometimes they are quite vicious, but on this and subsequent occasions when I rode after elephants on ponies, there was no sign of it. I can only offer as an explanation the fact that where they are used to being hunted by mounted men, as these were, they become so demoralized as to be an easy prey to anyone with a weapon sufficiently sharp to enter their tough hides. Their killing becomes butchery, and their only chance of escape is the falling of night or the reaching of dense forest or deep swamp.

In another kilometre and a half or thereabouts, we passed the tiring calves and began to draw up upon a cow or two. These offered no hostility as we galloped past them at a few yards' distance. I imagine that they were in-calf, for when elephants are near their time, they frequent the dark, cool places in the bush by themselves.

Had we been Arab elephant hunters, these miserable animals would have been our first prey. We would simply have ridden them along until they were completely beaten, and then we would have dismounted and either thrust our huge spears into the small of the stomach between the ribs and the thigh, or we would have hamstrung them. As it was, we passed them by.

Our speed throughout would not have averaged more than fifteen miles per hour, except, perhaps, at the start. This, however, was sufficient to take us into view of the main herd in another kilometre or so. Here, then, were we, on ponies still comparatively fresh, and as regards the humans, quite fresh, with a whole herd of elephants at our mercy. They were so completely cowed and dead beat that they never even turned their heads. With plodding, dragging steps, drooping ears and trunks, their pace was now little better than that of a fast-walking man. I was filled with astonishment. I asked the Arabs if all was normal about the whole thing. They assured me it was, and my subsequent experiences confirmed it.

These, then, are the methods of hunting that spell death to all elephants except those inhabiting the dense forests. Nothing can save them from complete extermination except either a world-wide boycott of ivory in any shape or form or the domestication of elephants for commercial purposes. This latter solution of the problem would, I think, appeal to everyone as the best.

With India as an example before us, why should it not be possible to tame the African elephant? Everyone knows that a young elephant becomes tame after a day or two in camp and no longer needs to be confined in any way; in fact, it will follow one about like a dog. I am convinced that African elephants are only wild because they are so continually harried by hunters. They are naturally of a most docile and kindly disposition.

If all harrying ceased and plantations of foodstuffs were provided, in a very short time the elephant would be as tame as or tamer than the black-faced sheep in Scotland. It would then be a comparatively easy matter to corral them—as in India. Besides catching the young males for work, the ivory of all males and females might be sawn off beyond the hollow, and this alone would afford a considerable revenue. The expense of such a scheme would be great, and should probably be undertaken by the State.

The fact that wild elephants can be ridden to death by practically unarmed men on very inferior ponies in "fly"-infested country and steered hither and thither during the course of the hunt is surely a hopeful fact to start with. The Roman Empire domesticated African elephants for war purposes. Why should not the British Empire do so for peaceful purposes? The Belgians are trying it on a small scale in the Congo where the nature of the country is against them. Now is the psychological moment to begin this great work. In a few years it will be too late.

I have already mentioned that five hundred licenses to hunt elephants had been issued from one administrative post alone. Say that there were one thousand hunting parties out—and it must not be forgotten that many natives hunt without taking out a license. Say again, that sometime during the hunting season of four months, each party encountered a herd of elephants, just as we did, and that they managed to kill three elephants only, and we have the frightful figure of three thousand elephants killed. A much truer figure would be about ten heads to each party.

I met three of these hunting parties. One had twenty-one elephant tails, another twenty-three, and the other seventeen. And most of these animals would be females, many of them in-calf. Others would leave suckling calves unable to live without milk and unable to defend themselves.

I found one such case. My notice was attracted by vultures. Under a spreading tamarind tree a lion lay with his back to me busily eating something. I planted a bullet in the base of his skull, and found that what he was eating was a young elephant freshly killed.

PART V

ONE can scarcely imagine the destruction of elephant life going on in Africa now. Owing to the great rise in price of ivory of the last few years, every man has become a hunter. Add to this the fact that ivory is mostly bought by pounds sterling, American dollars, and even depreciated francs, elephant hunting has become all the rage.

In the past the big men of the tribes would think it beneath their dignity to hunt, deputing it to slaves and underlings. Now it is so well worth their while that they not only take to the bush but they also organize the hunting parties and look after the products of the chase. For with this universal fever to

A lion eating a freshly killed young elephant.

kill elephants for their ivory, there has arisen a parallel fever to buy ivory and, consequently, to sell it also. Traders will buy it and ask no questions.

Then, again, a few years ago a cow elephant bearing tusks of seven or eight pounds was hardly worth the trouble of killing. Now the prices paid to natives in the parts of which I speak are fifty francs per kilogram for small tusks and one hundred francs per kilogram for large ones. The franc's loss of purchasing value is not apparent to the native. Therefore the elephant is a veritable gold mine to him.

******

So far I have talked only of one method by which such numbers of elephants are being destroyed, i.e., that of riding them to a standstill with horses and then spearing them. But there are other methods of destruction that have become intensified of late by the rise in the price of ivory. I speak now of the muzzle-loading gun known generally in West Africa as the Dane gun.

There must be tens of thousands of these guns distributed over every part of Africa. Their possession by natives is agreed to by the Powers, it being considered, and rightly so, that the African requires them for the protection of his crops. It has always been accepted that a muzzle-loader is not a very deadly weapon in any case. But before we agree to this, let us examine the part these contemptible weapons are now playing.

Take the Dane gun, put into it as heavy a charge of powder as experience will allow you, put over this charge a long cushioning wad of fibre, and ram this down on the powder with a hardwood stick. Make sure the stick is an easy fit into the barrel and long enough to protrude an inch or so from the muzzle.

Bore a hole in the protruding end. Then purchase a ball of fresh poison from the poison vendor. Knead about three ounces of this on a barbed iron head that you can obtain from the village blacksmith. Fit a covering of skin over this poisoned head, for, if it should scratch you, it might cost you your life.

Then with a percussion cap or two wend your way to elephant-frequented bush, find your animal, approach as near as you dare. After fitting your poisoned dart into the hole in the end of the stick protruding from your gun, place a cap on the nipple, hold well for the middle of the elephant, fire, throw down the gun, and race for your life.

Then come back next day, pick up your gun, and take up the tracks of your animal. You will find him dead, sooner or later, provided your aim was good, your range short, your poison fresh, and your powder charge sufficient. It matters not where you hit him so long as the poison enters the circulation. And this is what thousands of Africans are doing now.

Then there are the game pits, suspended spears, poisoned arrows, elephant snares, and modern rifles all hard at work. It is futile for those responsible to say that the game laws are strictly applied, that trade in ivory is stopped, and that all is known that goes on in the districts. The stuff comes upon the markets, as anyone can see who takes the trouble to visit the ivory marts. And that is the proof.

In the case of the rhinoceros, things are even worse. Throughout my journey of about eight hundred miles in the bush, I saw not so much as a single track, and only four years ago rhinos were so numerous as to be a nuisance. In fact, the only sign of there ever having been rhino in the country was afforded by the horns in a Greek trader's store at N'Délé. And even those were not all from the country. Among them I noticed some with the larger dimensions and the unmistakable square base form of Burchell's or the white rhino.

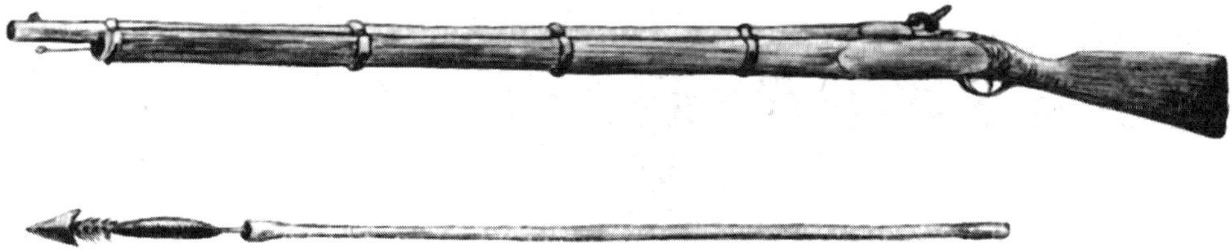

The Dane gun and its poisoned "arrow."

I immediately became interested in the origin of these horns. As far as I knew, the white rhino does not occur in the French Congo. From what I could gather, these horns had come from the country of the Lado—from the middle of one of our carefully preserved game reserves! Here they were several hundred miles from home, percolating through native channels to the traders' shops. Up to seventy francs a kilogram was being paid for rhino horns.

The export of ivory from N'Délé, I was informed, had dropped from 25 tons [a British ton equals 2,240 pounds] per annum to about 11 tons, and one of the largest buyers of it told me that the average weight per tusk was now 4 kilogrammes. I write of 1923. This means that 1,443 elephants—for about 10 percent have single tusks—were destroyed for this post alone. There are many other posts where much larger quantities of ivory pass through each year.

When one considers that this slaughter has been going on now for many years, one cannot help wondering at the numbers of the original stock. This original stock must have been almost countless, but now it is at last showing signs of depletion. Although the total weight of ivory exported is now less than formerly, it is made up of smaller stuff. The deadliest thing about the whole business is that most of the animals killed are breeding females.

One would have thought that the business aspect alone would have created some effort to stay the destruction of these herds, the value of which would probably run into millions. In no other part of Africa is there such fine bush grazing for pachyderms, nor is there anywhere else such large areas of it. With a sparse human population, abundant water, thousands of square miles of bamboo forest affording green food when all other bush is withered and burnt up, sufficient dense forest for the breeding operations, innumerable mud baths, an abundant supply of earth licks, and extensive patches of fruit-bearing trees, this was, par excellence, the veritable home of these valuable animals. What a tragedy that it has fallen to those who cannot, or will not, look ahead, whose sole object is to bleed it dry so long as the revenue does not fall during their particular tenure of office.

While on the subject of killing elephants, I would like to say something in defence of the genuine white hunter of elephants, more especially as it may appear rather like the kettle calling the pot black, for one who has killed as many elephants as I have, to condemn others for doing likewise. But the point is this. The real hunter seeks out and kills only the large bulls. He may have to shoot a cow or two in self-defence sometimes, but, as a general thing, he does not trouble the breeding herds except to take from them some of the larger of the bulls. His chief object, and the most profitable, is the large, solitary bull that is past the breeding age.

******

Continuing my search for just such bull elephants, and with the boys now anxious to find them, we headed straight for the bamboo country lying about the sources of the tributaries of the Aouk. The bamboo country undergoes the purifying scourge fire at the same time as the other bush, but whereas the shallow-rooted grass requires rain to make it sprout again, the deeper-rooted bamboo soon throws off its withered leaves and becomes green and succulent. At this season elephants distribute themselves all over the bamboo country and fill themselves with the tender shoots. As soon as we reached the first bamboo country, we saw numbers of elephant tracks and, unfortunately for us, numbers of mounted elephant hunters' tracks also.

On the second day we fell in with some Arab hunters. They were in a bad way. Their horses and ivory had been taken from them by armed robbers of the Banda tribe, and they were making their way home on foot. We continued south along the Goro River. The next day we sighted mountains south of us and still very distant. While riding on ahead, I heard voices in the bush.

The Arab with me said they also were Arabs. I sent him by himself to intercept them, and when he had made contact with them, I followed. This was necessary as the sudden appearance of a white man would have stampeded them. As soon as I came in sight of them, they dismounted, and when I rode up I saw that they were returning from a hunt. Every horse had freshly killed tusks lashed to the saddle. Most of them were female tusks. I asked how many they had killed, and they showed me twenty-one tails.

Continuing south on what was now a well-beaten Arab hunting trail, we sighted vultures circling over a spot apparently on the trail ahead of us. On arriving nearer, we saw vultures and marabou storks on the ground in great numbers. Thinking to get a shot at a lion or leopard, I dismounted and approached on foot.

The first thing I remarked was elephant meat drying in strips on sticks, then the remains of fires. *Simply an abandoned camp,* I thought. Then I saw a dead horse to one side and, a little farther on, a dead man. I beckoned to the Arabs, and we examined the corpse. It was that of a young Arab, and my people recognized him at once. He had a bullet through the neck.

While the Arabs were burying the body, I examined the camp. There were man tracks leading away from the camp along the trail we were following. They were quite fresh. Thinking to surprise the robbers and to show them that a white man was about, even in the heart of the bush, I followed the tracks. It was then late in the afternoon.

I had with me a native who felt convinced that the robbers must be Bandas. He was very nervous and kept imagining he saw people hiding in the bush. Toward evening we came to a stream, and I saw that we would have to camp there for the night. Choosing a decent ground, we waited for the safari to come up.

Time passed, and nobody showed up. I thought they must have missed our tracks and followed some others. I told the boy with me to shout. He did so, and we had an answering shout from our front. They had passed us. We waited. Then the boy shouted again. This time there was no answer. I fired my rifle.

Presently into camp came riding two of my Arabs. They were almost inarticulate from excitement. I finally gathered that they had passed me, together with the interpreter and my personal boy, that they had heard the voices in the bush, and, thinking they were ours, had walked right into the robbers who had murdered the man we had found earlier in the day. The robbers had immediately covered them with their guns and had intimated forcibly to them that they—my people—were about to "enter the earth." All indications were that their number was up.

Luckily at that precise psychological moment I fired that all-important rifle shot. This so heartened the interpreter that he found tongue and told the robbers there was a white man with them, and that if they carried out their threats, there would be trouble. This made the robbers think a bit. They had no idea there was a white man within hundreds of miles. Meanwhile, the two Arabs came for me. I jumped on one of the ponies, and, with the other Arab to guide me, I soon arrived where the trouble was.

My boys were all bunched up, while a row of twenty-five kneeling Bandas looked at them along twenty-five guns of all descriptions. Although they were in no great danger from anyone purposely firing into them, they were in considerable danger from some heavy fingered native touching off accidentally one of the murderous-looking guns. I myself felt pretty hot with all this business, so I rushed up with my rifle and called for their headman.

Such is the power of a white skin that he came, and when I told him to tell his rabble to quit their ridiculous nonsense, he did so, and they got up from their menacing attitude. Then I ordered them all before me, and got them pretty tame.

A runner was sent off to their chief, who was in camp a few miles farther on. Meanwhile camp was prepared nearby, for it was almost dark now.

The headman explained that he was acting under orders from his chief, and that I should wait until I saw him for answers to my questions about what they were doing shooting Arabs and threatening white men's servants. The robbers had with them some horses and the ivory of the Arabs they had attacked. They had made one Arab a prisoner, and when I asked this man what had occurred, he said that the Bandas had attacked them while they were at their prayers. They had simply poured in one volley at them, and everyone had stampeded for the bush. Through bad shooting, only one man had been killed.

On the following morning I met their chief who was apologetic about the whole affair. He hinted that he was acting under the orders of the administrator at N'Délé. How true this was, I cannot say.

We continued our search for elephants, covering in all some eight hundred miles of grand bush. We actually saw five herds of elephants, numbering from twenty to eighty individuals. Throughout the whole time we never saw a decent bull, but we found four dead elephants with their ivory intact. All were cows, and immature at that. The heaviest tusk would weigh four pounds. The only solitary bull we fell in with was solitary from wounds and not from age. After tracking him a short way, we sighted him in bamboo.

I never, in all my long experience of elephant hunting, saw such a picture of misery. He appeared to me to be a very high elephant. This was because he was gaunt. His skin was covered with corrugations and scabs measuring square yards in area. Running sores oozed from the folds of his skin, and his tail had gone. He had been caught in a bush fire, filled with gun-shot wounds, and smothered with spear thrusts. In spite of all this, he was recovering. While we tracked him, we saw abundant signs of his robust appetite.

Such is the work now going on in Africa.

******

After rejoining my friend at permanent camp on the Bahr Aouk, we decided to return via the Soudan. Luckily, all our petrol had not leaked away, and we reckoned that we had enough to see us to El Fasher. Paying off our boys and after arranging for our heavy baggage to go home, we set off with all our petrol and stores in the Fiat.

Wounded by fire, shot, and speared—but still alive.

We soon reached the Dar Fur frontier at Geneina and met with the usual Soudanese hospitality. Pleasant as this was, the news of the road ahead was anything but good. We were told that it would be impossible to get through one particular pass unless we put lthe orry on its side and slid her through. We pushed ahead and passed this place without knowing that it was the bad pass referred to. By the simple expedient of building up with stones, we passed over rocks that had been described as precipices or cliffs. From Geneina to Fasher took us three days.

At Fasher we sold our Fiat and went on in the two other cars. That is to say, we started to "do" the stretch from Fasher to El Obeid in two cars. But it would be more truthful to say that we pushed the cars from Fasher to El Obeid because the sand held them up more often than not. How we regretted selling the good old Fiat. From El Obeid, the railway carried us to Khartoum.

THE SAHARA ROLLS SOUTHWARD

On our motor journey from Kano to Khartoum we were struck and saddened by the encroachment of the Sahara on the good lands bordering that frightful ocean of sand. One could see in its relentless roll southward, the myriad tiny particles sweeping ever onward before the hot, dry wind, slowly but surely engulfing good soil in its advance.

Our route lay along the very edge of the advance, especially between Abeshe and El Fasher. One saw trees with two feet of sand up the trunks with their tops still alive, while toward the north we could see the whitened tops of dead trees still sticking out like the skeletons of prehistoric monsters. At Fasher itself the sand had invaded the streets and the tennis courts had to be swept every day.

What the final end will be I do not know, but already game is retreating southward before the blighting invasion. Perhaps de Lesseps[2] had something after all when he proposed to cut a canal from the Mediterranean into the Sahara and thus flood it.

[2]The architect of the Suez Canal.

Contribution to a Christmas Feast

Chapter 16

Christmas was still a month away, but this did not deter my French friends from inviting me to their Christmas party. I knew it would be a terrific affair. Every Frenchman seems to be a born cook, or, if not that, he seems to have a very decided opinion on what any dish should taste like. Away in the wildest country, he insists on a homeland standard of living. This achievement leaves the Briton gasping.

Having concluded that the bare necessities of life for a white man include white flour, sugar, lard, coffee, and wine, the French go about in a new land by first of all laying down large stocks of those useful commodities. But where they prove themselves above all other races is in making these stores available to all white men, and at cost price. As if that were not enough, they establish gardens, with gardeners and irrigation, at stated points on all routes. Any traveler may call upon these gardens to provide vegetables, salads, and fruits at a fractional cost.

Now I was living tough. I had nothing that I could contribute to the feast—not even whisky. Away over to the north-west lay Nigeria. At the head of navigation on the Benue River, the Niger Company had a store at Garoua [Cameroon], four hundred and fifty miles away. They were reputed to have considerable stocks of white-man stuff. They should have, as their steamers reached Garoua in the rains. I determined to send for something that I could contribute to the feast. I would explain my predicament by letter and see what they could do. I secured a *laissez passer* [1] from the commandant for a runner, and I sent him off with a promise of a liberal reward should he return in time.

Meanwhile I continued my bush-whacking ploy, returning to the fort just before Christmas. Great preparations were afoot, everyone bringing something.

[1] An official permit, like a passport.

The commandant provided champagne, others gave liqueurs and even whisky. My runner had not yet returned. I still hoped he would be in time. Christmas eve arrived and so did my runner. He bore in his bag a single very much dented tin of dry red herrings, the comestible much in demand by our forefathers and commended by them as a cure for a hang-over when taken with bitter ale.

My French hosts were charming and made a huge joke of it. "We provided the hang-over, and you provided the cure," they roared.

Gorillas and Chimpanzees

Chapter 17

My next try was the German Cameroon. They had on their statute book a hunting permit that costs Reichsmarks 5,000 [£244.75]. After one hurried trip inland on a bicycle and over excellent roads, I decided to apply for a permit. The law laid down that the permit was only granted by the governor. It was the time when Kaiser Bill was working up every kind of hate for the Englander. Apparently it extended even to innocent hunters. My application was turned down flat. Off then to the liberty loving French once more. . . .

I was on one of those nondescript cargo steamers that go snooping slowly along the West African coast on the look-out for any chance of trading or picking up cargo. If they see a man on the beach they slow down, in case he may wave a towel, thus indicating that he may have need of something or perhaps he may have a few bags of copra [dried coconut kernels] or whatnot to sell.

These boats do not carry passengers as a regular thing but will do so by "arrangement." You state your wants to the purser; he asks you if you want a receipt; and if you say "Please," you are done. His company must get their whack and so must the captain and purser, too. In the other case everything sinks smoothly into a pocket and no one is the wiser!

We were passing or stopping along gorilla and chimp country. Very often country that suits these gentry is found to be favoured by forest-dwelling elephants also, so I was eager to learn all I could of the hinterland.

When you are the sole passenger on these boats and can convince the skipper that you are "safe," you have a great time. You are not "safe" if you are a missionary, journalist, rival trader, or any kind of functionary. I had taken the necessary precautions!

Thus, it was that my skipper invited me to go ashore with him when we anchored off a solitary trading establishment, commonly called a "factory" on that coast. Needless to say, these factories make nothing unless it be victims of trading practice. We were to dine with the solitary white man, and Skipper hinted that we could expect good entertainment.

I was eternally on the look-out for new hunting grounds, and Skipper intimated that the owner of the factory had been forty years on the coast and knew everything that was to be known. I was told he never sat down to a meal without six or seven gins under his belt and was, in fact, one of the real old soaks that nothing could kill.

"He has a tame gorilla, and if he is in the mood, you'll see some fun," Skipper told me.

Wherever you go in gorilla country, the natives have persistent stories of these apes carrying off native women. Most of these stories are fables, no doubt. Almost certainly the ones that claim progeny resulting from these unions would fall into the fable category, in spite of the strong facial resemblance one sees among forest-dwelling humans. Even among the whites, instances spring to mind of a strong family likeness!

We were bidden to a *chop* (dinner). We landed in daylight through a nasty surf. In the expert hands of a surf crew and in a stout Liverpool-built whaler, we were safe enough. All the same, Skipper announced he was not returning to his ship that night. Like Jorrocks,[1] "Where he dined, there he slept."

The liquoring-up started right away . . . without preliminaries. Straight gin with or without. Skipper introduced me as an elephant hunter on the look-out for pastures new. This caused suspicion; I don't know why. I caught our host drooping a very sly eyelid at Skipper, as if to say, what does that mean? But Skipper quickly reassured him on that point, roaring, "If he ain't that, I don't know what he is. I have his rifles under lock and key and his ivory in the hold. Is that good enough?" Apparently it was because our host opened his heart and liquor store from that moment.

Anon our host asked us if we would like to see his gorilla. We followed him out to the back. There he was, an enormous beast. He was confined in a

[1]Jorrocks was a creation of Robert Smith Surtees (17 May 1805–16 March 1864), an English editor, novelist, and sporting writer. Jorrocks was a cockney grocer who loved the sporting life in the country, and with his vulgarity and good-natured artfulness, he was a great success with the public. These tales first appeared as comic stories in a magazine and were later collected in book form in 1838 as *Jorrocks's Jaunts and Jollities; or, The Hunting, Shooting, Racing, Driving, Sailing, Eating, Eccentric and Extravagant Exploits of That Renowned Sporting Citizen, Mr. John Jorrocks, of St. Botolph Lane and Great Coram Street.*

flimsy-looking bush cage. This fact seemed to surprise Skipper. Apparently the gorilla had been loose when he had last been there.

"Had to lock him up, I see," remarked Skipper.

"Yes, he's gone savage—can't bear the sight of women. Never used to be like that," replied our host.

Just then that colossal ape sprang onto the bars of his cage and started rocking the fragile-looking contraption in such an alarming manner as to threaten its immediate destruction. Skipper and I nearly fell over backward, my hand groping automatically for my rifle. However, our host seemed to be used to these outbursts. He told us the beast used to be quite gentle but now he thought he would have to shoot him.

"But what's exciting him?" we asked.

"Look over there," and he pointed. "He really can't stand the sight of women at all!"

An Unusual Hunting Incident

Chapter 18

An unusual hunting incident once cropped up when I was in the N'Délé country. This is how it happened. There were to be found stowed away in the furthest recesses of the bush, fugitive communities who had fled from the activities of the great chief Senussi. Just as with Buba Gida, this tyrant had "gathered in" all the outlying villages so that he might control their destinies more closely and efficiently.

It was by mere chance that we came across one of these bush occupations. As may be imagined, great secrecy is observed in these matters. No worn path leading to the location is allowed to develop, and no information about them is available to strangers, not even to an elephant hunter.

Lying so far out in the bush, any cultivation that was achieved was completely at the mercy of elephants, for you cannot fence against such predators. So the people were glad to see us once they had recovered from the shock our discovery of their secret hide-out had caused them. They hastened to show me the extensive damage to their growing crops already caused by the ponderous marauders. They said there was certain to be another visitation during the night. As it was nearly always bulls only who raided gardens and as all the tracks I saw were large, I thought the prospect was bright for the morrow. Of all forms of hunting, this is the most exciting.

After a night very much disturbed by hyaenas, against which we did not like to lay on the usual counter measures for fear of alarming the raiding elephants already at their fell work, we visited the scene. Such destruction you never saw. The sorghum crop was just ripening, and it would have made any farmer weep to see such work.

Now elephants when in this state of ascendancy over man are impudent, to say the least of it. Certainly they leave the fields before daylight, but they do not trouble to go far for their daylight siesta. They choose some dense thicket quite close to the village and lie up there the whole day, not emitting a sound. The great ears still fan away, but the action is controlled so that there is none of that resounding whack as the ear meets the shoulder that you get with conscience-free elephants. The belly rumblings, sighs, wind-breaking, and belches are all absent. In dead silence the day is thus passed while cocks crow, children shout and play, and people gather firewood or cut sticks, all within yards of the almost invisible and guilty hiders. Should a native spot them, he silently withdraws from the scene while warning others not to approach that part of the bush. The word goes round and the hiders are left in peace.

One might think this was a cowardly attitude on the natives' part. But if you have ever disclosed to a waiting bunch of bull elephants that they are suddenly discovered, you will, I think, admit that the natives have some reason for their actions. For one thing, elephants den-up close together. You can at most see one or perhaps a part of another. But you are pretty certain from the tracks you have been following that there are a dozen or more. The range is at most ten yards and maybe less. It is dark. All are listening intently to the rustling you have unavoidably been making. You know that at the first sign of their being discovered, they will instantly launch out into the craziest stampede, and it is heavily odds-on that some of them will come hurtling straight at you, not in vicious attack, but in panic-stricken flight.

I consider the hunter runs his greatest risk during the instant of the first shot. It is not an orderly flight these bulls engage in, where large objects are avoided, but a mad stampede over or through anything or everything for the first fifty or sixty yards, anyway. Great trees are broken off short and displaced sideways, to fall straight down on their suddenly acquired new splintered ends, while their upper works are still entwined with their neighbours' branches. Time after time such a performance would be gone through without mishap. This time, however, the unusual happened.

It is best to go in alone after bulls on these occasions. I had found my culprits. The village noises were all about us. The elephants were not five hundred yards from it but hidden in that frightful growth that takes the place of abandoned plantation. Anyway, I could see but one of them, and he was about eight paces away.

Taking the precaution to place between us as large a tree trunk as I could find, I kept my eyes on my prospective victim and got ready for the explosion I knew would follow instantly on my first discharge. All the while I wondered just where the others were, for I knew from the tracks that there were at least a dozen of these animated tanks within twenty yards or so of me.

I got the first one down and instantly fired into the lowered forehead of another one coming directly toward me, about four or five paces hence. He, too, fell very close to me, and I turned my rifle on a third one. By that time the whole place was rocking, and the show was over. Nothing would now pause that headlong flight, and they thundered off in a whirl of leaves and broken branches.

Turning toward where the first one had disappeared when falling, my face nearly came into contact with something hard. It was a tusk sticking through the tree trunk behind which I had been standing. How it set there without my being aware of it remains a mystery.

Then I found that the second beast in falling forward had pierced a tree trunk with his tusk, and, as the tusk was quite a large one, it had split the trunk from near the ground up to a height of twelve feet or so. How this had happened without my being aware of it was a mystery.

Only once before had I seen this happen. It was in the dense thorn strip of the East African coastal belt. I had shot an elephant in the body, he had launched out in a death-rush, and one tusk had pierced a tree trunk as he fell. So, to have this happen twice in one morning was, truly, an unusual hunting incident.

******

Once caught, the raiding elephants were too wise to return. The plague was lifted from the fugitive community, and now the natives could tend their crops unmolested. The poor devils gave me a ringing send off as I departed on my hunt.

ELEPHANT CONTROL

CHAPTER 19

When I finally overcame all obstacles in my path and embarked on my elephant-hunting career, I unwittingly forestalled what is now known as "Elephant Control." This body consists of some white and a large number of native African hunters. It operates in the Soudan, Uganda, Kenya, and Tanganyika. The object is primarily the protection of native farms from the visitation of crop destroyers such as elephants and buffaloes. It has been found that only by killing the predators can they be deterred from ravishing banana and other crops. The meat goes to appease, somewhat, the justly infuriated farmers while the ivory helps to pay the necessarily high expenses of such a government-run concern.

In my day there was no such thing as elephant control. Elephants came nightly to the native gardens until ruin faced the cultivators. True, they had some flintlock and percussion smooth-bore guns, and they did their best. Their utmost efforts just about kept the marauders at bay in full daylight. But by night they would be at their fell work again.

These conditions made it ideal for the hunter. Not only was the game near-by, trusting to high grass or dense thorn thickets for protection by day, but it made the resentful farmers eager to help the hunter so as to avenge their losses. They got the meat while the hunter got the ivory—so the poor saps thought they had got their own back. Now I understand that farmers swarm into the Posts demanding that "government cattle"—as they call elephant and buffalo because they are protected by law—should be shot at once. Thus is one more grievance added to the growing list of many held against the white man.

Among the most persistent and determined of raiders there would be found in most districts one or two very old bulls living a solitary existence. Their tracks were of outstanding dimensions while their weight caused the print to impress itself more deeply than that of their lighter kin. Some of these gentry were very experienced in the ways of man. They seemed to know when to bluff it out if confronted by a woman or an unarmed man. In this case, the old bull would make a dash at them, terrifying them, and giving rise to all sorts of stories of their charging propensities and general hellishness. Only very occasionally would someone be knocked about or trampled, for primitive man is very quick at realizing what to do and doing it pronto.

Some of the very best hunting was achieved in following these big fellows into their daylight lie-ups. It was fairly easy tracking them owing to their size and weight. Once the probable site of the hide-out was reached, it was found best to follow in by oneself, leaving the Africans to await events outside as even one extra hand on the trail added to the difficulty of a silent approach. I will now describe a typical hunt that will serve for many such.

We had been roused at early dawn by villagers whose plantations had suffered that very night. The elephants had just left and could still be heard crashing about in the neighbourhood. We could generally manage to have a cup of tea or native-flour gruel mixed with honey or tamarind before checking over the rifles and then setting off. For those hardy ones able to face up to it, there nearly always was meat in some form, perhaps roasted on the spit or plain boiled. Best of all, perhaps, was the centre of a chunk of elephant trunk measuring several cubic feet that had been roasted in its skin on hot stones in a deep pit for a night. This treatment seemed to tenderize it and the juices were kept in.

The daily ritual of looking over the rifle was not neglected, either. This included wiping out the oil from the barrel, seeing the action worked sweetly—whether a .303, .275, or .256—looking over the sights to see if they had suffered injury, and then checking over every round of the thirty-five "solids" in the belt just to make sure there were no faulty rounds, no split necks in the case of the .256, no ruptured or dented cases, and that all were free from dried mud or dust. Then when all was snug inside and out, I would fasten the belt round my middle, load the magazine from it, insert a cartridge in the chamber, lock the safety, work my arms a bit with the rifle, take a few sighters, and off we would go.

The native in front would have, perhaps, one or two reputed hunters to help disentangle the trail while my personal hunting attendant followed me. He carried a calabash of milk rapidly souring and churning with the motion, a second rifle—generally the .256 or a .22 L.R.—tobacco, matches, his own chunk of roasted meat, a half ounce of tea, and a little sugar. All were conveyed in a cartridge bag. Tied around his shoulder he would have a waterproof ground sheet. This would serve as a cover overhead or as a sleeping mattress when laid on long grass.

I cannot remember ever going hungry on these hunts. If we did not kill an elephant, we could always secure something: guinea fowl or francolin, dove or duck, duiker or dik-dik, bushbuck or bustard—what a varied menu awaited one. While the food was varied, there was surprisingly little difference in the taste of the different viands, for once your bush boys had them roasted on spits, they all tasted of burnt meat.

Within a short distance, we arrived at the village that had been raided. The headman welcomed us with enthusiasm. He said this particular elephant was well known to his people and was very "hot," meaning savage. He resented any interference while he was blasting a banana plantation to pulp. Often he chased an intruder, and once he had smashed up a hut from which someone had fired a percussion gun into his stern. The only good word for him was that where he elected to feed, all other lesser beasts retired to some other garden. His tusks were said to be enormous—they always are. This is common everywhere I have been in Africa and is meant to stimulate the hunter's cupidity, I suppose.

There was only a short delay while some native beer was consumed,[1] and then off we went with the plantation owner and the headman now in the lead. All the medicine palaver had been gone through earlier. Almost at once we came on some really outstanding tracks and much mangled crops. There had been other elephants in the patch, but they had left when his majesty arrived. The diameter of a fore-foot I guessed to be twenty-four inches.

It was in the rainy season, so tracking was easy. The grass was the usual elephant stuff, about twelve feet high. The sun was relentless till about noon, and then it would become overcast with thunderstorms and deluges of rain in the afternoon, merging into a fine evening sometimes. It was useless to take

[1] Thinking in terms of food, it was commonly held that the white man ground down ivory tusks into flour to make bread. Sometimes when handling large tusks, someone would remark "that lot will take some grinding." The only grinding known to them at that time was the grinding of corn between two stones, which was always done by women; thus, their idea of us conjured up a comical picture of a fashionably dressed white woman on her knees trying to reduce a huge tusk to powder by such primitive methods.

any precautions to keep dry. If you could manage to have some dry matches at the end of such a day, you were lucky.

For not only does the rain beat down on you from above, but it comes at you from every angle off the bush or grass and even up from the ground. It does no one any harm until the human skin oil is washed off, and by that time, the march has become exhausting.

The ideal time, if not the only one, to get close to these cunning old elephants in their chosen hide-outs is when rain is pouring down in solid deluges. (I cannot see any form of wheeled motor vehicle operating in such conditions.) If there are blasts of thunder rolling overhead, so much the better. Fizzing lightning neither helps nor hinders, I should say.

On that particular day, we were heading in searing sunshine but glued to the tracks of our choice. There was the added hope that we might stumble on others of a like type—supremely bold and impudent by night, and shy, cunning, and retiring by day.

By the general direction of the trail, it soon became evident our bull was making for a very dense patch of high bush. This patch has since become famous or notorious—whichever you like—as the Masindi Bush, and it still holds big elephants, I am told. Even now in 1953 in spite of scores of license holders wanting to kill their one or two elephants and wanting them big, some hoary-headed old rascals that may well have been about in my day continue to play hide and seek with their hunters there.

Most people prefer to hunt in the dry season. For one thing their cars can function, and it is much more comfortable generally. That is why these devilish old elephants continue to pursue their marauding careers. And also some people do not like the close quarters of these hide-outs in spite of the formidable rifles they carry.

As we forged along the lane of trodden-down grass, it was evident that the old fellow was making some haste. There were no piles of dung as there would have been had he loitered along the way. Only single huge segments spaced five or six feet apart indicated that long steps were in operation, and it is a gait that is hard to keep up with, let alone to overtake. It is useless to try to overtake an elephant walking at this speed if the start is considerable, as it was in this case.

Even the centres of the dung dollops were cold and already oxidized, indicating he had passed this point about three hours ago. Already dung beetles were rolling away their balls of dung, heaving their weighty cargo over with their hind legs as they stand on their front legs or arms. This recalls the case of a famous best-seller.

The author wished to illustrate his book competently, so he employed a very good artist to do the job. Having no knowledge of the subjects, the artist naturally turned to the London zoo and to the museums for his models. He turned out a first-class job, too, far better than one would expect. But he got that dung beetle rolling its ball along just as a man would roll a huge snow ball, standing on his two feet and pushing with his hands. That mistake of the artist's served to distinguish the first edition of the book and enhanced its value quite a lot.[2]

About mid-day, scattered clumps of bush began to break the monotony of the eternal elephant grass. Thundery-looking clouds could be seen rolling and piling up, while distant thunder warned us what we were in for. Still our great thief kept on. I don't suppose we were relatively any nearer to his back side than when we started, unless he had already found some dense, dark hole in the thickest bush where he thought himself safe.

Presently, we were confronted with a larger patch of bush and a considerable number of tracks, some old and some fairly new. But this patch proved to be but an outrider to the real thicket. Our trail led straight through and on. Such small patches are easily driven and the ancient knew it. He had probably learned that one when we were in our cradles.

It now became a matter of some urgency to come to closer quarters. Soon the imminent downpour would obliterate the tracks. Therefore, instead of stopping for some much needed refreshment, we gnawed our corn cobs and redoubled our speed.

Just as the heavens opened and the first cascade of rain was on us, there loomed ahead a wall of bush over the grass tops. Thunder crashed and rolled while lightning sizzled around as we ran for the shelter of the bush.

As we entered, there was the added roar of the rain beating down on the dense cover. Here was no forest with giant trees meeting overhead and a pleasantly clear carpet under foot. Instead the whole thing was solid dense bush from top to bottom. Only the high grass was missing. An elephant passing

[2]Bell was referring to *Jock of the Bushveld* by Sir Percy FitzPatrick.

along makes no impression on this stuff as it closes in behind him, and it is as if nothing at all had disturbed it. From brilliant sunshine to these thickets is like entering the gloom of a tunnel. A glance at the large ivory (wart-hog) foresight was reassuring.

So on, on we went with not a moment to spare until we made some sort of contact with our elusive character. If only we could catch up sufficiently now to have fresh tracks underfoot, we still stood a chance. Luckily the downpour that was now undoing the tracks outside was in here so delayed and broken in its fall that it did not work the same mischief. Thus, we were still able to follow at a fair pace.

Naked Africans are at their worst in heavy rain once the natural oil on their skins is pierced. So I now led the chase, and every now and then I let a keener-eyed lad forge ahead of me. Then if I caught sight of any slight sign a yard ahead of him, I would pass forward again. It is necessary to do this not only to keep them keen but to instill in them the feeling that once the old devil is sighted at a few feet range, the white man with the rifle will be on the spot and the tracker may retire. Sometimes a young native will forget himself and, suddenly seeing a bit of tail moving in front of his nose, will panic right into you. But they are slippery beggars and quickly disentangle themselves from your rifle, arms, and legs.

If at all possible, it is best to be ahead of everyone. Your drenched khaki cotton makes a horrid noise when wet or dry, but with the roar of the rain, the rumble of the lightning, and the dripping of the rain, slight noises go unheeded. These wily old devils rightly reckon that no human will be about in such weather unless he is crackers, and they allow themselves a freedom from caution that is amusing.

Suddenly we became aware of treading on fresh dung. At the same time we became aware of the fresh, warm, near-elephant scent. Motioning the boys to retreat, which they were already doing, I started a slow parting of the bush while peering in all directions. Nothing could be seen and nothing heard. Thanks to the roar and pitter-patter of the rain, nothing now should spoil it for me except an unlucky slant of wind. Step by step with the safety off I moved forward. Blowing a rain blob off the back sight and with a wrist motion to shake off the rain drops gathered about the foresight, I crept on about one step in five seconds, synchronizing my bush-partings with any extra noises from the elephants that I could now hear.

Even then I was surprised to feel a movement of the bush as I pushed it aside with my right arm. At the other side of the branch some animal was in contact with me, and yet I could distinguish nothing. Stooping gently I could see what might be part of an elephant's leg. It could not be more than seven or eight feet away. "Which way was he facing?" became an urgent question. Luckily, it was solved by the unsuspicious beast evacuating.

He was stern on. Immediately he had finished—a matter of some seconds—he moved on straight away. It was now vital to keep in touch. It was unbelievable that such a monster could move so silently. One step and he simply disappeared.

How I cursed the noise made by the all-embracing bush slithering off my wet khakis. But I doubt if even he could have heard such sounds amidst the racket overhead. So emboldened, I pushed along in his hot scent all the while hoping for a sight of anything forward of his middle. I was ready to test my knowledge of his anatomy against his knowledge of the human and of the human's many weaknesses.

Wriggling along as fast as I dared, and keeping my eyes too low on parting the bush, I found myself staring at a very unfamiliar object. For a second or two I was at loss. It resembled no part of an elephant at all. Raising my glance, the whole picture crystallized like a flash. Here overhead was his outstretched trunk, and the end was almost over my head. What I had first seen was the junction of neck and body. Like another flash I fired and was immediately pushed aside, falling in the yielding bush.

Some colossal body brushed past, trailing bush along with him. I got entangled with some of this moving stuff, and this delayed my second shot. But it caught him in the neck from behind and down he went on his knees but still up on his hind legs. He had made a bit of clearing, and I soon gave him a settler, infuriated as I was by his rough treatment. In a case of this kind, you should approach from the rear, allowing you to fire from the hip with the muzzle almost touching the back of his head. That is if you are not carrying one of those double-barrel cannons so favoured by many.

At the three shots and then the sudden silence the boys guessed it was all over and heads began to appear, peering cautiously through the bush. They were hardly able to believe the massive brute was dead. Soon a fire was going, and we all warmed up. We cut out some gland meat from the head, and spit-roasting soon started. One native went off for the women, and soon my little safari would have all the comforts of home. The ivory went 134 and 98 pounds.

******

You may say, "What shocking bad hunting to get oneself in under an elephant's head." And so it was, but what do you think of a man who dined directly under the outstretched trunk and tusks of an elephant, and when asked what he thought of the dining room trophy—for, of course, it was a mounted head—the type replied, "What elephant?" He had not spotted it.

The owner of this superb trophy was one of those lucky mortals born to great wealth. He had a large house in London. Fired by my descriptions of hunting these solitary old bulls and having exhausted every pleasure that comes so easily to the really rich, he betook himself to hunting in that very same Masindi Bush. By that time game licenses were in sway, and only two elephants might be killed in a year.

My friend was well over the seventies when he first took to what he declared was the finest sport he had found in a life devoted to sport of every kind. Indeed, he was over eighty when he killed his last two elephants. The last few years of his life he spent in boredom waiting to take out another license. He was a real hunter born if ever there was one.

Two months before sailing for Uganda, he would go into training. He had a walking stick made to resemble exactly in weight, balance, and length his one and only rifle, a Mannlicher Schöenauer .256. With this stick he would walk sixteen miles in all weather just to get into training. Always alone, he never had any trouble.

Every year he returned with his two hoary old bull elephant heads all intact—skins, ears, skulls, and tusks. Having no need to sell his ivory, he gave them away to museums where they may be seen to this day. That is, he gave away all except one with two unblemished tusks, which was the choicest of them all. This one he determined to mount in his dining room.

Now an elephant's head takes a lot of holding up, so he let the job out to contract. First ordinary doors were found to be too narrow and had to be enlarged. Then ordinary walls were found too weak to support the enormous weight and had to be reinforced with steel beams. What that job must have cost! But it was worth it. A more magnificent trophy you could not imagine. It extended fourteen or fifteen feet from the wall over the sideboard right over the centre of the dining table. The ears alone spread out well over twelve feet. It was so vast that one could easily miss seeing it altogether especially at night by candle light.

That man was one of the giants of old. Hunters of his character and pluck are now very rare.

******

A dry-season hunt is different because the elephant adopts quite a different pattern of behaviour. It must be remembered that all those old marauding bulls had collected in their hides a wonderful assortment of missiles, ranging from round lead balls, bits of cast iron cooking-pot legs—a much favoured projectile this—to modern 8-bore slugs and falling spear heads. Mostly all would have been shot into him during the dry season. So it is little wonder that he had evolved a technique to meet this menace.

This was simply to keep moving during the hours of daylight with noiseless pauses for intensive listening. Every so often the bull will stand for two or three minutes in rock-still silence with ears motionless, catching every slightest sound in those enormous sound collections. Should monkeys move or chatter in an excited way, he will make a noisy rush, thrashing the bush as if he had seen or winded you. Should this demonstration happen to point in your direction, it is very hard to discard the notion that he has spotted you by sight or sound or scent. Most times it is nothing of the sort. It is simply his normal method of continuing to live.

If any hunter happened to be near him during one of these rushes, ten to one he would think he had been discovered and beat a retreat. Who can blame him when all he carried was a single-shot muzzle-loader or maybe a flintlock. But with a modern rifle, these blind rushes are sometimes the undoing of the old rascal. Generally two or three sorties of that sort are sufficient for a poorly armed African hunter, and he retires to spread the rumour that this particular beast is very savage or "hot."

I remember once hunting just such a character. Everyone had had a go at him, for he carried enormously thick ivory. It was the very middle of the dry season, and time after time I got close to him only to be balked of a shot by a sudden nervous rush. I knew that the patch of bush where he had denned was joined up with a more extensive patch by means of a narrow but quite short tongue of bush. All the grass outside had been burned off, so it was little use to try to drive him out. I thought he might be induced to leave the smaller patch for the bigger one by way of the tongue of bush where I would be stationed. With luck I might get a shot.

I explained the scheme to my boys, and they entered into it with keenness. I told them they might fire at him if they saw him or heard him close-by. They were to make him as uncomfortable as they could so as to induce him to move in my direction.

The wind was right, and I stationed myself in the middle of the connecting line of bush and awaited events. I heard a terrific din and then two or three shots. He would be on his way, but he might try bluffing the boys before deciding to shift his quarters. Sure enough, he was trying his bluffing tactics, for I heard a further fusillade and then silence. He came quite silently along that tongue of bush and was within a few yards of me without my seeing or hearing him. How long he stood there intently listening, I don't know.

Suddenly he started one of his short rushes, making a terrific uproar. This purely bluffing manoeuvre carried him toward me but slightly to one side. My first intimation was a commotion in the bush as if an express train were coming. It stopped as suddenly as it had begun, and there he stood, motionless as a rock, listening. All I had to do was steer my bullet between the screening branches.

His tusks taped twenty-four inches outside the lip. Later I would realize that they had earned the name—and realized an extraordinary price—of "Cristus" tusks.

Canoe Journey to Bahr Aouk

Chapter 20

The First World War had ended at last. Wynne Eaton and I had secured our discharges, and it only remained for us to try to get together some provisions for our proposed canoe trip. We planned to go some 3,000 miles up the Niger and Benué Rivers and then across about 80 to 100 miles of portage down to the headwaters of the Logone into the Chari. From there we would make our way up-stream into the Bahr Aouk. It was there we hoped to find some new elephant country.

Before setting out, however, we were reluctantly roped in for some formalities. Although we had both been surprised and faintly disgusted by the scramble for decorations, we had not entirely escaped the inundation ourselves. Hence, it was that pressure was brought to bear on us by our families, and we were compelled to submit to some delay in our preparations.

Rifles and ammunition were easily procurable and were ordered forthwith. Wynne ordered a double Rigby .450 and a .318, and I ordered a .318 and a .22. We had cabled the Peterborough Canoe Company of Canada to provide canoes for our journey: a large 18-foot by 4-foot freighter weighing 150 pounds and two smaller ones to nest inside the large one. This was done in order to save on freight cost as this important item was charged on the cubic capacity of the package or on its weight. The canoes were to be shipped direct from New York to Nigeria, West Africa. There we hoped to connect up with them. Indeed, we were optimistic enough to expect to find them waiting for us when we arrived.

As usual in wars, poor old Blighty[1] had nearly run her cupboard dry. Nothing was obtainable in the way of provisions. So we bought a 12-bore shotgun and plenty of ammo, determining to live on its proceeds and such grains and vegetables as our rifles could secure for us through barter.

[1]Another name for England.

I had covered the Chari River country and knew what could be done in this line with buffaloes, hippos, and elephants. Sugar was our main deprivation. Salt we could get. It meant that honey would find itself enjoying a very important position in our commissariat. Even tobacco was unobtainable other than in the form of cigarettes, its most harmful form from the hunter's point of view.

I wondered how the rather fastidious Wynne would take to the native variety of this precious commodity since the tobacco is bound with a mixture of cow dung. I need not have worried, for we both discovered that the sun dried tobacco flowers without any leaves whatever were far more potent and satisfying than any other form of tobacco we had ever smoked. It tickled the spine and sent the head spinning after a few puffs that would have satisfied the most addicted, and yet it passes off almost instantly and had no bad after effects.

Of course, we arrived in West Africa long before the canoes, and the inevitable wearisome wait ensued. But it had its compensations, too. We were able to learn something of the natives and their pleasant little ways.

We found the Niger Delta country reeking of palm oil, sex, and money. As you approach from seaward, you see what looks like the Rocky Mountains except that the shapes are too symmetrical, Next you appear to be viewing the pyramids; they are, however, mountains of huge tins of palm oil awaiting shipping or a rise in price, or both. Unfortunately this elixir of joy, if not of life, does not allow itself to be transported. It must be ever fresh. Were it not so, there is no telling the fortunes that would follow upon its introduction to the outside world.

With the world shortage of fats, the palm oil industry reached a new high. Prices were soaring, production was elevated, and everyone was in great spirits. All you had to do was try to cash a cheque at any of the banks. You joined a long queue of mostly blacks. You then saw the most astonishing transactions: coal black mammies paying in hundreds of sterling pound (£) notes or drawing them out, as the case might be.

There was only one motor road in those days, and it was about three miles long. Every afternoon this three-mile stretch was packed from end to end with every car filled with opulent, rolling-fat coloured merchants lolling gently along at two or three miles per hour in the latest procurable automobile. What a contrast this was to the war-blighted Britain that we had just left.

Once the canoes arrived, it was with a sigh of relief that Wynne and I once more embarked. From now on we would be independent of all, beholden to none. One round a day from Wynne's 12-bore would provide guinea-fowl, duck, and teal enough for all hands, for in some places birds were literally in the tens of thousands. Wynne once killed twenty-eight whistling teals with one shot, a record I should think. They were tender and fat enough to cook in their own juice, and their flavor was exquisite. With our rifles we could obtain all the meat we needed to buy flour and oil from the natives.

While there were many fowl in thousands, none were so good to eat as the whistlers, except for the tiny and beautiful "butter-ball" teal. These were rather rare. The spur-winged goose and the Egyptian goose were also very numerous, but tough and strong in the pot. Guinea-fowl were very common, and the young ones were delicious, while the old ones made capital soup.

Once we heard guineas making a tremendous noise in the bush by the river bank. We peddled over to shoot some for the pot. Wynne fired from the canoe at one in a tree. At the report a large lioness slunk away through the bush. We let her go unmolested.

Besides all the fowl, there were fish in abundance. Wynne was a great fisherman and had brought a good assortment of hooks and strong sea lines. We were seldom out of fish. As soon as we arrived at the camping ground, Wynne and the boys would bait their hooks with teal-guts or a piece of buck meat and in a very short time either the tackle was broken or a fine fish landed. Wynne could never resist for long the temptation to bait a hook with a small fish of half-a-pound or so in the hope of catching that most sporting and excellent fish, the tiger or "capitaine."

It always ended in his hooking a tiger, but it could also end in the complete loss of hook and most of the line. No gear, however strong, seemed capable of holding this fish. We often admired them as they leapt feet into the air when in hot pursuit of some smaller fish. They presented such an air of activity and energy on these occasions as to make the movements of running salmon appear tame and slow in comparison. That they are equally good on the table we had many opportunities of testing, for we always chose them in preference to the others when buying from the natives, who catch them in clever traps.

We once had a "capitaine" served up with mayonnaise and the most perfect wine; this was when we lunched with the French. A more delicious fish could not be imagined. We were told, as a tribute to its excellent qualities, that it derived its name from the fact that it was considered so excellent that no-one below the rank of "capitaine" was worthy to eat it.

We had six boys, all pretty expert with canoes by this time, and in splendid order. They were all of different tribes or castes. We paid them well, but, what was of far greater importance, we kept them in tip-top condition. Living at the time entirely on native food, we appreciated the many and various grains, nuts, oils, etc., we could obtain from local markets. Whatever we had, our boys also shared. Fish and meat, millet or maize meal, rice and ground-nuts, palm oil, sim-sim oil,[2] ground-nut meal, and honey, all were to be found in the capacious hold of our cargo canoe, and all at a trifling cost. Whenever we were compelled to replenish our store of foodstuffs, we killed a hippo or two, rolled it up on a sand bank, and immediately a market would spring up.

The consequence of this high living was a state of high efficiency and contentment among the crew. As none of them had ever been with a white man except the cook, who had been with a German, they were all unspoiled and all willing to do anything that turned up. The cooks were boys one day, tusk choppers the next, canoe carriers the next, and so on. Everybody had to turn his hands to anything, and all were crew.

[2] Sesame oil.

Man Tracks—or Ape-Man's?

Chapter 21

The recent discussions about the Taung skull and the British Museum's present search for other prehistoric remains in Africa brought to my memory a curious find I once made in the French Congo. I will give a short account of it, for what it is worth. I do not pretend that the actual footprints were made by any animal, prehistoric or otherwise, or that they are anything more than a freak of nature. The sight of them, however, produced on me such an impression, and their presence causes such fear among the natives of those parts as to make the inspection of them a thing of awe and uncanniness, in spite of one's common-sense, however robust.[1]

The country where these queer footprints occur used to be the haunt of large and good elephants. It consists of belts of swampy forest with strips of open grass between. On many of these open strips dark red conglomerate rock crops out in bare, smooth reefs, and it is on one of these that nature, or some ape-man, has left its mark.

Holding, as it did, such good elephants—I once took sixteen hundred pounds of ivory from ten elephants in three days without moving camp or going more than five or six miles—I came to know this part extremely well. It was curious country because it never seemed to contain any elephants at all. This I put down to the hard and rocky nature of the bare patches where, in more normal country, elephant tracks would have shown up. Even droppings were scarce, possibly due to the ravenous, and certainly very numerous, colonies of white ants.

Anything might have existed in these forest belts, and its presence has remained unknown. Water, mud, mazes of slippery roots intertwining a foot

[1]Bell tells of an uncanny and inexplicable experience that befell him in the then-unknown heart of the French Congo. Were the enormous tracks that Bell found those of a giant ape-man? Perhaps. Bell mentions the discovery of the Taung skull in 1924 because at the time of the discovery it was widely accepted by scientists that humans had originated in Asia, not Africa. The Taung man is now considered to be a very early human ancestor.

A sketch showing the large and small tracks of the man/ape-man and the gigantic baby.

above the soil like gigantic cobwebs, spear-pointed and razor-edged palm fronds, clinging thorny tentacles, dank smells, and impenetrable thickets enshrouded in somberest gloom meet the hunter as soon as he enters the forest portals. Once inside, the hunter leaves behind him his visible shadow and the blinding glare of the outside world.

There was one section of my hunting domain that seemed to be closed to me. Whenever the hunt led toward this part, some excuse on the part of my boys was forthcoming for discontinuing it. The tracks would be lost, or the tracker would switch to another leading elsewhere. But so cunning were the natives, and so obtuse was I, that it was some time before it dawned upon me that the natives viewed the area as forbidden territory.

My enquiries, pushed openly in stupid, white-man fashion, brought the reply that there were no elephants there. This was obvious nonsense. Every lie was given a chance to stop my going. There were hunters already encamped there—this did not go well with the alleged absence of elephants—but finally it came out that there were spirits there, and bad ones at that.

Being young and impulsive then, I announced that there I would go on the morrow. A deserted village greeted my eyes at dawn as I rose to probe the mystery of the tabooed area. I could see it was a serious affair and that I would have to play my part with cunning. While having food and wondering what to do, two of my deserting natives came in. They told me that they had met elephant nearby while hiding from me.

They came because they knew I would sooner go after their find than probe a thousand mysteries. They were right. I met their find after an hour's struggle in the damp and gloom of the early morning, certainly not more than eight hundred yards from the edge of the clearing where our camp lay.

After a few more days of hunting in this neighbourhood, I said I was going to shift camp on the morrow to another village some few miles away. The men of the village were to help move the ivory. My intention was to get everything on the move, all the people together under my eye and rifle, and then to simply bluff and threaten them into the mystery country until we found water in it, and there we would camp.

I must explain at this point that I had no inkling whatever as to the reason for the native reluctance to take me there. I simply thought it was some of the usual magic nonsense; in fact, I was not greatly interested in the cause. What I thought was that here would be fresh elephant ground that would hold, perhaps, some outstanding big fellows, as it was undisturbed by men. Once we reached water in the area, the natives might—and probably would—desert, but that did not matter much. The great thing was to get to new country.

We moved off in the morning with our already imposing line of gleaming tusks, all nicely sand-scrubbed and glistening in the sun's rays. Our course would allow us to skirt the country where I hoped to camp that evening. I brought up the rear. About 10 A.M. the usual morning halt and rest found us all together on one of the smooth, rocky outcrops so characteristic of this part. I thought that at the move-off I would announce my determination to leave the track and head for the new country.

Now, in dealing with these kinds of situations, it is no use explaining in quiet tones that one has the intention of going in such-and-such a direction. If one is quiet and reasonable, it lays one open to argument, and that is fatal. Reason after reason will be produced why we should not go there. Night will creep on before a move is made.

The only chance for a lone hand is to assert himself so suddenly and so ferociously so as to stun the opposition. Then, with suggestive flourishing of death-dealing lethal weapons, accompanied by the most atrocious shouts, oaths, and orders, I intended to so snow-under and smother the smouldering hostility that the opposition would have no time or chance to combine and unite. This strategy, combined with ugly and menacing gestures, would, I believe, overcome the single mind.

"Everybody must get up at once. Now! Hurry! Off! Nobody must speak! Not a word! Keep close together! Anyone dropping out will be shot!"

How tame these sound when written down, and how lengthy our language seems. All the foregoing orders were expressed in about six words—barring curses. All pure bluff, of course, for if the natives had simply refused to budge, what could I have done? Nothing!

Loads were resentfully but hastily shouldered while this ridiculous scene unrolled itself before the eyes of the astonished guereza monkeys hard-by. My only chance was to keep everyone on the move. The leader asked where-away?

"To the magic—march," I replied.

He began to say he did not know the way.

"Forward," I shouted, with appropriate oaths and gestures.

He hurriedly turned and headed away, more or less in the right direction. How useless one's personal boys seem at such times. They, too, were under the sway of that deadly African fear of the uncanny or unknown, to overcome which requires such an expenditure of energy.

I had to be alert all the time. Any show of slackness and someone would stop to pretend to take a thorn from his foot, lay down his load, move backward a step or two, then take a flying leap into cover and be gone! On turning round, the left heel of the last man would be seen disappearing in the opposite direction, otherwise a blank . . . and there you are, pretty effectively anchored.

I had been through all this before and managed to so bullyrag my gang along that no one dropped out. I kept directing the leader in what I thought was the direction, and hour after hour the game proceeded. Water was abundant, and I had no fears on that score. Soon I began to wonder if we had come far enough. We had seen no signs of natives, and I did not wish to be too far from villages and food supplies. I knew that as soon as I halted, all the natives would desert.

Who made them—man or ape-man?

Presently we traversed one of the numerous belts of

forest in the usual way on an elephant path. We came out onto grass, crossed this, and came to a smooth rock out-crop. As the forest belt contained water, I thought that here would be a suitable spot to camp. I halted the line, but it would not halt. Instead, it broke into a kind of fast shuffle.

In return for my frantic questions, all I got from the man nearest me was "No! No!" in a fear-stricken voice. On we all pressed, I wondering what it all meant and what to do about it.

Presently the leader stopped, and I asked what it was all about. They said that it was the evil spirit. I asked them where. All eyes were cast down. They were all fear-stricken. My boys were the worst, for they did not know so much about it as the natives.

But where was it? Nobody would answer. There they were, completely cowed. Nobody even glanced about. They seemed to be expecting something awful to happen.

However, I made them all sit together on a bare open patch of rock, and over them I placed my two rifles in the hands of my cook and boy. These I told to shoot anyone who attempted to run while I was away. Then, taking one of the elder natives with whom I had hunted much and who was my fast friend, I led him away. Then I explained that I must see what caused all this bother and that I was spirit-proof and would protect him.

I so worked on him as to cause him to lead me back to where I had tried and failed to halt the caravan. Presently he stopped and said, "There!"

I looked about but could see nothing unusual. Then something caught my eye. I walked toward it. The queerest feeling came over me. There, on the solid rock in front of me was an enormous man-track deeply and sharply defined. Leading away from this track, but less sharply defined, were depressions about equally distant one from the other, for all the world like a man makes in softish but yet firmish clay.

As if that were not enough, there was a baby man-track as though the big fellow had been followed by his little boy. I can honestly say that nothing has ever made such a queer and uncanny feeling rise inside me.

"What on earth is it?" I asked the native.

No answer. Turning, I saw him sitting doubled up with his back to me. Then I took a real good look at the track. In the perfect footprint I placed my large foot. There was room all round and to spare, although I take size ten in boots. But what struck me most was the squareness of the front portion of the foot. Certainly no living race of African could have made those tracks.

I wondered how they came to be there. How could they have been impressed upon rock? If molten and plastic, no life could have survived the heat. It was all very curious. I wondered how I could cut out and carry away one of these tracks. It would be the devil's own job without tools, even had there been no reluctance on the natives' part. I could not help smiling when I thought what would happen if I should suggest work of this sort to my friends.

Rejoining the boys—much to the relief of the native who had been with me—I told them to stay where they were until I came back. Then I got paper and indelible pencil so that I could sketch those tracks. I had no camera in those days; I despised them then . . . such is youth and ignorance.

The sketches finished, we went on. The native heart becoming gayer and lighter the farther we left behind us those haunting tracks. I tried my hardest to get the native idea about them, but with no success. The natives would not talk about those tracks—openly, at any rate.

Years after I showed my sketches to different people. One, a geologist, pooh-poohed the whole thing. He said life could not exist when rock was plastic. But may not that great man and gigantic baby have been escaping from some imminent volcanic catastrophe when they stepped upon that fast-cooling surface, only to be encindered in a few steps?

The geologist suggested that the tracks were merely the outcome of natural erosion or gas bubbles formed when things were moving. That there should be a baby track following was merely coincidence, in his opinion.

I wonder.

Another I spoke to—a learned padre who knew the country and natives well, but not well enough—pooh-poohed it because he had never heard from the natives about the matter!

Perhaps some reader may have come across the like elsewhere. I never have.

THE DOMESTICATION OF THE AFRICAN ELEPHANT

CHAPTER 22

Is it possible? That is the first question. "Yes," must be the answer because we know that the ancients used African elephants for war purposes. We also know that a fully adult African bull elephant can be domesticated because we had "Jumbo" for years in England, as tame as need be. There is no reason to suppose that "Jumbo" alone of African elephants was of sufficiently docile nature to become the friend of man. I cannot help feeling that nearly all the elephants I have killed in Africa might have been jolly old "Jumbos" carrying London children every day on their backs and eating buns as a reward for simply being their placid selves, had they but chanced upon a kinder fate.

There were, of course, a few that were anything but friends of man, but they were the exception and not the rule. One I remember vividly was a regular devil of a fellow. He was on a hill-side and I was down in high grass when I first saw him. He got my wind almost at once, but instead of rushing away, as a normal elephant would have done, he charged headlong down into the long grass with an air of determination most impressive to see. When he reached the foot of the hill, I lost sight of him, but I could hear him coming like a brewer's steam wagon, smashing all before him. Meanwhile I ran toward him, for I had seen fine ivory sticking out of his head. I also wanted to get down-wind of him, for I recognized that he was out for blood.

We drew rapidly together, until perhaps twenty yards separated us, and then he stopped, and I did likewise. He was listening and trying to get my wind. The twelve-foot-high grass still prevented us from seeing each other. It was frantically exciting. I dared not move because I knew he would hear me and charge immediately. Once or twice I saw the tip of his trunk flitting furtively about the grass tops like the head of an enormous snake. Luckily, I was not directly in the wind stream.

After a few seconds of silent tension, the bluff began. He began to thrash the grass, making a terrible commotion. This suddenly stopped, but it had

I could hear him coming like a brewer's steam wagon.

allowed me to get another ten yards or so toward him and still more downwind of him. Complete silence followed. I would not have believed that an animal of his size could be so near without giving either sound or sign. What I did get was his bull scent and warm at that.

His next move was an electrical "swopping of ends." He had been facing away from me and was now facing toward me, for I could see, dimly through the grass, his trunk waving aloft and part of his head. Any shot but the brain shot was out of the question. So far I had had no chance. He was too close, his head was too high, and I was too much under him. But I was Oh! so ready.

Then he came! With a low sideways sweep of his head and trunk, the better to make a good row, I suppose, he offered the easy side shot at his brain. I took it kneeling, thereby fulfilling his domestic role as smoked meat in many a native larder and, maybe, as hair-brushes on some bedroom table.

That kind of elephant nothing but a bullet will tame, but they are few. The ordinary elephant is nothing but a simple-minded old grass-belly. His chief aim in life is to keep himself filled, and he is only worried by having but twenty-four hours a day in which to do it. If he is allowed to roam in suitable bush, he will produce in, say, twenty-five years two tusks weighing

The tip of his trunk was like an enormous snake.

sixty pounds apiece. His keep meanwhile costs nothing, except the cost of protecting him. Make imprisonment the penalty for killing an elephant, and the expense of protecting him will not amount to much. His ivory will more than counterbalance it. The solid ends of his two tusks should be removed with a saw, about two-thirds of their total length being cut off. It will not hurt him. Then let him go about his feeding and breeding business.

For these two tusk-ends you will receive about £90 at present prices. That is, in the case of a young bull in good elephant country. He pays a rent of £3 12s per annum for being allowed to live.

In the case of a female, the return from ivory will not be so great, but she will breed with steadiness and regularity, and provide no one can say how many bulls with ivory for the saw. Her own little tusks might be left uncut so that she could the better feed herself during her breeding life—if elephants ever do outgrow that useful period. Think of the hundreds and thousands that have been killed since firearms arrived, and yet there are elephants still. But there will not be for long unless some scheme is devised to protect and utilize them. Otherwise you cannot hope to save easily killed animals in wild country when they roam about with £200 worth of ivory sticking out of their faces.

But how are you to catch your elephant, people will ask. I can only offer suggestions. I have caught young elephants by the trunk and taken them to camp with a few boys. I had them following people about two days after, perfectly tame. But this method will not do because you have to kill the mother before you can catch the baby.

I have also ridden elephants down on a pony, and been in perfect command of them, and able to drive them hither and thither. I and my boys could have corralled them as easily as not. Do they not drive whole herds into stockades in India and Burma with men on foot beating kerosene tins and drums?

I am convinced that the African elephant could be as easily handled if once the appalling massacring, burning, trapping, spearing, poisoning, and shooting they are now subjected to were stopped. Will my readers believe that foot-running men are actually tiring them out daily and spearing them to death with two penny ha'penny iron spears? I have seen it. It is going on now.

By way of helping the forming of opinions on the practicability of the domestication of the African elephant, my easiest way will be to quote a hypothetical case. To begin with, we will suppose that wise statesmen have decreed

He offered an easy side shot.

that all harrying of elephants must cease. Protection from elephants is afforded to native plantations. Every village is served out with Verey signal pistols and cartridges. They are permitted to fire these at marauding elephants as they do in India. Suitable country is selected and a scientifically constructed elephant-proof stockade is erected. A body of native men is formed and disciplined. No better material for this work could be found anywhere than the natives of certain parts of Africa. They will serve as drivers or beaters. A separate corps with small portable signalling outfits will act as a Game Intelligence Service. An aeroplane could be used by this corps.

Suppose then, everything to be ready, stockades completed, men drilled, ponies fit, and elephant handy. Off go the mounted corps. They surround the herd and drive it toward the stockade. By the time it reaches the stockade, all fight will have left it. It enters and the gates are closed. The inside of the stockade has been cultivated and sown with millet and sugarcane. Good crops are assured by the manuring of the elephants. A stream runs through part of it. Human beings are constantly about. The taming has commenced.

Then the real difficulty begins. The bulls must be driven, like the wild-range cattle of the United States, into "squeezers." The only difference would be that everything would require to be on a much more massive scale, and, whereas a horse-man would be employed for cattle, a small and active tank would enter the stockade and drive the elephants where wanted. Held immovably and painlessly in the "squeezer" by equal pressure all round, instead of branding them, as in the case of cattle, they would be painlessly de-tusked. If it were desired to retain some of the younger bulls for domestic work, it would be an easy matter to tie them up and train them as they do in India.

Personally, I lean most to the ivory as a commercial proposition. Elephants eat too much for plain people to keep. Only rajahs can do it. Besides which, the future of African transport is bound up with motors. Motors can go anywhere in Africa. The matter, however, is urgent. Something must be done and soon if we are to retain the African elephant on the globe. The supply of ivory is dwindling steadily and the price is as steadily rising. Every African is now out to kill elephants, for it means a fortune to him if he succeeds. He is a bold, cunning, and determined man.

Besides all this, why should we allow the production of such a good and beautiful material as ivory to cease? At present ivory brings to the State but a trifling return in revenue, and elephants a still more diminutive return from the sale of licenses to shoot them. Why not look upon them as extremely valuable self-supporting livestock? It is the breeding cows that are now supplying the ivory markets. And that way lies extinction.[1]

[1] Bell's subtitle for this article was: "The Necessity of the Elephant Farm—Otherwise the Speedy Extinction of the African Elephant."

An Elephant Drive

Chapter 23

From the heights of Elgon a clear-day view of the country to the north, east, and west shows miles of plains with abrupt and rocky hills rising suddenly here and there. Away to the north-east can be seen the beginning of a ribbon running through a vast plain toward the north-west and ending in what might be taken for a mirage, if one did not know that there lies Lake Salisbury. The ribbon we used to call the Kilimi River.

Years ago I sat down on the tiny seat attached to one of the legs of the tripod stand of my large telescope. It was mounted at the edge of a native clearing on the northern slopes of Elgon, and perhaps 3,500 feet above the surrounding plains. The day was clear, the view superb, the season right, and I had plenty of leisure as we were camped close-by, trading banana flour from the natives for the journey north to Karamojo. This trading was a lengthy business in those days, as everything had to be paid for in trade goods, such as iron, copper, or brass wire of varying lengths. The goods had to be filed off, or cloth torn up, or beads measured out.

I nearly always started an examination of a piece of country by optimistically fitting the highest power eyepiece to the telescope, but the occasions when this could be used successfully were extremely rare, and then only in the wet season after rain. On the occasion of which I write, I found at once that the haze, although imperceptible to the naked eye, prevented the use of the +60, so I substituted the +45. With the focusing screw I soon had the banks of the river, twenty miles away, in sharp definition, and I began to sweep the plains on either side of the river with the glass.

I do not know of anything more fascinating than this hunt for game. I used to spend hours at the eyepiece. The field of the glass nearly always contained game animals of some kind, and, of course, they were completely at home and unsuspicious. One used to see some really charming sights, such as two rhinos making love—a truly quaint affair. But the country must be open, the elevation of the observation point sufficient, and the visibility good.

Through the telescope.

On this occasion I had not swept more than a few miles of country when I encountered a few elephants in the telescopic field—in addition to the usual stuff, such as hartebeests, a rhino or two, and some eland. Evidently stragglers from some herd, these elephants were stalking nakedly over a burnt plain, away from the river. How gaunt and tall they appeared, visible as they were from toe-nail to top of their heads. They were cows, half-growns, and calves, and all headed leisurely in a straight line.

Sweeping the glass slowly along the line and ahead of the elephants, I soon discovered their objective. A great, long, dense, black line of elephants appeared, stretching clean across the field. It was one of the immense herds, or dry-season gatherings that annually took place on those plains at that time.

From the hunter's point of view, these great herds were not of vast importance. They consisted of cows, immatures, and herd bulls carrying lightish ivory. What the hunter most desired was to see the bunches of mature bulls that roamed the country. These might contain any number, from two to fifty, and some immense ivory might often be seen in them. It was in the hope of seeing some such bull herd that I continued to sweep the country, only to encounter more and more cow herds. I hardly like to say what number of elephants I might have seen that day because I did not count them, but there certainly must have been several thousand visible with a strong glass from that point of Mount Elgon.

I was not greatly disappointed to see no bull herds. They dislike and avoid the neighbourhood of cow herds. I thought I should find them in the crater of the Debassian Hills, which showed hazy blue forty miles to the north. I hoped to have them driven to me as I occupied the middle of the exit from the crater to the plains.

As soon as sufficient flour had been traded, done up into approximately watertight and thorn-proof packages, and loaded into the donkey saddles, the great trek north began. First the steep descent from the cool, humid mountain air to the dry and pantingly hot air of the plains. Then the long, scorching march across the plains to the river. The water flowing swiftly over sand, straight to the west, was quite hot to drink during the day. But how jolly to have clean flowing water, no matter what the temperature.

This would be our last "cheap" water, with the exception of the crater stream in the Debassian Hills, until the coming of the rains months hence. From now on it would be a case of laboriously winning it from deep holes in the sandy river beds, from pools of damp mud, from springs trickling at the rate of a gallon per hour, or from almost inaccessible rock pools, filled with what might have been water before the baboons got to it.

This difficulty about water in a hot and parching climate might be counted by comfort-lovers a drawback, or at least a possible source of irritation. But who, living the life of an elephant hunter, would care two pence about that or any other thing?

Only once was I really worried, and that was the time when I had four days of what I believe now to have been nettle rash. Anyhow, it was raging hell, red-hot, and covered me from crown to sole, and stopped me sleeping, eating, sitting, or lying down. I could not wear any clothing, not even a rag, and I must have covered, in those ninety-six long, weary, and mostly agonized hours, a great many miles on my eight-yard beat under a mimosa tree.

Then one of my old native boys, named Kilassa, gave me a basin full of what looked like cooked spinach, and told me to rub myself with it all over. I did so, and in fifteen minutes I was cured. I thanked Kilassa for his promptness

The inquisitive hartebeest.

in recognizing and curing my illness, but, as the old man could not see the sarcasm of this, I cursed him soundly for not bringing me the remedy ninety-five hours before. This he understood and chuckled, saying I could count myself lucky that he had been able to find the proper herbs in the vicinity.

Elephants bathed and rumbled, shrieked and trumpeted all round us as we lay in the still and wonderful moonlit air of a perfect African night on the banks of the Kilimi River. Tomorrow's march should see us camped on the crater stream among the foothills of Debassian, and we should be passing through elephants all the time.

At 2 A.M. the loading of donkeys, with its usual uproar of braying jacks and Swahili curses, dimly penetrated my sleepy brain, and shortly after, a cup of tea succeeded where noise had failed, and I woke up. Strangely enough, when well-trained donkeys are once saddled with their loads, they subside quietly into a kind of a doze until their companions are ready, and all move off together on the day's march.

As we were now trekking through game country, the donks waited until the man-part of the safari had moved off so that the rifle should be ahead of everything. But had we been making a passage on a trail from one point to another, the donks would have left camp first around 2:30 A.M., followed by the man safari at 5 A.M. or so.

Dawn found the killing part of the safari, consisting of myself and my Nyamwezi gun bearer, miles ahead of the main safari, well out on the open plains. Right ahead of us the foothills of our objective looked close in the clear morning air. As we approached, the open grass plains became more wooded, with belts of light bush between the barer spaces. All the grass was burnt off, as these arid plains take a running fire weeks before the moister parts. I knew, for instance, that the grass in the crater we were making for would be still unburnt and comparatively green, and that is why I expected to find elephants in it.

Passing along at a good pace through the cool air, we were surrounded sometimes on all sides with herds of game. There would be a line of topis, perhaps one hundred strong, standing gazing intently at those two strange figures shaped like men, but grass-coloured instead of black. Here would be a bunch of hartebeests, similarly transfixed with astonishment, one looking at us from the top of a ten-foot ant-heap, as if he had never seen the like before—and probably he never had. Occasionally wart-hogs would be seen digging in the dry mud of wet-season elephant baths, enveloped in clouds of bluish dust, and once wild dogs ran leisurely across our path thirty or forty yards away, some of them standing on their hind legs to bark at us.

Arriving close to the foothills, we joined a great elephant path worn as smooth as, and much cleaner than, a London street. This perfectly graded and good-conditioned prehistoric high road followed a line along the lowest slopes of the foothills. It led straight toward the breach in the walls of the old crater, where the running stream issued onto the plains. It was there we would camp that night.

A difference was now observable in the vegetation. Clumps of unburnt grass and large patches of badly burnt grass alternated with parts where the fire had done its work cleanly. These latter were already beginning to look green—the shoots of deep-rooted grass just bursting through the ash-strewn soil indicated more moisture-retaining conditions and perhaps a more humid mountain atmosphere.

The smooth surface of the elephant road added another mile per hour to our speed. We strode over masses of buffaloes, elands, and elephant droppings, much of it polished, damp, and warm, while fantastic visions of colossal elephants falling to my rifle one after the other in a mountainous pile, bristling with tusks of quite impossible length and size, filled my dancing brain.

In this state of mind any other game animal might have done what it liked; I would not have stopped to fire at it. A record buffalo head, with horns too wide to enter Rowland Ward's shop, might have fanned me with its ears, or a lion with a jet-black mane so long as to make him walk sideways,
or get it shingled, might

Wild dogs ran leisurely across our path thirty or forty yards away, some of them standing on their hind legs to bark at us.

Fat elands.

have smiled at me, and I would not have stopped. Nothing but big old bull elephants with huge teeth drew fire from my little gun in those days. And I thought I was nearing the place where such worthies were to be found.

As we came in sight of the dark line of evergreen bushes marking the course of the crater stream where it left the hills, elands became visible in good numbers. They looked very fat and good to eat, and I wished we had met them on the day before at the Kilimi River instead of those dry and tough old hartebeests I had shot. Now I dared not fire for fear of alarming the elephants ahead of us. About mid-day we arrived at the stream and drank our fill of its cool waters. I was over-joyed to see that the water was quite muddy. This meant that somewhere along its length elephant had been busy bathing.

After a short rest and a home-made cigarette of strong shag tobacco shared between us, we went up-stream toward the crater mouth to see what we could of the game inside, from a viewpoint of two hundred feet up the side slopes. The safari would not be along for several hours yet, and everyone knew from bitter experience what would happen should any noise be made in camp with game about. We soon reached our observation post. We sat down on grass-covered, red-hot rocks in the futile shade of a leafless bush and began to sweep the level expanse of crater bottom that lay below us.

As I expected, the grass had not yet taken fire, and still showed a tinge of green. In the wet season it is very high, ten to twelve feet, and extremely dense owing to the abundant moisture and the richness of the soil. Now it was withered and breaking, and it had been thoroughly churned up and trodden down by the great herds of elephants, buffaloes, and elands that frequented it. As it was mid-day or thereabouts, no buffaloes were to be seen; they would be lying up in the cool and fly-less dens of those black-looking forests on the opposite slopes.

What we did see were elephants almost everywhere. Some were bathing and some were standing dozing drowsily in the shade of evergreen clumps on the banks of the stream, often with their mud-covered backs sticking out of the dark foliage like great mounds of earth. Some wandered freely about the greener patches of grass, while others sauntered leisurely toward the cool shade of the forest with their freshly applied anti-fly mud coatings, the still wet parts showing black or glistening in the strong sunlight.

The place was full of them. A lot of them—most, in fact—were cows and their followers. Two or three decent bulls were with them, it is true, and one or two large bulls had entered the forest. There might be more; there might be dozens; there could be scores of big bulls hidden away in those dense black thickets on the slopes. And yet, all those beastly cows, with their screams and agitations, their noise, bluffs, and feminine bickerings—how could any respectable hundred-year-old remain in the neighbourhood and preserve that calm and peaceful demeanour so essential to the attainment of a further hundred years? The morrow would bring the answer.

The idea was simply to drive those on the crater floor toward the breach in the walls where the stream left it with as many of my Nyamwezi porters as were obedient enough, greedy enough, or foolish enough to undertake the job without arms. The rifle, meanwhile, would occupy a ten-foot ant-heap in a position of great security, commanding the neck of level land where, it was hoped, would pass the animals scared by the beaters.

That evening I chose my ant-heap, and as a stance it was a beauty, quite twelve feet high with gently sloping sides and a decently spacious top. The stream was thirty yards to my left with a level strip on its far bank, twenty-five yards wide, and then the rocky hill-side. On my right the level measured fifty yards to the hill-side. The only obstruction to a perfect view on any side was ant-heaps similar to the one upon which I stood.

As I overtopped these by my own height, I thought all would be well. The grass, of course, in this neck was thoroughly trampled. If they came as expected, it seemed to me that nothing could prevent me making a really good bag. At the same time I quite saw that anything might happen.

Very few portions of the surrounding slopes were unclimbable for elephant; consequently, they might break out almost anywhere. They might refuse to be driven or they might charge the boys. If that were to happen, I knew that they in turn would refuse to drive or would stampede into the forest where it would be impossible to dislodge them. Or there might be no elephants in the crater to-morrow. Anything, in fact, might happen, and I went to bed in a queer state of mind but hoping still to get that stack of tusks. A silent camp sank early to sleep with at least one anxious breast soothed by that best of music, the belly rumbles and belchings of care-free elephants.

PART II

Dawn of the day found everyone supping hot gruel or blowing on it. Then most of the lads took off their shirts, seized their knives and clubs, and were ready for the drive. Kilassa might be seen putting a prodigious amount of snuff into his calabash snuff-box, which he had suspended from his neck by a sinew cord. Its liquid content might have been a quart, and this would last him a day or two. As he had once been an elephant hunter, the drive was entrusted to him. Besides which, he had a Snider rifle and a great reputation for "medicine."

The beaters were to go to the far end of the crater by way of the side slopes, spread out, and bring all before them. They took with them some of the safari guns and also my spare rifles, and I told them to use them if they saw any reluctance on the part of the game to face the narrow opening where I hoped so many were to meet death.

As the beaters had several miles to go and I only about one and a half, I breakfasted well before making for my stance. I had taken an outrageous number of cartridges, two rifles of the same calibre, and my gun bearer for loading the rifles, so I felt fully prepared for anything that might come, and certain we would do well.

On reaching our ant-heap, which we did by softly threading our way between scattered groups of buffaloes, we perched ourselves aloft and took a survey through the glasses. The whole floor seemed to be crawling with buffaloes, all making toward the fly-free forest. Then I saw elephants in the grass about four hundred yards away. They were cows and calves, with one herd bull that had tusks of forty pounds or so. I wondered now what I should do if this lot came along first, as seemed likely. Would a shot at that herd bull prevent others behind from coming forward? I thought that the luck of the day was in the hands of the gods and that I had better take what presented itself.

No more elephants were visible from the ant-heap, and I feared to leave it for the hill-side in case something might move in our direction. There was nothing for it but to wait, and this was made rather uninteresting because all the game had already moved into the crater. Presently even the cow herd moved off and was lost to sight.

About ten o'clock things began to happen. A large spotted hyaena sloped away past us on the far side of the stream. He only became visible to us when he crossed the breaks in the line of evergreen bush fringing the stream. I began to hope that no big elephant would follow that line and perhaps escape me. For a long time nothing moved. Then I saw what I thought was smoke rise on the air at the far side of the crater bottom. I judged the boys would be there or thereabouts by this time, and I thought they must have fired some dry grass to frighten some beasties that had refused to be driven. But I was all wrong—it was not smoke but dust, and clouds of it. Something was astir evidently!

Looking into the crater.

Then elephants appeared heading straight for us and coming at a good slashing pace, but not stampeding. There were not many, seven or eight adults and some followers, but among the former appeared the broader forehead of our acquaintance of the morning, the forty-pound herd bull. It was indeed the same little herd, and they had caught some suspicious sound, perhaps, that our duller ears had failed to gather. At any rate they were determined to reach the great outer plains, and the tall, gaunt, haggard-looking leading lady had decided that right past my ant-heap lay the road to freedom.

While they approached, I sighted my rifle on the bull's forehead, and I was astonished to find that the hitherto disregarded ant-heaps were going to have a most important effect on the day's results; they interfered most damnably with any shooting at all far out. At one hundred yards the animal was either engaged in swerving about to avoid them—resembling somewhat the pip in that game where it collides with 10,000 pins before settling into the pocket you have not backed—or the tops of the intervening heaps were completely obliterating the few vital points of the animal's anatomy. I had, indeed, to shoot this bull when he was five yards from the foot of my ant-heap and perhaps eight yards in an air-line from my rifle to his head.

This is going to be bad, I thought, *if they come in a bunch and fast.*

This fluttering but disturbing suspicion was soon converted into deeply impressed and irrefutable fact by a close and surging mass of elephants suddenly appearing as a broad brown front pushed along by a huge wedge of rising dust. This lot was moving, and the front parts were upon us seconds sooner than I anticipated. In the fringe a broad forehead indicated a bull—there was no time to look at tusks—and at this I shot, again at a range of feet.

Now there was simply hell let loose all over the place. Past us on all sides rushed closely packed masses of shrieking and trumpeting elephants. Trunks waved in our faces or blasted dust clouds about. Dust rose around and over us in denser and denser pulsations. The elephants were mad, and so was I, especially when my demented gun bearer jerked my aiming arm and roared that a big one was passing. I knew. Big ones were passing on all sides at a range of feet.

I seemed unable to do anything. My rifle never seemed to be loaded, all I seemed to do was to cram cartridges into the magazine, and yet when my fingers closed over the fore-end on to the barrel, they got burnt. Sweat bore dust into my eyes until I was blind. I pushed the boy nearly off the ant-heap when he joggled my arm again, only he seemed unaware of it. Suddenly all was over.

The tornado had passed and could be heard shrieking and crashing away fainter and fainter. I turned to my companion, slapped him—*whack*—on his muscular shoulder, and then I burst into roar after roar of laughter.

"Well, I'm — !" I said, and I expect he understood, although he knew no English.

A quick glance round had not shown many carcasses, so a sort of subconscious disappointment made me sit down and roll a cigarette. I handed the pouch to the boy, and as I did, I thought to myself that I had put in a good many heart or lung shots and that these would not be in the immediate vicinity. A little tobacco and I felt strong enough to face the music. I was very much afraid that I had made rather a show—got too excited—and had made a regular hash of it, in fact.

It seemed to me I ought to have dozens down. The litter of spent cartridges was not great as they were mostly invisible down the slopes of the ant-heap, but I knew I had fired a lot. It seemed to me that elephants had been barging past me for hours. This was not so at all—probably three or four minutes would have covered the whole period. Anyhow, it was time to get the tails of the slain.

I was certain of two, for there they were, one of them with a tusk buried in our ant-heap, our friend of the morning. And on the other side we found a third—all three brain shots. Then I remembered firing at the very large head of an elephant rather far out, and directly facing, as he rushed toward me. At

Here they come!

A dense and surging mass.

the shot, a great cloud of dust had risen, and I vaguely wondered if I had hit the ant-heap, but then I recollected that his head had disappeared suddenly behind it. I made for this and sighed with relief when I saw him lying there.

He had magnificent ivory that looked like 100-pound stuff. That made four, all brain shots. Now I needed to look for the body shots. They would be past the stance and might be some way off. Here came the beaters; they would soon find any dead elephants about. I thought I would have a look about with the glasses from the hill-side while the boys searched the trampled grass that was, however, still high and thick enough to hide the carcass of a dead elephant on its side.

I reached a point and swept the far country to see the fleeing herd we had been mixed up with. They were nowhere to be seen, although it could not have been more than twenty-five or thirty minutes since they went crashing through the neck.

Soon I picked out three more dead elephants, aided by the presence of some of my boys beside them. I began to hope that I had done not so badly after all. I thought that they ought to be able to find perhaps five or six more. But I was disappointed, for only one more body was found, although the boys searched on foot and I looked over the miles of plain surrounding us with the big telescope. I consider that I made a bad job of that drive, just through getting over-excited. But those few minutes on the ant-heap were a glorious and nerve-stirring time.

THE WILD HUNTING DOGS OF AFRICA

CHAPTER 24

There is, of course, no spring proper in equatorial Africa, but the season that most resembles our spring is that which follows immediately on the long dry season. Here, spring comes gradually, but there, it arrives in a night. One good downpour of rain and the world is changed. All plant life takes on a new aspect. Young grass and flowers with entrancing scents burst from the ground. The gray and grim-looking thorn bush changes to delicate green and golden haze. Everything starts growing with a sort of triumphal hum. Even the air changes. It sheds its skin-cracking dryness and its dust-laden haziness to become cool, moist, and clear.

In the animal world the transformation is just as great. To the casual stranger a stroll of twenty miles through the bush in the dry season would convey the impression that it was almost lifeless. He would see a few dry-country hornbills see-sawing through the air, a few dik-diks, maybe, and a lesser koodoo or two. All the great game tracks would appear to have been made during the last rains. He would wonder where on earth all the animals that had made those tracks had gone. He would certainly not believe that all the animals that gladden his eye in spring were about him then. The fact is, the tracks are there, but the ground is hard and dusty, and the mid-day wind sweeps over them an almost impalpable covering, destroying the sharp-cut edges of a freshly made hoof print.

Once the rains have fairly set in, pools of water are formed wherever the ground is sufficiently close to hold it. These pools become the centre of attraction for all the mud lovers, such as wart-hog, bush-pig, rhino, and elephant. For now there are myriad flies, ranging in size from the tiny sand fly and the minute black bee, not more than one-sixteenth of an inch long, up to the huge stinging fly of an inch or more in length, which pesters man and beast throughout the day.

Against these, mud would appear to be the only protection. These pests can penetrate the thickest hide with their brown steel-like probes. I have stood

Wild dogs in pursuit of a hartebeest.

close to mud-covered elephants watching the stinging horrors busily scratching at the thick mud covering, trying to find a place for their stab. When, finally, they succeed, holding tight with all their patent gripping feet meanwhile, they launch the thrust with a convulsive heave of their bodies. If the down-penetrating lance encounters no nerve centre, suction is applied, and in a few moments the abdomen is filled with the host's life-blood; however, if a nerve is touched, the host is electrified into action.

It is a wonderful sight at such a season to watch from a hill-top the great game at their ease. Dik-diks will be seen chasing each other, sometimes racing full split from one patch of sansevieria to another. If in gerenuk country, these strange-looking antelopes may be seen contorting their long necks in the most fantastic way. Giraffes browse sedately on the fresh foliage while in every pool some animal bathes. If elephants are about, most attention will be paid to them probably.

At such a time and in just such country that most beautiful of African antelope, the lesser koodoo, may be seen at home. To my mind, no other animal can touch it for grace of form and movement, nor for beauty of colour when its delicate tints are closely observed. It presents a picture of scintillating immobility when at rest, perfectly camouflaged with its light stripes against the light thorn stems, its dark eyes sparkling with perfect health like the many sun-reflecting points about it. In movement, it is a flashing joy as it bounds through shade and sunshine, blending equally with its surroundings except for that tell-tale patch of white on its stern.

It makes one think that, perhaps, Nature found she had succeeded too well with the lesser koodoo's colour scheme, and, in order to save us from a deluge of them, had clapped a white hand to the fleeing stern. Or was it to enable its greatest enemy—after the head collector—the wild hunting dog, to sometimes capture, by the most strenuous and clever running, its swift prey?

For, to run down a koodoo in its native country by sight can be no easy task. The antelope can and does dive through the most appalling thorn thickets—thickets that must be avoided by anything shod with pads. Dogs must go round, and, maybe, it is just that fast-disappearing flash from the white stern patch that enables the chase to continue to its legitimate end. Or is it to afford the night prowlers a better chance?

A picture of scintillating immobility.

Pyjalé and I once viewed a pack of dogs running lesser koodoo, I through a telescope supplied me by its makers in return for a goodly number of sovereigns, my companion through the lenses supplied him gratis by his mother. I would not like to swear that I saw more or better than he. We were perched on a hill-top and had searched the bush for elephants without success. This was not so surprising as it would have been had we not killed forty-four bull elephants in the preceding three days in the country lying around us.

Then Pyjalé pointed, and I looked at something surging along past our front. Getting my small glasses on it, there appeared a single dog, then behind him three others, then, well astern, a considerable number. They were all legging it hard. The sun was up and their tongues were out. Then, looking for the object of their chase, I at last caught the koodoo in my field of view. He was a fine buck, and appeared to be going quite leisurely along, except that he seemed to be leaping a prodigious number of thorn thickets. Then, on sweeping the glass back to the dogs and again to the koodoo, it became apparent that they were not closing the distance between them, although the speed of the dogs seemed to be vastly greater than that of the buck. They, poor devils, were busy running round, while he flew superbly over the close but narrow thorn strips.

A flashing joy as it bounds through shade and sunshine.

He flew over the close but narrow thorn strips.

The chase led them across our front, and we had a grand view of it whenever an open bit was reached. Now the dogs seemed to gain ground, and then the koodoo would "lift" a dense thicket in a superb leap and give those dogs some exercise getting round. I was looking for the relay system in the dogs' running, but this was not apparent. What did happen was a constant change in the leading dogs because of thorns penetrating their pads. One could see the leader suddenly stop and bite savagely at its uplifted foot before going on again. Meanwhile, such was the pace of it all that other dogs had passed on.

Hardly ever were their heads down, and only then when they had run round some unusually difficult bit of bush. The end of the chase we did not see, for the bush prevented it, but the impression left on my mind was that this wonderful buck was complete master of the situation. I would have put my money on him rather than on that scrofulous-looking pack, but Pyjalé said they were certain to have him.

On another occasion I saw an actual attack taking place. It was at some distance from me, but with powerful glasses and fairly open country, my view was almost uninterrupted. The prey was a large cow eland, and I noticed that she appeared to be in milk. What had happened to her calf I can only conjecture. As there were only a dozen or so dogs with her, and as this number was unusually small—for that area, at any rate, where one often saw several score of dogs in a pack—I think that probably her calf had been devoured early in the chase, and that the unsatisfied ones had continued after the mother.

When the affair came within my view, the leading dogs were close up to the tired and bleeding eland. They seemed fairly fresh, and yet not very anxious to close with their prey. Possibly they wished to still further tire her out. At any rate, the chase continued thus for some time without much happening. Occasionally the cow would launch a vicious kick at some dog as it dropped back with a chunk from the inside of her thigh, where the skin is thin and tender. I noticed that she was bleeding profusely from both hindquarters.

Meanwhile, more dogs arrived from the rear. Now the eland was staggering in her gait. With a lightning leap a dog fastened on a hind leg and clung to it, in spite of her efforts to get it free. He was, I take it, gnawing his way through the exceedingly tough leg sinew. Anyhow, when he came loose, the eland was more or less anchored, and now completely at their mercy. They all took part now in a general attack. Her flanks were torn to shreds. One fastened on her throat. Her efforts to defend herself rarely got home. The poor thing was done. Presently she was dragged down and torn to ribbons.

The last two scenes before the final curtain.

It was early morning, and the scene around us lay calm and beautiful, except for the small area of the tragedy. The air was fresh and cool, and game in countless numbers mixed in their play with each other in perfect harmony. It almost seemed that they were elated at the thought of one more night passed, at having at least one more day to live. Generally speaking, a killing as just described rightly belongs to the night, and I fancy that herein lies the reason these hunts are so seldomly witnessed.

I have often seen packs of hunting dogs in the daytime, but they always seemed to be returning from a hunt. The apparent indifference shown by game to the presence of a large and scattered pack running through them by day would seem to confirm this. Just so one may see game staring with curiosity from close range at lion returning by day from their nightly work.

It seems to be Africa's desire to show us her pleasant side under the intensest light, her abounding wealth of animal life of the most beautiful forms and colours, and to hide away in shame under the pall of darkness her other side.

AN ELEPHANT HUNTING CAMP IN AFRICA

CHAPTER 25

In order to be convenient to the hunting grounds, I once established my base camp away out in the wilderness, remote from any human habitation. Meaning to spend the whole of the wet season at this camp, I had constructed quite elaborate quarters for myself and my men. It pays to do so, as sickness—fever and dysentery—is very prevalent among the porters during this season.

The camp was well situated at the foot of a solitary hill, rising in the midst of, and overlooking, grassy and bushy plains, which extended for miles in all directions. From the top of Base Camp Hill an elephant could be seen, with glasses, up to ten or twelve miles away. It seemed so easy from that look-out to go straight to them. But it was not so, for between lay miles of stubborn, ten-foot-high grass and many deep watercourses.

We had moved to Base Camp with the early rains. While the construction of our grass-thatched houses was under way, the donkeys were busy bringing native flour from the nearest villages forty miles away, as, once the rains set in, they would not have been able to reach any provisioning centre.

I had picked a sandy ridge at the foot of the hill for our camp, thinking that drainage would be good and that, consequently, there would be no place for mosquitoes to breed. But it turned out to be one of the most heavily infested spots I ever had in that country. Owing to the greater warmth of the hill, I think, millions of swamp-bred mosquitoes flocked upward at night. Luckily for us all, everyone was provided with a mosquito net.

Every morning at dawn I climbed the hill and sat at the eyepiece of the powerful tripod telescope and systematically swept the country for elephants. In traversing those immense plains, hundreds and hundreds of game animals of all sorts would pass across my field of view wherever the grass was not too high to hide them. Great troops of giraffes were always to be seen, besides rhinos, buffaloes, and most of the lesser stuff. But it was only the gray top-sides

Looking through the glass.

of elephants that stopped the swing of the glass, that is until it was decided whether they were bulls or cows.

It is curious that I never saw a cow elephant in all that stretch of country, except just after the first rains. Then a migration took place, preceded by a gathering together into immense herds. Anytime during those few days several thousand elephants could be seen from my look-out hill, but once these herds had moved off, only bulls of the solitary description seemed to use the country. It was too wet and boggy for the calves, and the mothers were now bent on reaching the hillier and drier country to the east. In this way it was an ideal hunter's country, for not only were there only bulls, but they were old and carried big, heavy tusks. There were no rival hunters, as natives shunned what were at this season mosquito-infested swamps.

I had for gun bearer at this time a very tall Manzema. I chose him because he was very strong and could lift me with ease by putting his head between my legs and then standing upright. This brought my head about level with the grass-tops, and I could then see my game. I weighed a good 13½ stone [182 pounds], and with rifle and cartridges about another stone [14 pounds] more, yet he never got tired of heaving me up, and there he would stand like a rock. His great, wide-spread muscular toes would sink deep into the mud in gripping it, where a boot-shod foot would simply have slithered about.

As a sunshade to his very bloodshot eyes, he wore a strip of giraffe hide round his head, with the stiff, bristly mane standing out all around as a brim, while his shaved and corrugated skull stuck up in the centre like the dome of a bashed bowler hat. He was certainly not a beauty, but when it came to standing steadfast with infuriated pachyderms crashing around, or straight at him for all he could see, he was in a class by himself.

I will now take just an ordinary day's hunting. The spy round showed elephants about eight miles south-west, slowly feeding toward some swampy and inundated parts. Careful examination showed five bulls—all there were, apparently, unless others were hidden in the grass. So, back to camp we went for some breakfast, and then for it.

After some native meal porridge with honey and milk on my part, and some gruel and elephant fat—about half and half—on the gun bearer's part, we set off to follow some drier ridges that we knew from former experience. Once

The camp well situated at the foot of a solitary hill.

The Manzema, with sunshade of giraffe hide.

down on the flat, I wondered how I was ever going to find those beasts. Visibility was about thirty yards in the open and as many inches in the thick parts.

I was out of footgear of the conventional type at this time, and was wearing home-made moccasins made from the hock pieces of giraffe. The heels were very neat and fitted perfectly as they exactly corresponded to the knuckle or elbow, or whatever it is called, of the animal, but the toes were quite the reverse. The skin, being more than a quarter-inch thick, had to be kept moist by filling the moccasins with wet sand at night, and this set up a kind of slow putrefaction in the untanned hide. The hair soon came out, and a very unpleasant smell greeted one in the morning. This, however, quickly toned down once they were in the mud and water, and altogether they were not at all bad as long as they were wet and pliant.

On the way we passed by the carcass of an elephant we had killed some days previously. It lay in long grass and was not visible until we were right upon it. As we appeared, a great cloud of vultures rose with a noise like thunder, and an old leopard sprang out of sight with a snarl.

So far we had been following the sort of faint path a small gang of boys had made in de-tusking the elephant. We had no great native gathering for the meat we killed as we would have had in the dry season. Now we had to break fresh ground; except for elephant, the African bush would be almost impassable for man off the beaten track. They trail about all over the place, and wherever they pass, they leave behind a track amply broad for a single man. By zig-zagging about in these paths you can generally arrive wherever you wish to go, provided, of course, you retain your sense of direction.

After some hours of groping along, we finally arrived about where we thought we had first seen our game. It was not in sight, and we did not expect it to be. The sun was well up now and the elephants would probably be in the mud and water of the swamps. Now we had to find their tracks, and then follow them.

Getting the bearing of our camp from the gun bearer, who shinnied up a tree and pointed out the direction of our hill, we plunged on and came soon to a dry ridge. This was literally covered with game and a much sparser and finer growth of grass. On the top of the ridge we found the tracks of our game. Now we had merely to follow them—an easy matter in the wet season—and hope to find them in dry country.

The tracks showed abundant evidence of their leisurely feeding operations. It is surprising how far this slow gait will take them. The excitement made miles seem short, and the smell of bull elephants became hotter and stronger as we ran on their trail.

I suppose to a keen-scented animal like a foxhound, the smell of elephants would, probably, be overpowering, but to such blunted noses as ours, it seemed just pleasantly perceptible. The freshly crushed herbs of the dry parts gave out a delicious perfume, equalled only by that of the smoking dung—in the elephant hunter's estimation, at any rate.

We passed occasional pools of rain water held up in hollows. Here our game had bathed, churning up the mud and smearing it over their great backs and sides to keep out the blood-sucking flies. In this process, mud had reached the surrounding vegetation for fifteen or twenty yards all around, and was at first dry or semi-dry, but later as we drew near our game, it became

An old leopard sprang out of sight with a snarl.

An old cow rhino was rolling in the mess.

moist. At one of these baths an old cow rhino was rolling in the delightful mess, her peculiar physiognomy suiting exactly her surroundings. We slid rather apologetically past her as she peered at us out of her tiny eyes.

Presently we heard that nerve-thrilling sound, the regular *clop! clop!* of the elephants' great ears as they swing to and fro. A few yards more and we came in view of a fine bull elephant that was about twenty yards away. He was standing by a tree and had been rubbing his sides and back against the smooth-worn, mud-encrusted trunk. He re-commenced to do so as I peered around for his companions. He looked just exactly like a pig rubbing itself on a post, with the exception that here the tree—a stout one—seemed in imminent danger of being thrown to the ground, for its top was swaying and quivering in the upheaval.

There was no sign of the other four, except their tracks leading on past our friend here, so I shot him in the brain, and ran on as soon as I saw the quivering and jerking of the legs, without which sign there is no certainty of the shot having reached the brain. The gun bearer would have off his tail in a second, and would catch me up on the tracks of the other elephants.

He was, indeed, the only boy, except Pyjalé, who ever grasped the fact that after the brain shot one could do so with perfect safety. The others could never believe that death could come so suddenly to so huge an animal, and they would stand well back until every quiver had subsided. Even then they would bolt when some anxious sprite would catch a glimpse of the little rolling eye, mistaking a wink of the eye-lid for a sign of returning life.

The tracks led almost directly into real bad grass and, presently, into water. The gun bearer came up with the tail, and I got him to heave me up to see if I could catch a sight of what lay ahead. Ten yards from me were the head and ears of a listening elephant, while beyond him were several backs sticking up out of the sea of grass. We had been making quite a noise floundering through the mud and water, but our noble game had no suspicion that the noise was caused by anything other than their companions.

At any rate, when my arms and rifle followed my gray hat and muddy face into his purview, he mildly felt toward me with his finger-ended trunk. It seemed almost to reach me as I tried my rifle on his brain. The trunk interfered badly, but I was ready instantly to take advantage of a change of position. This came with a sudden side-sweep of the head and cocking of the great ears. He had got a whiff of our scent, but before he could do anything that would have stampeded the others, he had a bullet through his brain—it could be heard whining away in the distance. It was a .275, the only bullet I have found capable of traversing a fully adult bull elephant's skull from side to side.

Down he went with that suddenness so up-lifting to the hunter's heart, and down I went, too, for, by arrangement, I pressed with my hand on the boy's head and he simply dropped to his knees and I to my feet. I ran quickly to the prostrate elephant, up his gangway of a quivering front leg, and thence to the great arched ribs standing six or seven feet from the ground.

From this vantage point I looked eagerly on for the other elephants. There they were about two hundred yards away, but stern on. They were moving slowly toward a belt of trees, denoting drier ground. The grass came too high up their sides for a shot at their hearts, and the distance was too great to shoot at their brains, so I slid to the ground by the stern of the elephant where the boy had hacked off the tail, and we both plunged into the grass and water on the tracks of the remaining three elephants.

A fine bull elephant . . . rubbing his sides.

This sort of ground is the very worst one can encounter. Added to the broken down, but floating, grass twining round your legs, there are the innumerable deep pot-holes made by the elephants' feet sinking into the mud. This latter has not had time to settle, and the pot-holes are, therefore, invisible through the troubled water. Consequently, with every other step you go right down to the armpits—that is if you are not thrown headlong into the morass. The more you hurry, the worse it is. You are drenched in the stuff from head to toe, which does not matter, but your rifle is also drenched. This does not matter in the case of a Mauser or similarly efficient engine of warfare, but should you be carrying one of those beautiful and expensive double-barrel creations, so dear to the London gunmaker's heart, you will probably be unable to close the breech should some of the all-pervading mud succeed in reaching the faces, as it is almost sure to do.

After an exhausting half mile or so of this kind of thing, we were relieved to see looming over the grass-tops the branches of trees, and in a few more steps we were once more on dry land. Now we legged it hard to try to catch our game before it reached another swamp. We were overjoyed to see the tracks leading along the crest of the ridge where the bush was thicker but the grass much thinner.

Panting along like hounds on the trail, we suddenly came to the edge of one of those open patches of fine, silky-looking grass. There, about in the middle of it, stood the three great sterns in line abreast.

I was pretty well done, and wanted a minute's rest to steady me. While we waited, the three great animals suddenly wheeled round as if it had been part of their drill. After a minute's pause they came straight back on their tracks at the run. They were not charging, but merely coming back to the companions they had left behind them, I suppose. But they looked simply grand in their massiveness as they bore down upon us. They were most impressive.

I ran out to meet them so as to have as good a chance as possible at them before any of them could reach the high stuff surrounding us. We rapidly drew together.

My first shot brought the centre one slithering head to ground, legs tucked back under him. The two others swung across his front broadside to me, one covering the other, heads high in the air, wonderment in their whole attitude. My second shot reached the brain of the nearest, and down he went, too, disclosing behind him the third and last, whose massive head and gleaming tusks swung high toward his fallen comrades.

I was on the point of pressing the trigger on him also when he suddenly swung away, with a bang of the ears, and started to rapidly diminish in size as he fled from us. We were now in for a devil of a chase, in all probability, and I hoped it would lead us homeward. Getting the tails of the fallen, we set off as hard as we could on his tracks.

After about three hours of hard going we caught sight of him. He turned neither to right nor left, and the direction led straight to Nopak, visible on the horizon, miles away. It was evident that a foot-runner could do nothing toward getting up for a broadside shot, and evening was drawing in. I determined, therefore, to try a shot I had discovered some time previously.

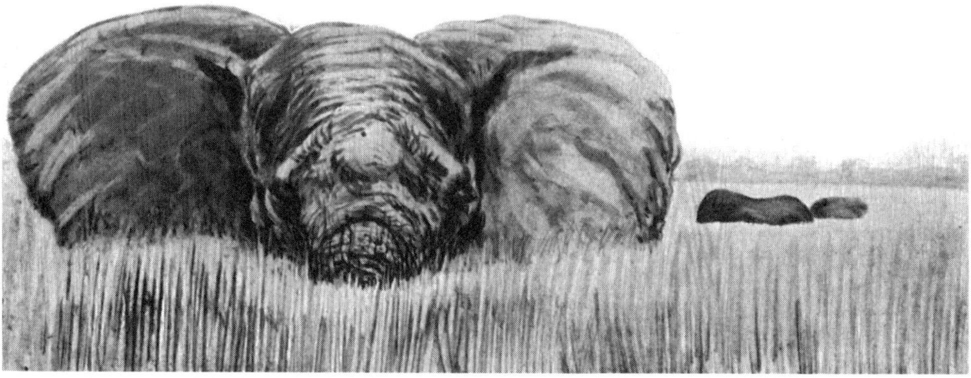

Ten yards from me were the head and ears of a listening elephant.

It was a risky shot that should only be tried as a last resource—that is, the shot from behind, rather to one side and placed accurately under the short ribs, and high. If properly executed, the bullet rakes forward into the lungs without encountering the dense, bullet-stopping wad formed by a ton or two of grass in the stomach. It will be found most successful when the animal has had time to evacuate a few hundredweight of intestinal contents, as they so rapidly do when fleeing. It was just such an animal as that before us, in fact.

It was not long before I had a chance to send him three rather long, but pretty well-placed shots, as the dust puffs on his sloping stern showed. For twenty or thirty yards there was an increase in speed, but after that a diminishing one until he came to a slow walk and then a stop. He was ours, and it only remained to run up as quickly as possible and finish him with a shot in the brain.

We were miles and miles from home, and the sun was practically gone. Soon the mosquitoes would be on us. Firewood and a dry spot were what we required. Luckily, both were near at hand. I started collecting wood while the boy cut off the elephant's ears to lie upon if the weather was fine and to cover us should it rain. Soon we had a good fire going, with chunks of elephant trunk grilling on spits before it as I lay on one side and the Manzema lay on the other, tired but happy.

That is the kind of day we had throughout that wet season. Sometimes less successful, once or twice more so, but seldom blank. The spy from the hill-top saved us from that. Of course, on many days I saw nothing at all. And then there would be breaks in the hunting when food had to be bought for meat from the distant villages. For this purpose the common game, such as zebra or hartebeest or topi would be shot as near to the temporary meat market as possible. Once giraffes were found and requisitioned, and fine trade they brought, being very fat and consequently popular with the native women.

Then, as the rains began to fail and the country began to dry up, native men would drop in on us once more. I remember one such day some natives were discovered bathing in the pool we had scooped out in the spring for drinking water. As it was not by any means the first time, I thought it necessary to make an example of the culprits. So they were brought to camp and ceremoniously beaten by my head man. They seemed to take it extraordinarily well, and when it was explained that it was for polluting our drinking water by bathing in it, they simply laughed. They seemed incapable of understanding our dislike to such a harmless custom, and innocently asked why. The unsanitary nature of the proceeding, when pointed out to them, did not present itself to their minds as the real reason for our behaviour.

"No! No!" they laughed, "you simply want to show us that you are our father and we your children. And so we are!"

And they all crowded round offering to be beaten again if "father" would only give his children some iron chain or brass wire or beads.

"Look," said one old rascal, as he laid himself flat on the ground, displaying his fine, beefy buttocks, "you can give me ten strokes, if you will, then give me one cubit of iron chain."

As "father" was then about twenty-two[1] and his child about fifty, the position was decidedly awkward for the former. That sort of thing rather takes the wind out of your sails when you want to be firm and dignified!

[1] This would have been in 1902.

MAN-EATING LEOPARD IN THE FRENCH CONGO

CHAPTER 26

In these days of easy and comfortable access to the great game haunts of Africa, with its attendant disadvantages in crowded hunting grounds, costly licenses, and harried game, it will come as pleasant news to many shooting men that there still awaits their coming a new country and new game. During my elephant hunts in the French Congo I came upon a species of game new to me. The game is the leopard, but it is not the ordinary duiker- and monkey-killing sort. It is a race of leopard that has taken to man-eating.

This has happened through a variety of causes, chief of which would seem to be the presence of sleeping sickness in the villages and the native custom of segregating the victims in camps at some little distance therefrom. Unable to defend themselves and unattended by those able to do so, the miserable victims of Africa's scourge fall easy prey to leopard and hyaena.

As with lion, the habit of killing and eating man, once acquired, is never dropped by the leopard, and when I was in that country just before the 1914 war, leopards had become so numerous and bold as to form a scourge scarcely less deadly than the sickness itself. Their onslaughts appeared to stir no combative spirit among the natives. Attack after attack was received with an apathy incredible to the European mind, and no counter-measures of any sort were taken. In time the whole country fell into a trance of terror, extending even to the white men living there.

An instance of this occurred to me. I arrived one evening at a military post, where I received the usual hospitality of dinner and a house to sleep in. As usual, I had my camp-bed placed on the open veranda, but when my hosts saw my boys erecting it there, they were horrified. "Leopards are all over the fort at night," they said.

No man moved out after nightfall in spite of a formidable breastwork all around the place. Sentries and everyone else were simply terrified. The whole place was hermetically sealed up after nightfall, as I soon learned as we sat sweltering in the heat at dinner.

A good clean shot at leopard.

It seemed to me a comic situation. Here was a force of two hundred fighting men, white and black, armed with the deadly weapons of modern science—mitrailleuses[1] throwing streams of high-velocity bullets—all cooped up by a strolling cat or two. But so it was, and is, for all I know to the contrary. When I suggested they should follow the tracks into the bush, they had very many reasons why such experiments were bound to fail, but no one spoke from actual experience. It was very evident that no one wished to have anything to do with tracking pussy to her lair.

Among the natives the same lack of spirit prevailed; only here they had the excuse that, from time immemorial, leopards had been regarded as containing the spirits of the departed. Therefore, they would not undertake to hunt up and destroy the raider themselves, nor would they help anyone else to do so. Yet, with their assistance many of those devastating cats could have been bagged, although their dogs proved to be as poor spirited as their masters.

I arrived one evening at a village and pitched my tent nearby. They told me a boy had been taken in the night. In answer to the question, "Had he slept alone?" it was said others were with him. The others were produced, and one of them said he had jabbed a spear at the animal. The victim was a small child of six or seven years.

That moonlight night I lay at the end of the space of the village commanding a view of almost every hut. Crickets sawed away in every tree, full-throated frog croaks came from the swamp, and dogs barked, howled, and wailed. Hour after hour droned away. One or two men, overcome with the crowd and heat of the tiny huts, drew forth their mats and threw themselves down in the sparkling moonlight.

Suddenly there was a cough! Dead silence. *Cough! Cough!* Not a sound now from the valiant pack of dogs. The sleepers-out flitted silently off, dragging their mats. The curs had already gone cowering into the huts. The village was as if dead or deserted. *Cough! Cough!* Nearer and nearer.

In front of me was the quite open and clean space between the two rows of huts. If anything came out into that space, I felt sure I would see it and be able to shoot. I had had no difficulty in seeing and drawing a bead upon the

[1]A mitrailleuse, from French *mitraille* meaning *grapeshot*, is a type of volley gun with multiple barrels of rifle calibre that can fire either multiple rounds at once or several rounds in rapid succession.

A more usual glimpse of a leopard.

village curs before they withdrew. I noticed that those so standing toward me as to show some part of their body in shadow were the most clearly definable. The colour of the native dogs was a dirty yellow, not unlike the between-spots parts of a leopard, and I argued from this that I should have no great difficulty in seeing the enemy.

Meanwhile, all was silent—neither a whimper nor a sound emerged from the huts. One would have thought they would be piling up the fires or making some preparation. But nothing. The complete dread of a deadly nightmare gripped all. Cold shivers ran up and down my spine as my eyes probed the shimmering space in front of me, and my head came round with a jerk to glance behind me, for, of course, the leopard might approach from any side. I began to think those fellows in India who get up a tree with an electric torch were not such muffs after all. A nice safe perch has great attractions at such a moment.

Cough! Cough! Very loud and near this time—and in front of me, thank goodness. Surely he must be almost in the village now. But, of course, he would nose round and maybe come in behind me yet. It was devilish exciting. *God knows where my bullets will go,* I thought, *if he should appear between me and any of the double row of huts.*

What was going on now I did not know. There was not a sound and I was beginning to feel that sickly desire for something to happen. But nothing did happen for what seemed a very long time. Then, quite suddenly, without any movement being apparent, there appeared the beast silhouetted sharply against the shadowed wall of one of the huts. What a perfect snip! But the leopard is a thin animal, and so is the mud and wattle wall of a native hut, and my bullet would tear through both of them at goodness knows what velocity. . . . I held my fire.

He moved forward, left the shadowed wall, and at once became almost invisible. I do not believe I could have seen him at all, but for his shadow. From my low elevation, this appeared almost as a black line, and it was this black line with a gray shadowy thing above it that I saw move across the open space. Once it was clear of the huts, I fired into the forward part of the gray shadow and had him.

The shot had broken his spine. He made a devil of a racket—there was enough noise for ten—and he began biting at himself and kicking up dust. I ran up and the gallant beast came slithering at me, dragging his hinder half, paralyzed, behind him. But how near a miss was that shot. Curs first, then men came out when I had shouted the news a dozen times. Some old men came and almost held the dear departed's hand. They seemed more awe-stricken than glad to be rid of a pest.

That is the point I would stress in connection with this game. The Government has offered what is a large reward to natives for every leopard killed, but nothing will move the natives from their centuries-old attitude toward these ravening man-eaters. No wonder leopards find man-eating a safe and convenient

Leopard stalking a baboon.

In the moonlight.

form of running their commissariat. Anyone wishing to devote himself to the systematic hunting of these animals could not count on much native assistance. Information of their doings and the localities of their depredations would be about all one would get.

There are, however, motor roads and telegraphs. A man with a Ford lorry or two, a pack of native dogs from some other part not terrorized by leopards, his own personnel of good stout bush-country boys, and his own camp equipment and arms could move rapidly from scene to scene. In two or three months he would assemble quite a unique collection of man-eaters.

The town of Bangui, on the Ubangi River, is reached from Brazzaville, the capital of the French Congo. There used to be several services a month from Bordeaux to Brazzaville. At Bangui food of all sorts, petrol, Ford cars, Ford lorries, tyres, etc., are available. Tents, rifles, ammunition, camp-beds, medicines, fishing gear, and, of course, personal gear, are all that is necessary to take on an expedition to collect man-eaters.

Fire Hunt and the Islands of the Ubangi River

Chapter 27

So densely clothed in high forest are these islands that it was by mere chance that I discovered elephants frequented them at certain times of the year. So numerous were they that I made haste to equip myself for the job. I reckoned a small steam launch was required, capable of being carried over land in sections each weighing not more than 150 pounds.

Imagine what a gift this thing was. All transport problems solved. Fuel to be got everywhere for the cutting. Lubricating oil? A ten-gallon drum lasted six months, and if necessary, you could boil down hippo fat. It was a gift straight from Heaven, and made a paradise of that mighty river with its elephant-haunted islands. We soon rigged up a grass-roofed house on a platform built over two long native dug-outs. The platform occupied two-thirds of the length, leaving a space for the launch in between the two canoe hulls.

When we first tried this house-boat affair, we nearly sank the thing. Used to motors with their failing power with the drop in revs., it came as a pleasant surprise to find the very reverse with steam. We had not thought to cover in the ends of the canoes, so when we opened the throttle, we nearly went bow under, shipping a lot of water. We just got back to the sand bank in time.

Rapidly we decked in the ends of our catamaran, and shifting some weights aft, we set off for the island hunting grounds. Tying up at a lovely, clean sand bank each night, an hour's bush-cutting by all hands provided fuel for the next day's steaming. Life was reduced to its simplest elements. The meat of the elephants killed provided all our own requirements. We never touched money. When elephants failed us, there were hippos and buffaloes to be had.

As our hunting tactics developed, aided by this ideal transport, we began to use hundreds of natives from either the Belgian Congo side or from the French side, or even from both banks together, in clearing a space right across some good, heavily frequented islands. Of course they could not tackle the large trees, but they would lay low all the underbrush so that when elephants were moved down the island, they would give the rifle a chance when they came in view to cross the clearing. I had visions of mowing them down in scores. Far otherwise was the reality.

The first time we tried a drive, we had all the usual palaver with the medicine-man to go through. It is as well to exercise some patience with these gentry when trying something new, if only because the natives are more given to heed their word than that of an unknown white man. On our houseboat we could transport forty natives at a time, so we soon had a large gang whacking away at the bush. The medicine man, encouraged by a slug of absinthe, had promised them mountains of meat.

With drums beating and exhorted by the elders, who were comfortably installed in the shade with beer pots around them, they fell to with a will and soon had a strip of sixty yards broad right across the island. This particular island was about twelve miles long and a hundred yards broad at its narrowest point. The debushing lasted a day, and I told the natives we would try the scheme on the morrow. This was mistake Number One. We subsequently found we should have left the place quiet for at least a week. However, it was imperative to show results at the first trial as otherwise it would be difficult to get a labour force for any further job.

I had two .303 ten-shot rifles and, of course, the old round-nose "solid" 215-grain bullet. The launch went off at cock-crow to put the beaters ashore at the up-stream end of the island some six miles away. I took up my stance beside a large forest tree at the edge of the clearing and awaited events. In front of me lay the debushed space still littered with the cut underbrush and with all the large trees still standing. They were mighty close to each other, and I anticipated some pretty fancy shooting if the elephants came fast.

Nothing happened for a long time. I began to fear the elephants might have broken out and taken to the river. Actually they were bunching up in complete silence in the thick stuff at the edge of the clearing, evidently upset by the unusual look and smell of things. We should not have attempted a drive until the elephants had got used to the new surroundings.

We never saw a sign or heard a sound of an elephant as we waited expectantly. Yet they were there within shot and in numbers. They had on their quiet act. There was not a belch, not a sigh, nor a belly rumble, not even the tale-bearing *plop, plop* of evacuation. No flap of ears to warn the waiting hunter could be heard.

Just as I was beginning to think the thing was a flop, they came. Needless to say, not as I had hoped they would come, two or three at a time, but in a solid bunch. How many? I could not say. It was impossible to count. They came at speed, and for a few seconds all was just a confused mass of cascading gray heads. Had they come straight, something might have been done with two or three of the leaders, but they poured between the large trunks of the still-standing trees.

It was quite the hottest seven or eight seconds I can remember. Nothing but semi-automatic fire could have dealt with it, ordinary push-bolt fire was hopelessly out of it no matter how expert the operator might be. I fired three shots, two brain shots and an oblique shot through the neck, as they were going away. It was all over. Although I was disappointed they had not come quietly and spaced out, I was thankful to have got enough meat to satisfy the horde of natives. Had nothing been killed, I doubt if I should have been able to get any further volunteers for the bush-clearing jobs.

As we gained experience, we did not clear the whole cross section of an island. We merely thinned the actual field of fire, left it for a week or ten days, and then returned to it. We also learnt to move elephants quite quietly with only two or three reliable old boys. In time we attained a very decent level of bags, and we soon had people preparing sites for new drives, quite on their own. Once we tried bringing them back over the fire area a second time, but they came even faster. After an attempt to repeat the drive a third time, the herd left the island taking to the water and escaping into a few million acres of timber on the mainland. We gave it up and confined ourselves to one drive per island.

This was the easiest, cheapest, and most exciting hunting I had ever experienced. I would not have looked at any other, but unfortunately the elephants left the islands with the beginning of the rains. Not a single animal seemed to be left in those scores of islands. This was confirmed by all native sources, so very reluctantly I concluded I would have to do a little work and resume the endless foot-slogging required to come up with those cunning old rascals. This task is never easy, for a century of dodging man had injected these animals with uncanny powers of concealment . . . along with bullets of every description, pieces of iron, spears, and arrows. At that time I reckoned I had done about sixty thousand miles on foot in going to and returning from hunting grounds as well as on the actual trail of the elephant.

When our island hunting ceased from lack of elephants, I determined to ascend the Ubangi until a large-enough tributary running in from the north presented itself. This I hoped would lead to some convenient point from which a portage would land us on the Shari-Chad watershed. Thus we hoped to tap some new country.

The rains were on, making all rivers raging torrents. Above the town of Bangui the rapids began. Often it became necessary to break down the catamaran into its component parts and manhandle them through the worst parts. We found there were very few places where the launch could not navigate, but without the canoes, of course. Gone the comfortable grass-roofed house that had been so pleasant during the island hunting. Now we had to pitch camp ashore.

With some difficulty we got our gear up that rapid and came to a *poste* a few miles farther on. Over lunch the *chef de poste* asked me if I had seen the steamer.[1] On my saying yes, he said, "What did they give you?" "Nothing," I replied, at which he roared with laughter. "You are the only white man, then, who didn't receive something." I gathered he and anyone else who might have become witnesses had been squared.

This same *chef de poste* was a great friend of mine. These people do not hunt themselves, and if they do, it is mostly birds. They give a native one of their army rifles and tell him to go kill something. Their bullet was then the Balle D[2]—a homogeneous copper, very pointed spitzer affair—not at all a good killer except in expert hands. Consequently, they were generally short of meat. One day, having made a killing of buffaloes near his posts, I had sent a runner in to tell the *chef* that I had a buffalo for him if he would send out a couple of police to take charge of the meat. Ever afterward he introduced me as the friend who had sent him an entire buffalo for his dinner.

In this man's administrative area there was still a fairly heavy traffic in female slaves from the Belgian Congo side. The trade medium was chiefly cartridges, percussion caps, and gunpowder. The girls were brought over fat and sold either as wives or for the table. In that part of Africa the diet consisted largely of cassava.[3] Being deficient in protein, the hunger for meat

[1]See chapter 8 for the story about the steamer and insurance fraud.

[2]Local French for bullet; all natives in French Africa used it.

[3]Cassava is an edible starchy tuberous root, a major source of carbohydrates.

was appalling. Even the sex organs of bull elephants were consumed after the utmost fun had been extracted from the situation, of course. It always raised a laugh to see four or six old ladies carrying along one of those formidable weapons in pursuit of the young girls. East of the Nile, this particular tit-bit is only used for medicine-making.

After a few judicious questions about this slave traffic, I was astounded to hear from the *chef de poste* that all trade had been stopped. He based his assertion on no better grounds than that a law had been passed that prohibited the practice of trafficking in slaves or in eating them. As on the Nile and elsewhere, it was the government police who were the main purveyors of humans as trade goods. There are few so out of touch with the realities of Africa as those clothed with any kind of authority.

There is something that makes the owning of a human being an enchantment, especially so in the case of a young, unspoilt female. I could feel far more affection for such a one than for your equal-rights, "I'm-as-good-as-you" sort of creature, with her highly artificial bosoms generally cocked at the wrong angle and her false face and flaccid muscles. Contrast such a one with a girl who may be eaten if she has not the luck to find someone who will cherish her. Compare the service of the two: One with her head full of her "rights" kicks you around like a piece of dirt, refuses you this, refuses you that. The other—oh well! Perhaps I had better not say! No! Not even a peep at paradise.

Mind you, it is all strictly legal and above board. The chief has an adopted daughter surplus to establishment. The hoary rascal is in meat. He requires a marriage portion. All above board and not even a sniff of slavery, nothing but the actuality.[4]

When it comes to physical condition, the two will not bear comparison. I do not believe that a race that cannot breast-feed its babies can survive, or is fit to do so. When the Old Testament says, "The sleep of the labouring man is sweet," it was not necessary to even mention that that includes the woman. Automatically she is a labouring person as all women began as such. When neither man nor woman labour, that is the Finish.

[4]Bell is saying that cannibalism and slavery exist in parts of Africa. The adopted daughter is a slave taken in a raid. Since the chief is in "meat," he has no need to eat the daughter, so he sells her because he wants the money.

Raking our way slowly against the current and passing many rapids, we came finally to where a large river joined in from the north. It looked bank-high and much discoloured. Hoping to reach some point not too far from the Shari-Chad watershed, we bored our way into this new country. It is always exciting, just the fact of its being new. You always hope for something to turn up. Almost as invariably, you are disappointed.

Climbing steadily upward, the water being very fast, with occasional dashes into the high grass and gallery forest country, we just managed enough buffalo meat for all hands. There were few elephants here at this time, and we hoped they would be up on the watershed country. There were no native settlements on the lower reaches, only the remains. We suspected the dreaded tsetse-fly-borne sleeping sickness had been at work.

One day during my absence in the bush, one of my boys bet another he could hold in the bullet of a .22 L.R. by placing his thumb over the muzzle and holding it firmly. He was soon disillusioned. The bullet pierced his thumb easily and ended up in his guts. He died the next day.

Although in flood, soon the river began to look like one continuous rapid white water from bank to bank. We were nearing hills that appeared over the prevailing gallery forest. It was evident we would not get much farther by river.

I was out in the bush looking for elephants one day when I heard the twittering of honey guides. We were always on the look-out for these little birds as we used honey to make mead. We always carried an empty calabash with some seeds containing the necessary fermentative properties. When the calabash was empty, these seeds dried up and rattled about but did not lose their potency. If we came across or were led to a bee hive, we took the honey by means of smoking torches of grass, putting what we did not eat into the calabash. When mixed with water, it immediately came alive and started to bubble. If left a day or two, it became most refreshing and mildly intoxicating. It was often our sole source of sugar and liquor.

On this occasion, however, the birds were not guiding us to honey but to some natives. It was a wonder the natives did not see us; instead, we saw them first. This does not happen so often. Generally the more primitive see the less first. We watched them take the hive. They made a fire by rubbing sticks together.

The natives finished and evidently left the birds nothing or at best very little, for their feathered guides set up a most violent tirade at the natives' ingratitude. In leaving the scene they came straight to our hiding place. With that infinite capacity of the true primitive to hide emotion, they greeted us as if they were in the habit of meeting with white men round every bush. Only a slight trembling of the youngest's spear showed any emotion at all.

After sharing some honey with us, their eyes could not stray from a couple of elephant tails we had lying beside us. Pointing to them, we indicated we would give them meat. In return we wanted to be led to their village, indicating the fact by pantomime. Not one of that party spoke a word intelligible to another, yet they soon understood what we wanted.

First we required to know the distance. This we did by pointing to various positions of the sun in the sky. Then we imitated women—without whom no work gets accomplished in Africa—by holding our clenched fists to our breasts and pointing to the elephant tails. They understood perfectly, so simple are hunters' needs and wants. I have given the foregoing not as a major incident in a hunter's career but because I have been asked so often how I communicated with totally strange tribes. It never occurred to me that there could be any difficulty when wants are so simple.

In due course we reached the village and were well received. It is not every day that strangers come to town with a present of eight or nine tons of beef. Moreover, it was not far to the river, and we were soon served by the help from the tribe's numerous members in running down some quite good elephants. The rains were petering out, but the high grass still held the bush unviolated by fire, and elephants wandered freely into the ripening corn. Hardly a day passed without some infuriated farmer sending for assistance in handling these crop destroyers. Besides all these considerations, I wanted assistance in a big way to portage that steamer over the watershed that could not now be far distant.

They were a good-looking lot, these Banda, particularly the girls. The sex relations of these people differ largely from our own when it is a question of choosing a wife. I remember remarking to Pyjalé on an extremely attractive woman of perhaps twenty-two or twenty-three years of age who was still in a girl's dress—which is nothing but a tiny ornamental fringe slung on a string around the waist. To me she seemed to be one of those surplus women so rare in Africa.

It astonished me that such an outstandingly beautiful creature should be still unmarried, more especially as she appeared to be as full of sex appeal as a Scotch bun is of currants. Mostly all girls find a husband. But now and then you meet one who is not married. They are invariably good-lookers, in our eyes, at any rate. When you ask why they are not married, the men just laugh.

So I asked Pyjalé about her, and he seemed equally astonished that I should think of anyone marrying such a woman. Pushing him to explain, I asked him why she wasn't married, and he said to me, "Because she is married to all men." The species is not wholly unknown amongst us whites. Confirmed flirt is a feeble term. The tribes have a truer but more indelicate name for it.

Once we had killed, there came a horde of natives to the meat. Quite close to the kill they had captured some baby lions. They brought them to me in our camp some hundred yards from the nearest carcass. I wanted to try to rear these cubs, but I had no supply of milk. They had goats in the village some distance away. The cubs would have to wait until the morrow. Meanwhile they were hungry and set up a frightful din in camp in spite of the abundant meat.

The lion parents came to the carcass that night and kicked up a fearful fuss. Everyone expected them to come right into camp looking for their cubs. Those darned young squirts of blood dared this girl to go to the elephant carcass by herself unarmed. She went and returned without hesitation or haste.

Of course we had made huge camp-fires, and the whole scene was floodlit. As the girl coolly walked toward them, you could see the firelight reflected from the eyes watching her gallant figure advancing on them. They gave way reluctantly before her. Finally she seated herself on something until I went and brought her back. I did not like it and I had a rifle.

When I said to the boys, "What d'you think of that?"

They said with scorn, "Who would marry that?"

There are no flies on the African. If courage is required, the African reckons to provide it, but the last person he wants to show courage is his wife. So that nut-brown Venus remained a spinster but not a virgin. It is a curious sidelight on the inscrutable ways of Providence.

The villagers told me of a large military fort some days distant. Surmising this to be one of those establishments that one finds strung along the frontiers between the British and French, I paid no further heed to it. It is curious all the same to contrast the opposing styles: On the British side you find a single civilian official in charge of a small number of police, where his opposite on the French side will be a commandant with perhaps a dozen white officers and N.C.O.s and numerous regular troops. Presumably, the French felt that "Perfidious Albion" [5] might at any moment resume her treacherous tricks.

Once into the confidence of these people, it was easy to get news of elephants and of the country ahead. This latter sounded rough, but good, for elephants. It would only become traversable when the high grass had been burnt off, however. Then would be the time to tackle—for us—the stupendous task of transporting the steamer over the divide. With no roads and no inhabitants en route, it would be tough going, and only meat could induce natives to accomplish this task. Forced labour was the last thing we wanted to do, even if we had the necessary force.

We were shown some queer places while waiting for the grass-burning season. One place stands out because it seemed to be the headquarters of hyaenas. Close beside a village there was a great colony of the spotted kind. The villagers were scared of them at night and warned us to sleep in huts and not in tents. Hyaenas were said to seize a sleeper by the face or throat and drag him off.

At first all our energies were absorbed by the elephants. They browsed on the ripening corn by night and lay up in dense bush by day quite close to the village. They were hiding from the incensed farmers and made no noise at all. If anyone came around, they froze absolutely motionless. The ear-flapping that gives away unsuspicious elephants was absent. They relied on the thickest, darkest patches of bush to abate the fly nuisance; thus, would they stand all day long within a few hundred yards of the village. It was the most intensely exciting form of hunting.

They would let anyone come messing about within ten yards of them without moving. They were used to stick-gatherers, so it was easy to get near them. At the shot, the whole bush would erupt. Every suddenly animated tank would launch itself into instant flight in whatever direction it happened to be pointing at the instant the shot was heard. If there happened to be eight or nine of them, the fun was fast and furious. You could never see more than one or two of them before you fired, so draped and hidden were they by the foliage. It was here that I had the second example of a shot elephant piercing a tree trunk with a tusk in its fall. The other and first had happened in an East African coastal belt of bush.

[5] "Perfidious Albion" is a pejorative phrase referring to the British. It alludes to alleged acts of diplomatic slights, duplicity, and treachery on the part of England and the British.

In these crazy headlong rushes of guilty-conscienced elephants, the hunter stands quite a good chance of being trodden underfoot, or of receiving quite violent blows from falling, crashing bush. You see, too, the otherwise unique sight of considerable trees broken off short while still standing, their top-hamper held by creepers and vines to their neighbours, and their freshly broken ends thumping down solidly into the damp soil. It is difficult on these occasions to make a killing as time is so short, visibility so restricted, and their speed so much greater than anything the foot hunter can produce. But it is exciting while it lasts.

******

In camp preparations were afoot to deal with the hyaena menace. In all my experience I had never seen hyaenas so out of hand. They completely dominated the natives. At nightfall the natives were in their huts. These were heavily barred. No one stirred even to protect their crops from raiding elephants. They all agreed hyaenas would attack at night any solitary traveler while anyone sleeping out was certain to be jumped on and would be lucky to come out of the encounter with only half his face gone. Unlike the leopard, they seemed unaware of the deadly neck grip. As proof of all this they produced two men with their features badly mauled.

This all meant we would have to get out our 12-bore and buck-shot ammo. I hardly ever used this gun, preferring a .22 for bird requirements. But loaded with buck-shot, nine to the load, it was the gun for the job.

It was a moonless night, so we pegged out some fresh buck skin. On the far side we rigged up some white skulls and secured them so they could not be moved. You could just see the loom of white in the starlit night. The idea was to blast at the hyaena with the cone of buck-shot whenever one of the skulls was obscured. The buck skin had been folded up green and was in a suitable state of stink to attract these brutes. I intended to keep the first watch. The boys had prepared grass torches in abundance.

Almost at once a skull disappeared. I let drive both barrels. A boy lit a torch. There was something crawling away. Another shot anchored it. It was a hyaena. There were dozens of them around, but they were scared now. This was something new to them evidently. We dragged the dead one in front of the white skulls and invited them to come again.

Whether we had grown careless, or more likely had dozed off, I don't know, but they actually got the carcass away. There was an unearthly row as they fought over it. They had not got it out of range when a boy lit a grass torch and the 12-

bore slammed into them again. There must have been a good spread because several yelped and snarled and presently we could hear three distinct fights going on. They would be demolishing any wounded that might be weakening.

The boys dragged the evil carcass back to the target area. I turned in and left the gun to them to continue the good work, hoping the shooting would not disturb any visiting elephants in the corn fields. The boys certainly slept, for the carcass and skin was both gone in the morning. What wonders strychnine would have worked. Pretty safe too, as no other animal would touch a hyaena.

There was a great colony of their burrows not far from this village, and I tried smoking them out. It did not work; it was too deep, I think. Why they should have collected here, I don't quite know. Certainly they got the cadavers, but there were such from every village. These hyaenas were the spotted variety.

******

This certainly was a hard-luck village. Elephants raided their crops while farmers were confined to their huts by hyaenas. We were soon able to change the elephant portion of the infestation, and I pointed out to the farmers how neatly they were getting their own back. At first they were delighted, but after a few days of meat-gorging they seemed to lose their hunger. After a daily gorge of seven or eight pounds of elephant beef, they got that fashionable disease, jaundice.

As the dry season advanced, there was great talk of a fire hunt. I had never seen one of these devastating affairs from start to finish. Certainly, I had been called in to kill fire-blitzed animals that had proved too tough for the native equipment. It was nearly always elephants that had been blinded but otherwise unscathed by their ordeal. This time I would see the whole affair.

A most elaborate thing it proved to be and rather boring in the preparation. The medicine men ran the whole palaver. It was they who appointed and briefed the guardians and watchers. Without the aid of maps, they designated the area to be fire guarded. They commanded great obedience. The meat requirements of the whole country depended on the success or failure of this seasonal hunt.

Great was the "medicine" being made and tough the going according to the hoary old rascals. Innumerable the goats, sheep, and poultry required for the reading of guts. Only thus with a lavish supply of beer could the omens be weighed.

Meanwhile a few score villagers were busy cutting by hand a fire-guard twenty-five paces wide across a triangular piece of land between two rivers. The grass was eight to ten feet high and rapidly drying. The ground had to be clean; otherwise, the fire would jump the guarding strip.

As soon as this was accomplished, the grass outside the fire-guard was lit so as to burn back and away from the guarding strip. This safely done, the whole area was fired for miles around. Now watchers were appointed to see and report game entering or leaving the fire area. The "medicos" redoubled their gut-readings and omen-dodging while relays of beer-pots replenished their energies.

The game wardens' reports were highly favourable. Elephants, buffaloes, and antelopes were daily seen to enter the grassy area. Even lions were spotted, and this drew some wonderful manoeuvres from the magic mongers, the gist of which crystallized in more demands for chickens. No wonder they required conditioning. Your primitive African can become a murdering devil in an instant. If the game should leave the area or aught else go wrong, he will rise as one man and slaughter the medicine men, no matter what excuses they may offer.

There was a huge ant-hill just outside our camp, and daily one of the brotherhood could be seen up on top of it. He would be hung about with a veritable museum of charms. With a grave and weighty air sitting heavily on him, he would glance around the shining firmament. Should the tiniest cloud appear, he would transfix it with a glare while pointing a charm-hung wand at it. Some gibberish that no one understood then followed, while with great deliberation he began to wave it away from the direction of the fire area, having first adroitly chosen the probable course it would naturally take. His efforts would redouble until the sweat poured off him, until in the natural course of things the cloudlet became vaporized by the sun and so appeared to respond to the wand waving.

Just as we were all getting rather bored with these goings-on—they lasted for weeks—the word went round to warn all villages that the date was fixed. The longer this could be delayed, the better the grass would burn and the more game would be caught in the trap. But should an unseasonal shower fall somewhere, out would spew all the stuff in the fire trap. Game animals can scent rain miles away. Rain on parched burnt ground gives off a strong smell. Should this happen, the medicine men were in for it.

There are other snags, too. A high wind will let animals through by keeping down the flames. They will be blistered but otherwise unhurt. A flat calm is considered best. The fire itself then creates its own draught upward. This ensures that elephant will probably be blinded and so fall—after much strenuous work—to the natives' primitive weapons such as spears and large knives.

Soon people from the neighbouring villages began to arrive. Most of the new arrivals already carried green bark sandals for use on the burnt ground. I began to wonder how my boots would stand up to the red-hot ashes. I need not have worried because my eyes would not let me nearer than a hundred yards to the wall of flame.

Next morning we were off on the now well-stamped trail leading to the fire site. So also were hundreds of native men, women, and children. Every imaginable piece of ironmongery was borne along by the multitude. There were worn-down spears retaining only the merest trace of iron at their tips, and knives that consisted chiefly of handle were in the eager grasp of tiny tots willing to try their luck against the mightiest beast of the jungle. The young girls were in their element out to enjoy the occasion, while the elderly women showed their sense by carrying calabashes of water; they had been there before. Besides thirst to be quenched, there was blood to be caught.

Everyone now had the huge green bark sandals. How it was all arranged I do not know. Long practice and custom and wont, I suppose. At a signal, the whole area burst into flames.

I had got myself close to the chief medicine man. He seemed serene enough. I expect he had arranged his get-away should anything go wrong. Once he seemed to be perturbed by the strength of the wind. The game scouts had reported some eighty elephants and numerous buffaloes in the trap that morning, in addition to uncounted antelope.

As soon as the fire started, simultaneously on all sides the natives went quite crazy. They added what they could to the roar and crackle of the fire. The flames shot up thirty-five to forty feet, while clouds of sparks rose into the billowing smoke. What a scene from hell! Every yard of flaming front had some sort of native following it up close. How they did it, I don't know. I could not stick it nearer than a hundred yards back and even then my eyebrows and every hair exposed soon went. I began to wonder what I should do when it came to shooting with all these natives about.

Through watering eyes, I saw a native man raise his spear and dart it into a black lump on the ground. The lump unfolded in a flash, revealing a truly devilish creature. It was jet black on the top and sides while below it revealed the untouched brilliant spots and yellow of a satanically active leopard. In one flashing bound it was on the spear man, who missed his thrust at it, and bit him in the shoulder. It straightway sprang on another man who had come to the first man's rescue. He, likewise, missed with his spear and fell to the ground. Away sprang that gallant beast, apparently unharmed.

My bullet sped but passed him by. I am glad now that he escaped, yet he added one more missed leopard to that all-too long list. They seem too quick, too quick for 2,000 f.p.s. bullets, anyway. I wonder if a 3,500-footer would have shortened that list. I know a short-travel striker would have.

This was a bad beginning, but the uproar drowned everything. Next there was diversion on my right. Something was coming. By heavens! Buffalo! A mass of them. Instead of being fire-stricken, they were fire-stimulated. They came, with ginger under their tails, like a train. I could not shoot until they were nearly opposite me. One bright and hopeful lad thinking they were blind, laid hold of passing tail and was busy giving its owner the works when a following buff caught him in the stern and heaved him aside. He got into a sitting posture and swore at those buffaloes with such indignation on his face that it almost prevented me from engaging the passing target for laughing. They had found a break in the wall of fire and had come through untouched except for losing all their hair from body, ears, and tail. A lucky out-crop of rock had saved their steaks from grilling.

Although there was little or no ground wind, there was a strong up-draught. The isolated trees suddenly enveloped in heat and their sap turned instantly to superheated steam, bursting asunder with reports like field guns. Following the chief medicine man, we came on elephant tracks showing gray on the uniform black ground. They had evidently broken through but seemed to be cows, so we did not press the matter.

I was looking at something on their tracks, wondering what it was, when it suddenly took the shape of a mangled child. Hardly a recognizable item of its make-up remained. As we hesitated, some native men who had followed this bunch of cows now appeared to be running back to the fire. They shouted that the elephants were going hard. Evidently they had not been delayed by their fire ordeal.

Soon the fire trap became quite small. Now was when the fun should start in earnest. It was unbelievable the speed it went. On the trodden grass of the game trails, the fire ran along at express speed. The major trouble was the poor visibility owing to smoke. You simply could not see what was going on. This was a pity because plenty was happening. As the fire contracted, so did the noise expand. There were now masses of infuriated natives dashing in and out of visibility on all sides. Some unrecognizable beast would burst through the throng with the milling mass of people apparently hanging on to it, spears jabbing, everything going at it until it fell.

Then a large bull elephant badly burnt and deeply dejected appeared with drooping ears and blisters the size of tea trays—a horrible sight. I quickly dispatched him and examined his eyes. They were both scorched white in the eyeball. He could not have seen at all, and I doubt if he could have recovered. Just then a native plucked me by the arm and I followed him seeing his urgency.

They had three great bull elephants in a bunch. Every time they moved to get away, a spear would catch it in the trunk. They were completely done and showed no fight at all. I quickly felled them. Just then there burst past us a very different apparition, a bull in full possession of all his senses if minus every hair. There was no hesitation in the way he charged through the maddened throng. He must have found a weak spot in the now dying fire. I remember to this day speeding the bullet over the heads of scores of natives and not so much above them either. I watched that bullet kill him. A body shot would have been impossible; it would have become a head shot before it reached its intended target.

And so it went on that awful day, far into the night. It was a ghastly job. You could not leave those fire-blitzed animals to the fumbling native equipment. I never knew how many buffaloes and elephants I dispatched that day. All I know about it was the final count of tusks, the deadly tiredness after it was over, and the sore lungs that resulted from the inhale of smoke. The medicine men were in terrific form, and dancing was the order of the day.

Just as we were recovering from these debaucheries—they were free for the moment with their women—a runner arrived with a letter carefully wrapped in skin and held in a cleft stick. Passed on from village to village, it came from one of those large frontier posts the French are so insistent on retaining to guard against those perfidious and thrusting British.

It was to say that the commandant had orders to quit the country, that mobilization had been declared, and that "war had broken out between Britain and France on the one part and Germany on the other." It had been going on for five months, so you can imagine how communications were in those days. It was the Great War of 1914.[6] This news completely upset the apple cart. Gone were the plans for portaging that steamer over the divide to the Shari River basin. Gone, too, was the idea of hunting on those delightful islands and among those delectable but heavily forested strongholds of the wily elephant. All would have to wait.

******

When I come to analyze my motives in leaving these happy hunting grounds to join up in a war that could affect me but little, I find it difficult to describe them adequately. The country I was in would become even happier hunting grounds because nearly all the whites would be mobilized and would leave. It was partly just for the hell of it and partly a sort of fever that gets into the blood at such moments. It was unthinkable to stay behind.

I must also confess to a long-cherished urge to fly. Shortly after Bleriot had flown the English Channel and Farman had produced his biplanes, I had sent for one to be shipped out to me. I intended to teach myself to fly it on some extensive sands. It all sounds crazy now, but from my subsequent experience I personally have little doubt that I would have mastered it. After all, those early fliers had no previous experience of leaving the ground.

I also had a semi-automatic rifle that I wanted to try out. It fired only the spitzer-type military bullet and was not good for elephant. In all other respects, it seemed to me then a knock-out. I took on three sergeants of the French colonial army, all first-class rifle men, with their 8-shot Lebels firing the homogeneous copper Balle D, and my rifle licked them. All this happened long before the Garand was heard of. My secret ambition was to shoot down an enemy aircraft. So arranging my affairs as best I could, I got under way. I along with all the ivory went down to the river where the little steam launch lay snug in its grass-roofed house.

Here, to my astonishment, I met a great influx of steel whalers sent up to transport the troops that had been holding off those encroaching British. The commandant—the one who had sent me the letter—introduced himself. We dined and wined together. He asked how long it would take me to get to Bangui.

[6]World War I began on 28 July 1914, so Bell must have learned of the hostilities sometime in December of 1914.

If we hit nothing, I thought we could make it in two days provided we had nothing to carry. He proposed we should go in the launch while all the boys, ivory, and gear could follow in the whalers. I told him my commissariat consisted in living on the country. He said that would be all right. He had white bread and wine. The latter appeared in a ten-gallon drum. It was supposed to be sufficient for two days.

With such abundant man-power, it was not long before we had enough fuel stacked up to take us to the sea if need be. Early the next morning we left for the down-river rush to Bangui Town. Unencumbered by canoes and excessive baggage, we made terrific progress.

We had evolved a rapids technique that astonished our passenger. Instead of rushing these white water and rock passages under full steam so as to retain good steering, we turned our bow up-stream and steamed against the current. The man at the tiller kept one hand on the steam throttle and so by a turn or two could regulate the speed so as to lower the boat gently down between the rocks. A touch on the tiller sent the boat this way or that, and when on opening up a new vista, a closing of the throttle allowed the boat to drop gently down-stream. It was a queer sensation to see the roaring, foaming water rushing by, and the commandant enjoyed it, wondering why the steamers did not adopt it.

He asked me if I, too, had been mobilized. I told him we had no such system. He seemed puzzled and remarked that no Frenchman would voluntarily join up for war. He explained that mobilization meant that all ships would come under orders now and that I would have difficulty in getting passage on one. He said he thought he could arrange one for me.

He was able to do so, and after I sold my ivory and the launch to a trader at a very good price, I left Bangui on a steamer crammed with conscripts. There was only one thing wrong with that launch—the bronze bearings. Unlined with white metal and without forced lubrication, wear was considerable. In spite of running in an oil bath 1,000 r.p.m., such a system really should have forced lubrication.

AFRICAN CROCODILES

CHAPTER 28

I have often wondered why more is not heard of the hunting of crocodiles. In these days of close restriction to limited numbers of almost all African game and of the huge licenses demanded for killing those few bucks, it is pleasant to think upon one exception to this rule. I do not suppose even the most rabid of shooting regulations would place crocodiles on the protected list—at least, not until some considerable body of the public begins to find pleasure and recreation in their pursuit. Then the collection of licenses will come along sure enough. Meanwhile, however, the croc is fair game for all, and no license is required.

What is game and what is not I leave to others to decide. But, vermin or game, the wily old croc requires very careful hunting and very straight shooting. To anchor him to his sand bank, a shot in the brain is the only sure spot, and to make certain of hitting it, the hunter must get within reasonable distance.

It requires very little or no stalking to shoot the ordinary fish-killing croc. More often than not they lie like logs on the sand banks until shot at. These are poor fun, and may be slaughtered without more ado. But the big, old rascals that take a goat or a cow or even a native child or woman at the watering places—these are a very different matter. They do not lie on the banks much, and, if they do, they take good care to slip off into deep water the moment the sound of approaching paddle strokes or other noise warns them.

The sort that may be slaughtered.

Through the glass.

Should it happen that natives report a croc taking a toll, the best thing to do is to pitch camp close to the watering place and, if possible, on a commanding height. If the tent door faces the river, one may sit at one's ease and, with a pair of glasses, keep a close watch on the river, all the while paying special attention to that part of its surface covered by the reflections of the opposite bank.

Sooner or later a tiny gray-green spot will appear, hardly to be distinguished from a piece of anything, except that there is something tell-tale about it. It is rather too rounded, or it remains motionless when flotsam drifts slowly by. Sometimes it will move gently against the current, but so gently as to cause no wash. Maybe, should the glasses be good, the focus quite correct, and the distance not too great, tsetse fly may be seen trying to settle on the little protuberance but never quite able to do so. This interesting little island is the croc's eye, his highest point when afloat, and he is probably watching the watering place.

Before taking up this sort of game, it is essential that the sighting of one's rifle should be known to a hair. If you decide to risk a shot at that minute target over there in the shadows, most will depend on the elevation. A tick over or under, and he has won. If you are a good height above him and an inch low with your bullet, it will not matter, but if you are firing from such a position that the bullet's course forms a very slight angle with the water's surface, the merest trifle low will produce a ricochet . . . and one degree more wilyness in that croc. Unless you feel pretty certain of bringing it off, it is better to wait for an easier shot. If the croc has not been shot at before, he may show himself—floating with the current past the watering place and within thirty or forty yards of it.

When shot in the brain while floating in deep water and while not wishing to cause any disturbance, our friend will have so inflated himself with air as to float just awash. If you get a shot into the brain, the croc will remain in this position and can be retrieved by a canoe, which—by the way—should be all ready to do so. There is not any time to waste in getting a rope on to him, for even when shot in the brain, he may squirm about sufficiently to lose his air, and when he sinks like a stone, he is gone for good.

When attaching the rope, care must be taken not to raise his head or he will belch air, and down he goes. I was once nearly upset holding on to quite a small croc—about eight feet long. In my ignorance, I thought it a good idea to tow him by the head, so I raised it to put the noose over him. There was a waft of gas and he suddenly became like lead in my hands. I held on by the head while he bubbled away, getting heavier and heavier, and, of course, while my side of the canoe went lower and lower. Finally, when the gunwale went under, I had to let go.

Notorious man-snatching crocs are awfully well worth getting, but they are hard to bag. The reason for this is, generally, that native police have been detailed to deal with them. These imbeciles will fire any which way at such a croc. They are not so much concerned with killing him as with driving him away. Consequently, these crocs are extremely gun shy; it is hard, indeed, to get a sight of him even. Great patience and the very deadliest of shooting are required for these gentry. A second chance would be rare, but even here luck will sometimes chuck up the most unexpected things, as this instance shows:

The government representative told me he wished I would have a try for a croc that had taken all kinds of stock, including human, from one of his villages. He had been himself to see what he could do, but had had no sight of the enemy during a three-day vigil. I asked at once if he had put the native police on to the job, and he said he had kept a picked shot in the village for more than a month. I said it was hopeless, then. Although I thought I would be wasting my time, he persuaded me to go and have a try.

I found the village headman quite despondent. He said there was nothing for it but to move the village as soon as the crops were got. Nobody could kill that croc. Everybody had tried, including the Government, referring to my friend's attempt, I suppose, and that of the native police.

"Did anyone ever see the brute ?" I asked.

"Not now," was the discouraging reply.

It looked pretty hopeless.

The village was on the banks of a long, narrow lagoon. Only in the rainy season was it part of the river. There were several nice sand banks and long grass on all sides. That evening the watering gang set out, consisting of a string of women with the pots and men with spears to guard them. I went with them.

After arriving at the spot, I asked why they had not guarded it with stakes set in the water as is usual when man-snatchers are about. "And who is going in to set them?" they said.

Quite demoralized, it was evident!

While the watering was going on, I searched the expanse and under the banks with my glasses. Not a sign of anything. The lung fish even seemed to have left the pool. Late that evening I crept through the grass to where I could search the whole pool, but with no result.

The next day I watched the pool steadily from a grass shelter the villagers had made for

A visit to the larder.

the police, and by evening time I was sick and tired of that croc. Not a sign had he made. Where the brute came up to breathe, heaven only knows. Under some bank probably. The only sign of life in that pool was two turtles, and I came to know those two smooth heads pretty well.

Some strangers had arrived in the village on their way to Mecca. They had been seven months on the road and expected to be a year and a half more. Whether the headman had warned them about the croc—he swore he had—or whether they had not understood how things were, I do not know. But while I was off watch and having tea in my tent, a boy came rushing in with the news that one of the strangers had been taken by the croc.

It appeared that they went down to get water, and, seeing nothing, two of them began to wash at the very edge—they showed me the spot—in not more than three or four inches of water. Suddenly one had been snatched off into deep water and disappeared, leaving nothing but rings on the surface.

I had had considerable experience of crocs, and I knew their habit of eating only a part of a bulky victim at the time of killing, and then dragging the remainder on to a sand bank to devour it at their leisure. I enquired if it was a grown person or a child, and hope began to mount in my heart when I was told it was a grown slave man. *This croc may,* I said to myself, *have more left from his first meal sufficient to induce him to drag it to the bank.*

That night I lay watching by moonlight, but nothing came. The whole of the next day nothing came. But as dawn broke on the succeeding morning out came the grisly horror, dragging with him a human arm, and on to my sand bank, too. It was point-blank range, and even over-excitement could not cause a miss. I sent a bullet crashing into his skull net, as the French would say.

How I became so intimate with their habit of keeping something in the larder was from the time I spent on the fly rivers. There are no villages on those fly-infested banks, and the big crocs prey on large antelopes, chiefly waterbuck and hartebeest. I have frequently shot them in the act of finishing off a buck's remains that showed signs of having been kept a considerable time in water. How they keep others from their larder is their secret, and likely to remain so, I think.

The Mysterious Country

Chapter 29

I was feeling a perfect fool as I sat by my camp-fire. I had footled about[1] with a lion badly, wounding him in the jaw. He had nearly got one of my men and had treed me, and I was feeling humiliated. I drew consolation from damning my black-powder, single-shot rifle. But still it seemed to me that it would be a very hard and long road to travel before I could approach as a hunter any average native about me. I do not suppose that I was any worse than any other white man. I could run, hear, see, travel, and bear hardship just as well as the next man, but it was all so far below the standard of the native hunters I used that sometimes I despair of ever approaching their level. In my gloomier moments it seemed to me that my sole excuse for calling myself a hunter at all was the possession of a weapon far superior in killing power to that used by the native hunter. Their invariable habit of mothering me—adopted by my natives—was a source of secret annoyance to me, but I must confess that it often saved me from trouble.

My great ambition was to be able to leave camp, find worthy game, kill it, and return to camp all on my own, unaided by natives. Many of my attempts at this were frustrated by my boys finding me just when I was beginning to test myself. I could hardly ever leave camp without someone being told by the others to follow me and to see that I did not lose myself. After I had shown my annoyance a few times at this irritating watchfulness, telling them plainly I would not have it, they did stop following me openly, but I could never be certain that I was not being carefully followed by some of my devoted fellows. It was all very galling to the aspiring hunter, showing so plainly that they had no illusions about my woodcraft.

On the few occasions when I did manage to escape their vigilance, I must admit now that their judgment was not at fault. I found, to my astonishment

[1] Engage in fruitless activity.

Before me was the elephant—but stern on.

and chagrin, that I was worse than I had ever thought. I hopelessly lost myself in spite of my strenuous efforts to imitate the natives. After miles of wandering through the sea of bush, I would find myself confronted with my own boot-shod footprints—and only then would dawn on my confused mind that I had been wandering in a circle. At that point, I would sit down and curse my upbringing. In those moments it seemed to my mind that my situation represented a sheer and malicious irony: Civilization had placed in my hands such a perfect death-dealing weapon as a modern rifle and, at the same time, had taken from me the powers of using it to its fullest advantage.

Time after time nothing but luck saved me from death by thirst. Once, when hopelessly lost, I found fresh elephant tracks. With great difficulty and much casting about, I was able to follow them, for it was the dry season—that most difficult time for tracking. I finally managed to kill one and drink the water from its belly in time to save myself from a thirsty end. Had I had a few more miles to go, I should have given it up. It is on those occasions one fully realizes how much one owes to the native who usually accompanies the white man on all his hunts. It is not too much to say that that quiet little man who seems to thread the bush with such ease is indispensable.

Having killed that elephant, I was apparently no nearer finding my way back to camp. But next morning vultures came in the hundreds out of the blue, and they, in turn, drew natives to the kill. I got them to hack out the tusks and then lead me to my camp. Their bearing the tusks saved me from having to confess to my boys that I had been hopelessly bushed, but I suspect they knew.

Bitter experience is a hard but thorough teacher, and in time I came to be able to regain my starting-off point with fair certainty. It was then I found those solitary rambles in the bush gave me the greatest pleasure. There was no thrill like the exquisite one of setting forth on your own feet and legs to see what the untouched wilds had in store for you.

There was never a dull moment as there often is when trailing along behind natives. They never realize that their ordinary world is something quite new to you. They never explain anything to you, and if you badger them too much with what seems to them very odd questions, they either say they do not know or they answer in the way experience has taught them is the quickest means of satisfying your curiosity. As an example:

White man: "What is the name of that hill?"

Native: "*Murna.*"

You sometime later find out that *murna* simply means hill.

When in grass country, the surest method of returning to camp I found was to seize in my hand a bunch of the tall stuff and bend it over so that the stems broke but did not fall to the ground. It is wonderful how conspicuous a sign this makes when returning in the reverse direction. An elephant track is good so long as it does not rain. After a heavy shower it becomes like all the other thousand-and-one tracks.

Late one evening I spotted a large bull elephant about a mile away. I was close to camp, so I ran there to get some cartridges, etc., but I said no word to anyone. I wanted to bring it off entirely on my own. To reach the elephant I had to descend onto the grassy plains, and I soon lost sight of him, for the stuff was high enough to hide me. I guessed at his location and hurried on as the sun was very low. Meanwhile the elephant had moved on, and it was some time before I found his tracks. There was still shooting light, so I ran hard

He looked enormous.

along the straight lane in the grass of the traveling elephant without taking the precaution to mark my passage by breaking it over here and there.

Running suddenly to the edge of a watercourse, there, just in front of and below me, was my elephant, but stern on. I had been making a great clatter as I ran along, which had not disturbed him. When the clatter suddenly ceased and my image appeared against the sky behind and just above him, he bustled himself off in a great hurry, showing enough of his ivory to convince me that here was a monster.

Had he been an ordinary beast, I would have shot him with the lung shot from behind, but my reluctance to try it on such a prize delayed me so long as to make it out of the question to fire at all. He was soon out of sight. It would now be dark in a brief half-hour, but I simply could not leave such a monster to wander away. His ivory looked colossal, and I had to follow him.

On I went, then, until night fell without another glimpse of him. I dared not follow by night for fear of swopping his track for one of the many older tracks about. I began to wish now that I had not been so impatient. I could have followed him the next morning fully equipped to track him till Doomsday, if necessary. Now I was in for a beastly night, for I knew that I could never find my way back to camp without native assistance. There was nothing further to do till morning but to gather grass and firewood and hope it would not rain.

Two or three hours after this, as I dozed by the fire, what should I hear but voices. Looking along the flickering lane of laid grass, I saw my devoted safari headed by Pyjalé coming striding along in close formation and with very much the air of "You naughty child, why will you wander away by yourself in this idiotic way?"

They did not say this, of course. Instead they set about pitching camp, and soon I was enjoying the dinner that had been ready hours before—and jolly good it was. Then I turned into my camp-bed, and was altogether much more comfortable than any forethought on my part had earned for me. What grand fellows those were to turn out, pack up everything, and follow me through the bush at night like that. How they ever found me remains a mystery to me to this very day, for I had not blazed the trail as I should have done. As I wished to be off with the first light, I told the boys they need not set up the tents. However, they insisted on putting one up, for themselves they said. And, sure enough it started to pour. *Now,* I thought, *we shall never find that big fellow, the tracks will all be washed out.*

With the first light we were off on the trail. It led us, in course of time, into some quite new country. The farther we penetrated, the more signs of elephants did we see. The whole place seemed to smell of elephants. We crossed or followed great well-worn elephant roads all the time. Their mud baths occurred every mile or so. Salt licks, showing tusk marks as if made by the picks of some giant race, formed the centres of perfect mazes of roads, and finally all sign of our particular elephant was swallowed up in tracks made since the morning. We had tumbled on a veritable stronghold of elephants.

On striking water, the boys pitched camp in a secluded spot among the thorn bush, while I and Pyjalé went off to look for that monster bull. I knew it would be mere chance if we saw him, but, surely, with all those tracks about, we would find something.

I trod on air. The whole place seemed worn smooth by some gigantic traffic. The very bush was all torn, bedraggled, worn smooth, broken, and trampled. All was crushed except the euphorbias. Only for the myriad hosts of the white ant, our feet would have touched nothing but elephant dung. As it was, for twenty yards at a stretch they encountered nothing else. We had reached *nabwa* at last, that mysterious country I had heard about but which the natives seemed reluctant to lead me to. As far as I could ascertain, the word *nabwa* seemed to be used to indicate country unfit for human habitation and, therefore, given over to the great animals.

Lying as they do at some distance from inhabited country, these areas called *nabwa*[2] are seldom visited. They are decidedly eerie kinds of places and have acquired a reputation for evil spirits. They are almost over-poweringly dominated by the great game animals. Wherever you turn, nothing but animal signs meets your eye. Hardly a square foot of ground but has some track on it; no tree can be seen that is not broken, bent, uprooted, rubbed smooth, or stripped of its top hamper. My impression of *nabwa* is what a rhino or other African might have on suddenly entering London. From what I have seen of it, I should say that a human figure in *nabwa* is about as rare as a rhino would be in London.

Presently we came upon some very fresh spoor. The deep corrugations showed them to belong to heavy bulls. We started tracking them with Pyjalé leading, and going about six miles an hour, we hardly paused. His keenness to kill elephant made that splendid native very dear to my heart. He had no share in the result, and yet he was always tremendously anxious for me to get them. After ten months of hard hunting, I would give him two or three cows, and he considered this extraordinarily generous treatment.

We found our game by a mud bath. The ground was red and the elephants were, consequently, red also as they were completely covered in mud. They were quite unused to firearms and hardly moved between shots. The brain shot had them completely mystified. The big one was not among them.

I made for a huge rounded mass of granite where baboons were barking and screaming, and on reaching the top, I displaced perhaps two hundred baboons in the process. I sat down for a spy around, for that so often shows me game in that country.

[2]In other places, Bell describes *nabwa* as *wilderness*.

As I was examining the farther-off parts and just as I had taken the glass down so as to shift round a bit, my naked eyes fell on the sunlit back of an elephant just under me, some five hundred yards away. Putting the glass on him instantly, I saw he was my monster bull. Can you imagine what I felt? Anyhow, I cannot describe it. There he was, quietly feeding. Surely his number was up. He looked very big even when seen from above, and his tusks were a perfect pair.

Well, I funked[3] the brain shot at that massive head because it looked so impenetrable. Instead, I gave him one in the heart, when he squirmed together, and another in the same place as he unsquirmed and set off in his death rush. Then I raced hard at his heels, breathing in his dust, his bent-bush vegetation slashing me across the face—I was in a fever lest he should get away from me. So close was I that when he came to a walk, my rifle barrel touched his hind leg. It was all over with the old boy, and I killed him instantly with a bullet in the brain. There he lay, the finest trophy a hunter can get.

Try to imagine my feelings when I got back to camp that night. He made the seventh for that day.

[3]Avoided out of fear.

LEOPARDS AND CANNIBALS

CHAPTER 30

One day I returned to camp to find that a small native boy attached to my safari was wounded and required attention. His whole back was covered in blood. After washing him down, there appeared a series of long, parallel gashes or tears, not very deep but bleeding profusely, running from the neck and shoulders to the buttocks. Feeling the kid's pulse, I found it strong and regular.

"Is it sore?" I asked.

"No." he said.

After dressing with strong permanganate solution, I asked him what had happened.

"Well," said he, "I was gathering firewood when a leopard appeared close in front of me. He did not spring upon me. I knelt down with my face in my hands. He walked up close to me and then went round me, purring loudly. I remained motionless, for he was so-and-so." [He named a departed medicine man.] "He then began to tear my back. I still remained quiet. Finally, after urinating on me, he went off and I came back."

As simple as that.

I sent for the headman of the nearest village with a view of organizing a leopard hunt. The forest was such that only with the help of the villagers and their dogs would there be any chance of coming up to a leopard in such cover.

Now I knew in a general sort of way that man-killing leopards infested the whole of this particular country, but I did not know that they had acquired such an ascendancy. On questioning the headman closely, a terrible tale unfolded itself. Reluctant to speak about leopards at all and then only in bated tones, I dragged from him a description of affairs that astonished me.

Certainly I had often heard of people disappearing in mysterious ways. The jungle lies in wait for man, quick to pounce on the slightest lapse of alertness, and I had always attributed these disappearances to natural accidents or, in rare instances, to the few man-eaters. Now I learned that another kind of man-eater was at work—the cannibal. The acute lack of animal food and the appalling dearth of protein in their cassava diet had created a consuming passion for meat.

Without question the more important men who could no longer resist the craving were killing young women to satisfy their hunger. Presumably, they chose girls because they were easier to deal with than men, and also, perhaps, because they were more toothsome.

I am pretty certain, although proof is another matter, that many of the plump lassies I used to see about the villages, and who subsequently were not to be seen or heard of, were quietly killed and eaten. Most of them were brought from across the river from their capturers, while some of them had certainly been taken from far tribes of the Congo interior, as evidenced by their strange tribal marks or tattooings. Very often their disappearance was laid to the door of a man-eating leopard. No one would think of telling the true story.

Shocked as I was, I could readily believe the head-man's tale. I had all along in my mind put down this traffic entirely to the craving for meat. After all, I had ample evidence of this uncontrollable appetite. Whenever I killed an elephant, buffalo, or hippo, this irrepressible hunger for meat was all too evident in the way the natives wolfed down morsels of reeking raw flesh carved from, in some cases, still-quivering carcasses. It was an urge so strong that even the sex organs were eaten—a thing almost unknown outside the cassava areas.

So now it looked as if there were a second force at work—that of a real, honest-to-goodness man-eating leopard. I wanted to investigate this more closely, so with a view to this, I moved camp to a site close to a native village that was notorious for the disappearance of numbers of people in mysterious circumstances.

The village where we were camped was highly delighted with their medicine man and, in a lesser degree, with me because we had furnished them with so much meat. The old "doctor" was in terrific spirits. In the unusual bustle and upsetting of daily routine, caused by the sudden acquisition of meat, sundry plump and comely maidens had come to light who had previously been prevented from appearing under the enquiring eyes of strangers. They were easily distinguished among the natives by their unfamiliar tribal marks.

I determined to try to get one of these girls to tell me something about their future as seen through their eyes.

I knew that by merely questioning one of them whilst still in the village, I should learn exactly nothing. I would have to arrange matters so that the girl joined our safari on a permanent basis. Only after she had left the village would she talk at all. I arranged, therefore, that one of my personal boys should say that he wished to marry the girl. I, of course, would provide him with the dowry, as is usual on these occasions. As it happened, the particular girl selected for our enquiry belonged to the brother of the "doctor," as I will call the medicine man. Everything had to be done through this "doctor."

To my surprise, the "doctor" was quite willing that the match should take place. Whether it was the reaction to several days of meat gorging or whether there were so many prime candidates ready for his future needs, it is hard to say. For a modest dowry, my boy became the owner of an obedient and industrious wife.

Having arranged this affair so successfully, I set about the "doctor" on the subject of these leopard-killings. As it happened, I carried Pernod (absinthe) at this time, and, indeed, I found it one of the most economical of all forms of alcohol to carry about. With its 68 percent pure spirit, a litre bottle lasted much longer than an equal amount of whisky, and when taken with a lot of water to a small tot, it is a wonderful reviver.

Well, as a preliminary, I gave that "doctor" a slug of Pernod that would have knocked most people off their bases. But he was a seasoned cask and showed nothing at all except appreciation of the inward glow by rubbing his wrinkled belly.

"Now, what about those killings?" I asked

"Leopard," he said, "all leopard."

"But," I said, "the leopard did not kill my boy. He only scratched him," I pointed out.

"Ah, yes," the old man said, "he was not fat enough to eat."

"Does the leopard only eat fat people?" I asked.

"Well," said the doctor, "you ought to know that! You saw that boy killed and not eaten at such-and-such village. He was too lean."

This was in reference to a case where a youth had been killed instantaneously in a hut of a village close to our camp. We heard the hullabaloo and went over with lanterns to see what it was all about. On examining the body, only four neat little incisions in the neck could be found. When we suggested a leopard hunt with all hands and with the village dogs, the villagers flatly refused. They said so-and-so's spirit was in the leopard.

I next asked the "doctor" why no-one would help in destroying these pests. I said they could easily be chased up a tree with dogs and spear men and then shot.

Oh, no!" he said. "You can't kill these people." (He called these leopards people.) "And, besides, it would be murder! It would never do!"

I could not help laughing at this hoary old sinner talking about murder. I bet his whole body reeked of human blood if one could only have distinguished it among so many other blends.

"Would they mind if I had the next victim killed by leopard?" I asked.

"What for?" he asked with a keen look in his little eyes.

"As bait for the leopard," I said.

Drunk as he undoubtedly was, he saw through this scheme. Thoughts of strychnining the cadaver had certainly flashed through my mind, but he could not possibly have divined that—anyhow, I had none. *Wish I had,* I thought to myself, *it might have clarified the situation.*

After a pause, he said, "No, they would not like that."

"Why not?" I asked.

"Well," he said, "you see, these leopards are really departed spirits who have entered into leopards. They cannot be killed even by white men," he announced with seeming conviction.

"I would like to try to kill one, however," I said. "Now, you call your people together and persuade them to help me find one. I will do the rest."

But he only repeated that no-one would help.

"Well, what about the dogs? Can I have the use of them," I asked.

"They, too, would not help," he said. "Have you not noticed that whenever a leopard coughs, all the dogs are silent? They are afraid," he said.

This was true enough.

I could see it was hopeless. There was certainly some mystery behind all this. What exactly it was, it was hard to say. We knew that leopards certainly killed people—we had seen about a dozen victims with our own eyes. But none of them had been eaten. The doctor said it was because they were too thin. The fat ones were eaten, he emphasized. But we had never seen a fat one. No, because the leopard carried them off, was the answer to that one. It was evident that the "doctor" wished us to believe that leopard accounted for the strange disappearance of these persons.

Disgusted with the whole business, we left that country determined to find out from my boy's newly acquired wife more about these queer goings-on when she was far away from the fear of the "doctor." We hoped she would then shed some light on the subject.

As it happened, we fell in with some traveling elephants, or rather with their fairly recent tracks. As these appeared to have been made by a score of bulls and as we were fully equipped for a long hunt through the bush and independent of villages, a diligent pursuit was laid on. There was not only the prospect of coming up on the travelers, but also they were certainly too numerous to be anything but herd bulls. This might lead us to good hunting.

At this point I would like to note briefly the common error most animal lovers make in charging that the disappearance of game is the fault of professional hunters. Nothing could be further from the truth; only the amateur engages in wanton and wasteful slaughter.

For two days the going was good, and the herd kept more or less single file and laid behind it as perfect a track as one could reasonably expect to find in a cross-country journey. On the night of the third day, we heard the elephants. That meant we should with ordinary luck find them on the morrow. The camp was silent that night and fires kept down.

Toward dawn much crashing and rumbling was heard, showing the elephants were still about. And so it proved. A goodly number were slain, being caught in the cool early morning out in the open. During the ensuing pause in camp to get the ivory out and the meat smoked, my thoughts turned once more to that mysterious leopard business. I told my boy to tell me what he had learned from his wife.

It appeared from his account that she had been captured by surprise in the bush of her native land many days' journey from the river (Ubangi). She had been with her mother whom the raiders rejected and killed. She had been taken at great speed to another tribe not so distant from the river. There she had been built into a cage with other young girls where they had been lavishly fed many times a day and where they had no work to do.

After some moons had died, she and one other girl had been taken to the river bank. They crossed by night and arrived at the "doctor's." There in the "doctor's" village, she had been free but not allowed to work. She was again lavishly fed, as indeed anyone could see, for she was as fat as a little pig. That was her story.

"Now," I said to my boy, a native of those parts, "what was the "doctor" going to do with her?"

"Oh," he said without hesitation, "he would sell her if he was in meat, or eat her if he had meat-hunger."

"Do they all do that?" I asked.

"Certainly they do if they are rich enough," he remarked.

"But what about the white men? Do they allow that sort of thing?"

"Oh, sir," he laughed, "they never know anything about black men. Black men are bad. Why, the soldiers traffic slaves for cartridges all the time across the river. White men don't see."

Now for the girl herself. Would she answer questions?

"Yes," my boy said, "she is not afraid now."

"Can she understand your language?"

"Yes, she understands."

"Bring her here, then."

"Now ask her how long has it been since she was taken from home."

"Three big rains." (Roughly three years)

"And all that time, you were well fed and not required to work?"

"Yes."

"How about the men during that time? Were you pestered much?"

"Not much!" and here she tittered.

"What about that?" I asked the boy. "Don't they go for these captive girls?"

"No, sir," he said. "If she caught a baby, she would be worthless. Of course there were cases, but it meant the man would have to pay."

"What sort of price would a good, fat girl fetch (1) as a table delicacy? (2) as a wife?"

They conferred together for a moment and the boy then announced they did not know what the prices were. It was largely a matter of cartridges, powder, and caps (percussion). It was seldom money.

"All right. Did the girls know what their fate was likely to be?"

"Of course they knew!" (And she laughed!)

"And yet knowing this, they grew fat?" I asked in astonishment, thinking what condition a white person would be in under similar sentence.

"Yes," they both agreed that anyone would grow fat.

Undeniable digestion, I suppose! We dismissed the girl and I then asked the boy how they managed the business, the actual business of killing the victim.

One of them is simply told to follow a certain path into the forest, and that is the last anyone sees of her. Of course, her owner puts it about that she has been married off to a man who lives far away or that she was carried off by a leopard. Nobody believes it, but there it is. Nothing can be done about it. There are no witnesses, and the leopard takes the blame. So when you see in the press that men have been hanged for ritual murder, and of the doings of the Leopard Societies, you may guess faintly at what goes on behind the African curtain.

Even the poor old lion comes in for blame in this connection in the eastern part of Africa, probably because so much attention has been drawn to the activities of a few old lions that really were man-eaters, the Man-Eaters of Tsavo for instance, and would, therefore, serve as a more plausible cloak for the murders. But I'm still wondering why those girls allowed themselves to get so fat.

On Rifles and Shooting

Chapter 31

In my opinion and borne out by my experience, there are two distinct and separate ways of killing. They require different tools and techniques in their handling. I propose to call them Nos. 1 and 2.

In No. 1, the object sought is to penetrate deeply enough to injure a vital organ sufficiently to cause death. In the case of large animals, this calls for a bullet length of 3½ or 4 times the calibre of that same bullet and for it to travel at moderate velocity, if a jacketed one, so that the envelope will not rupture on impact with bone. If of the homogeneous type, the velocity may be raised. Speaking from personal experience, moderately fast bullets seem to hold a truer course than the ultra-fast ones.

In order to excel as a killer and to be even commonly humane to one's brother animals, a study of anatomy is essential. It is no use knowing where the vitals are unless you can hold your rifle steady enough to direct the bullet straight at them. This requires a considerable amount of muscle training, especially for off-hand or standing shooting. In jungle or high grass, most of the shots are delivered from the standing position, and to be proficient in this requires training and strengthening of muscles that are not ordinarily much in use.

The best way to attain this rifle control is to carry your favorite rifle yourself, not only when you are hunting but whenever you go out. Dry shoot it at anything and everything. Do all the exercises you can think of with it. Hold it out at arm's length for as long as you can stick it out, first in front and then sideways. Get your muscles thoroughly inured to holding it in any position you may choose. Let your will dominate your body and bring it into subjection. The reward of perseverance will be worth it.

The second method is best carried out with the later improved-velocity group of cartridges belonging to the era beginning around the 1940s, and still continuing [1952]. It is apparently only recently that the neck shot has come to be recognized as the deadliest and safest shot of all. Where our forefathers were content to aim into the front part of the body anywhere "behind the shoulder," this shot has ceased to be employed by discriminating hunters. The neck shot has all the advantages of the body shot and has an even more instantaneous effect than a brain shot. A quite light blow in the neck is sufficient to cause death. It is not necessary to hit the spinal column; in fact, the whole of the neck that is clothed in flesh is deadly for game, for all the nerves, arteries, and veins have to pass through this channel.

Besides these advantages, the neck is often exposed when other parts of the body are masked by grass or bush. If you get the habit of looking for the neck only and of disregarding the body entirely, it is remarkable how often the neck is presented to a vital shot even when the body is not in a suitable position. Rhino, buffalo, and all the antelope and deer tribe present a large neck target. Only the elephant comes somewhat short on presenting a suitable neck target. That's because it is very short and is much masked by enormous ears.

It is interesting to note that the lashing about of legs, quivering, and continuing heartbeats that follow on a brain shot are absent when the neck is hit. Perhaps, it was this fact that induced the secret police of the Nazi regime and other police states to employ it in getting rid of their victims expeditiously and quietly.

Whereas in reaching a deep-seated vital, it is advisable to have a long, parallel-sided bullet of 3½ to 4 diameters its calibre and of good sectional density such as the .315 calibre with a 250-grain bullet traveling at a medium velocity of 2,300–2,500 f.p.s. For the neck shot, however, quite a short, light bullet may be employed. Here velocity counts for a lot. Penetration is not so essential. The bullet should stay in the neck; that is, it should expend its whole energy on the muscular shield protecting the vital nerve channels: the arteries and, of course, the spinal column itself.

This is best ensured by a bullet that will expand suddenly. It should not break up into fragments. The greater the velocity, the better. It is not necessary to even touch the spinal column, but if this is achieved, so much the better. I personally have never struck an animal with a bullet traveling much over 3,800 f.p.s., and judging by the instantaneous death produced with a neck shot around that velocity, I don't believe anything higher is required. This opens a vast new field for up-to-date hunters. Gone are the old messy body shots. A quite light rifle, with perhaps a longish barrel, will be found adequate for the job with its consequential better shooting.

The neck shot is the only one where the vital area lies near the surface; this is in contrast to shots at the brain and heart where the vitals are deep-seated and carefully guarded targets. So let the aspiring hunter go light-heartedly and lightly loaded into the bush with his mind's eye fixed on the neck. There will be fewer wounded beasts around, and if you miss the neck, it will be a clean miss most times.

In off-hand shooting I always found that holding the barrel with the left hand as far out as was comfortable suited my style better than the close-in grip on the fore-end. I know this is not in accordance with the target shooters' practice. I found, too, that shortness of stock so long as it did not blur the open (iron) back sight by bringing it too near the eye was a distinct aid to steady holding.[1]

As for recoil, I deliberately ignore it because there is no earthly or other reason to employ a weapon that recoils violently. If a man is saddled with such a firearm, he has my sympathy only if he cannot get a decent one. A violent gun disturbs the whole lay-out of good rifle hunting. It flies up in the air, thereby wrecking any possibility of "follow through" or any other nicety of the art. It leaves you in a sort of "blast-happy" state when you should be attending to other matters, and it beats and bruises the air around you. It has to be heavy, and that means that it becomes a burden instead of a joy. Finally, it is totally unnecessary. In double form, they are extremely costly.

Of course, if you are going to use a scope sight, you will need to be careful about shortening the stock so as not to interfere with the eye-relief. Personally, I would prefer a large open aperture sight for thick stuff and so-called dangerous game. It is an aperture that disappears entirely when game shooting; that is, the sides of the aperture and the surroundings of the hole disappear to the eye, and you seem to be focusing on the front sight and target only.

In my case at age seventy-two, I find an aperture that is .1380 in diameter suits my eyesight, but everyone must discover for himself what best suits. The surrounds of the hole are, in my case, exactly .1000 thick. I regret that I cannot say what the proportions for younger eyesight might be as I never used anything but the open or iron sights in my hunting. It is true that I tried the aperture but found it slow and discarded it in favour of the open V, and then I later gradually drifted to the straight bar with a small notch.[2]

I don't know if others are afflicted with a super-critical sense of proportions as I was. Everything had to be a certain width in back sights. If they were too broad, I felt they were wrong. As they came straight from the gun-makers, everything was wrong. I find it difficult to define what exactly was wrong in so many words. They

[1]This can be overcome by using an aperture sight.

[2]Present choice.

just did not satisfy the feelings. I had to tinker with everything. Generally the back sights were too broad. They had to be of a width that corresponded to the diameter of the barrel, I think. Then with running shots, I found the V shape bothersome even when it was very open.

Finally, my last open-sighted rifle was a straight bar affair. From there I have since gone to very large apertures of .1380 that slope well backward with the hole bored out straight with the line of sight.

While discussing back sights, I may mention that even the rounding of the shoulders were found to have a quite important bearing on the completely satisfying back sight. There is no sighting device yet invented so fast and so accurate as the open back sight, for youthful eyesight anyway. A man with steady nerves and fit muscles can accomplish marvels. With no idea of boasting but merely to show what can be done, when so armed I will recount a little incident that happened to me. I will risk the boasting taunt.

I had 6,000 rounds of .318 ammo. This stuff was giving me a lot of trouble because it was defective. On an average, there were three misfires in ten. I wanted to get rid of the stuff. In this enviable state I found myself at Jinja, where huge Lake Victoria pours over a narrow rocky ledge. Every evening cormorants, flush with fish, homed over the centre of this outflow. They are straight-flying but fast birds. I used to buzz off .318 defective ammo at them.

They flew about three hundred feet above the rifle stance. During these shoots I once reached an average of eight in ten, which was unusually good. The general average would come not far short of six in ten. One evening I was so engaged when two on-lookers approached me. They were Goanese clerks from the government offices nearby.

They said, "That is a very fine shot-gun you have; it kills much better than ours. Might we examine it?"

I unloaded the .318 and handed it to them. They exclaimed when they saw it was a rifle.

In my experience haste in firing and flinch are the commonest causes of spoilt or inadequate shots—those requiring one or more subsequent shots to kill out-right. I myself am naturally of rather highly strung nature, and I suffered greatly from the eagerness that so easily leads to abortive shots. I found that if I kept in good training bodily and forced myself to count to ten slowly, I then brought off many good shots and a few brilliant ones.

Timing is of great importance. I don't know if this can be acquired except through physical fitness. Given that, I think timing follows naturally.

You would not at first think that "follow through" would find a place in rifle shooting. But it assuredly does so. This, too, will be found to follow on fitness of body and mind. The sense of visualizing the bullet's flight as you continue to stare, with both eyes open, over the rifle barrel constitutes your "follow through." This seems to give the feeling of confidence and power, of mastery of the tool that all goes to the make-up of a successful rifle hunter. It is an intoxicating thing not to be imagined except through actual experience. I don't believe it can be gained when using heavy, violently recoiling rifles.

When using a telescopic sight, I have found it very advantageous to rest the peak of the cap against the end of the scope. The peak should be the exact length of the eye-relief of your particular scope. Not only does this habit cut out extraneous lights, in itself a great advantage, but it steadies the head enormously. Besides it prevents an eye becoming injured should a recoiling rifle be held rather too loosely, as can easily happen in tense moments.

To sum up, I would advise a newcomer to the shooting game to study Col. Townsend Whelan's book *The Hunting Rifle,* select the rifle that seems most suitable, and practice carrying it everywhere to get the muscles in training by dry-shooting thousands of times at anything and everything. In other words, spend endless hours in every known posture and in every position peculiar to oneself until the thing becomes a third arm. Dry shooting, dry shooting, endless dry shooting will bring reward. To shoot off rounds and rounds is largely a waste of time at the beginning. A tremendous lot can be learnt from shooting dry. Target shooting is all very well if combined with this constant dry shooting. Alone it is but half the story.

The Hunting Rifle is by far the best book I have ever read on the subject, and by studying it carefully and with constant muscle training practice, you may hope finally to reach the stage where you can recline in the easy chair under a sun-awning and kill flying birds with your rifle through the canvas overhead. When you can sight in your rifle to group properly (target work) and you can bring down say fifty per cent of the flying birds, you may then say you are a trained riflemen . . . but choose straight flying ones.

This Killing Business

Chapter 32

What are we to make of it? If it continues, all wild animal life, apart from human, is going to be destroyed. Weapons are so deadly now [1952] that no animal has a chance. Take the .22 long rifle alone—what is its record? It has killed grizzly bear, lion, tiger, leopard, all the antelope and deer tribe, everything in fact except the very largest beasts, such as buffalo, rhino, and elephant, and even those are not too safe from a homogeneous bronze bullet.

How is this accomplished? Largely by the use of the motor car. The automobile has eliminated all danger and fatigue from the chase. From its safe interior nearly everything may be shot, if not by day then by the headlights, or spotlights, by night. What chance has anything got when staring into the glare that dazzles it while exposing its vitals to the searing light?

Some will say game sanctuaries and national parks form the answer. Yes, but for how long? With the increasing cry for more food for humans, how long will land capable of sustaining animal life be allowed to lie fallow? No! It would appear the only way to ensure a future on this planet for the lovely beasts that still roam what is left of their wilderness is to domesticate them. Nobody wilfully goes about murdering sheep, goats, or cows.

There would be no insuperable difficulty in catching the young of all the wild animals. The motor car that at present is the greatest threat to their existence would be the means of preserving their future. By its use, nylon nets of prodigious strength and astounding lightness would be borne to the scene, and others would drive the herds into them. What can be accomplished to make a film can surely be done for the preservation of species of specialized wild life. Instead of being done by Hollywood, the task will have to be undertaken by governments backed up by their people.

If anyone is skeptical about the catching of wild animals, let him take a look at any of the tribes who habitually use nets—their own home-made ones—for catching wild animals. The use of nets is widespread throughout Africa. Of course, the African uses them not to capture animals but to render them vulnerable to his spears and other primitive weapons by delaying their flight long enough for him to bring his deadly but short-range armament into effective play. But the technique is there and could soon be diverted to catching the young of buffalo and the large bovine antelope such as eland. Think what a source of meat that would promise. That is one side of the picture, the domestication of African wild life.

Instead of that picture, what have we? In Africa all wild animals are looked upon as carriers of the tsetse-fly-borne diseases. They themselves do not suffer from these diseases. But man and his present-day domesticated animals do suffer and die from these diseases. Therefore, the universal cry is to destroy all animals that carry in their blood the trypanosome or blood worm that causes the disease in domestic stock. Such destruction does not guarantee that when all wild life has been extinguished, the fly will also cease to exist or become innocuous.

When we examine the relative values as a source of meat and leather of the domestic cattle and the wild buffalo, eland, or hartebeest, it is obvious that the wild beasts win every time. They are larger and heavier than any domestic animal. *Bos caffer* could be likened to an Aberdeen Angus bull, while the eland would far outweigh the ordinary run-off native cow. Above all, wild life are immune to the endemic fly-borne diseases.

It is strange to reflect that this so wonderful civilization with its marvelous discoveries in the scientific field and its crying need for more food has, nevertheless, not added one single wild animal to its list of completely domesticated ones. India comes nearest to doing so with her keddah enclosures of wild elephants. The water buffalo, too, was carried from its native wilds, and look what a useful beast he has proved to be. Is it too fantastic to visualize keddah operations on a huge scale operating in Africa?

Let us look what happened when North America got scared her bison herds were about to be wiped out. Hastily the U.S.A. and Canada brought into being large tracts of country for the use of wild life. National parks they were called, and cavalry units and game wardens protected them from poachers. Soon the diminished herds increased to such an extent that official killers had to be employed to kill expertly such numbers as to keep the herds' increases within the grazing capacity of their territory. As the herds had not been hunted, wounded, or harried, they were not wild. Approach could be made easily to such a distance that they could be humanely killed by a shot in the head, as humanely, in fact, as domestic animals are killed in the slaughterhouses.

Canada, too, has had the same problem to deal with. It is reliably reported that one of these official killers has shot the almost incredible number of thirty thousand bison. He shoots them in the head with a soft-point .303 at an average range of sixty yards. He is followed by a team of skinners who skin and butcher his victims. Only as many as this gang can deal with are shot in the day. Nothing is wasted. Indeed, the "robes" are quite valuable.

Why cannot something of a similar nature be at least tried in Africa instead of slaughtering everything off? The fear of contracting "sleeping sickness" by the bite of tsetse fly is, I feel sure, very much exaggerated. At any rate, I must have been bitten thousands of times when following night-drinking elephants back into the bush for twenty to thirty miles. A hatted man bears along with him what can only be described as halo of tsetse while jabs from their fierce probes would average out at fifteen to twenty per minute in a ten-hour day. I refer, of course, to pre-motor car days. Of my total seventy thousand miles of foot hunting, I reckon at least fifteen thousand miles were done in known "fly" country, and never have I suffered the least sickness from "fly" bites. This all brings us back to this "killing business."

Many people feel uneasy about it. The modern rifle is so deadly, its sighting so refined, and its lethal properties limited only by the wobble of its firer. Even so, this generally results in a ghastly wound. Total extinction or, at best, a few museum pieces struggling along under the blights of restricted grazing, inbreeding, and curtailment of centuries-old migratory habits, with, perhaps, the latter being the most serious handicap of them all.

It is unbelievable how far game wander in search of their food in different seasons. Low-lying country becomes waterlogged during the rains while semi-desert thorn-bush country two hundred miles away becomes a veritable paradise for grass and tree-browsers at the time. It is well nigh impossible to contain within a national park all these requisites if a stock is to remain permanently healthy. Only under domestication of a very advanced kind could these weird animal forms be preserved. Our present treatment of cloven-hoofed animals in domestication needs drastic overhauling as evidenced by the 1952 outbreaks of foot-and-mouth disease.

Should all attempts at domestication prove to be unsuccessful and should all the land be required for human occupation then, and only then, should you study this book so that you may help to remove painlessly with the least bother what will have been decided to be useless forms of life.

World Record Tusks

Chapter 33

With Shundi in camp, it seemed a good chance to learn more about those fantastic tusks, one of which now lies in the South Kensington Museum.[1] Incidentally, it may be observed here that to exhibit such a tusk lying down is bad showmanship; they should always be shown standing up. Only thus can the exceptional dimensions of such a tusk be properly exhibited.

This colossal tusk weighed fresh 236 pounds; it has now dried out to about 226 pounds. It would appear to be the elephants' right-hand tusk. Its neighbour was acquired by Joseph Rogers & Sons and weighed fresh 225 pounds; it has now dried out to about 216 pounds. These weights have never been exceeded as far as is known. The dimensions of the larger one are given as 10 feet, 1 inch long along outside curve and has a circumference where the solid ivory begins of 23⅓ inches. So far as the writer has been able to learn, no mammoth tusk of comparable weight has so far been discovered.

Whether there are African elephants that attain a shoulder height of 12 feet is a much-debated question. It is not easily settled because of the difficulty of measuring the animal when it is dead. If it falls on its side, the knee is always bent, and it is extremely hard to straighten. Should it fall kneeling, as with a brain shot, when all four feet are under load, it is impossible to measure; one can only guess at it. In fact, all measurements of the living height are pure guesses.

But it is only reasonable to suppose that an elephant with two such formidable tusks such as Shundi's must have attained sufficient height to enable it to carry them free of encumbering bush, ant-heaps, and other obstructions, especially as they were not unduly curved. When pushing a tree over for better browsing, an African elephant pushes it with the base of his trunk. If his tusks

[1] Today both tusks are once more united in this same museum.

are inordinately long and fairly straight and his stature restricted, his tusks would be in danger of fouling the ground. I would suggest, therefore, that Shundi's elephant may well have been 12 feet at the shoulder and perhaps a bit more. The museums tell us that *Elephas imperator* reached a height of 13 feet, 6 inches at the shoulder while carrying tusks of nearly the same length as those of Shundi's elephant, but admittedly they are more curved.

The commonly held belief that elephants with exceptionally long tusks, finding them a burden, rest them in the fork of a tree or even drag them along the ground in reverse is, it would seem, but a fable born of the wish to do so when the load is transferred to human shoulders. Tusks of these great proportions take many years to grow. The muscular development must also grow to suit the load.

Shundi was the owner of these remarkable tusks and sold them in Zanzibar at the current price of ivory. He did not realize, in fact nobody did, what a prize he had got. Perhaps they will never be surpassed. He told me a slave of his, of the Chagga tribe, had killed the elephant on the forested slopes of Kilimanjaro, working singly in his backyard as it were. The Chagga inhabit these regions, so he was familiar with the territory. He fired his muzzle-loader into the body and fled—it's appearance and size had so frightened the hunter. This great elephant traveled but a short distance; nevertheless, the body was not found until the next day.

When first viewed, it had been looking straight at him, and it was when it turned away that the M'Chagga[2] had let drive with his smooth-bore percussion gun from about twelve paces. Thus was the world-record beater laid low.

I have several times killed elephants with tusks exceeding in diameter those of the world-record ones, but they were all broken. Once a very aged character bore the remains of tusks that taped 24⅛ inches outside the lip. What they might have weighed had they been intact it is impossible to say.

[2] We assume, from a linguistic standpoint, that Bell's use of *M'Chagga* refers to an individual while the term *Chagga* refers to the group or more than one person.

Some Bullet Experiments on a Buffalo Head

Chapter 34

The head under discussion was that of a young but mature buffalo killed in the Shari-Chad region. It was by no means exceptionally large and may be taken as a representative head of an ordinary, average animal that might be met with in great numbers in that region.

For these demonstrations, I used a Springfield .30-03 action on a .318 barrel rifle with an interchangeable .30-06 barrel. A large aperture fixed-peep sight was mounted on the action bridge sloping back and the hole was filed out round. There was no windage or elevation movement provided as the aim throughout was the utmost simplicity. As the rifle was primarily intended for big game, any adjustment of a back sight was eliminated. The foresight, of course, can be adjusted laterally, and a higher or lower one can be fitted. It is my idea of the proper weapon for big stuff, and it is one that may probably horrify other hunters.

The rifle was sighted to hit the spot covered by the foresight at eighty yards. In order to achieve this result, a black circular mark needs to be constructed—a pencil will do for this—of such a size as to contain and show a black margin around the foresight. The metal surrounding the large-aperture back sight must be narrow so as to almost disappear in cool, deliberate shooting and to totally do so when the attention is concentrated on game. There is then nothing but the brilliant foresight and the vital spot on the animal to think about.

There is a soft deer-skin cheek piece on the stock, moulded and shaped to fit it, and it is filled with deer hair. Rubber solution like that used in upholstery is used to keep it in position. When not required, it is simply pulled off. It does not blemish the stock. On the foresight block or ramp there is a simple protector hinged by a pin through the ramp. It cannot be lost and may be used up over the sight or folded back on the barrel. There is a spring-loaded ball to keep it in position.

The first shots fired into this buffalo head were frontal brain shots. I used first a "solid," lead-filled .318, then a soft-nose .318, and then a solid-copper, homogeneous .220 Swift. I placed a long sack of sawdust behind the buffalo head to trap the bullets. The lead-filled "solid" 250-grain .318 bullet penetrated the brain but disintegrated completely. I recovered only fragments from the sawdust. The soft-nose 250-grain bullet also penetrated the brain and also disintegrated, but at least one fragment could be recognized as the base of the bullet. The .220 homogeneous copper bullet of 48 grains penetrated the whole shooting match, but was not recovered, unfortunately.

I next ran a series of trials using a log of dry oak. I fired a 250-grain .318 solid, and then I changed the barrel to a .30-06. I then fired into the log a 168-grain naval bronze homogeneous bullet driven by 50½ grains of powder, then 130 grains of the same construction and material. I next increased the charge of powder and repeated the performance. The log was then cut up, and, unbelievably, all the bullets were found at the exact spot indicated and all were intact. They had all done about equally well in penetrating 18 inches of dry Scottish oak with the grain without deforming. We then tried an M2 with 150-grain standard military bullet. It stopped after penetrating thirteen inches of the same log.

So far only the lead-filled bullets had deformed. The .318 had flattened at the base and squeezed some lead out. The M2 round had flattened seriously and lost a good deal of its lead, some of it adhering to the outside of the gilding metal jacket as if it had been in a molten state.

None of the homogeneous bullets had deformed or lost any weight.

Now for the buffalo head. We set it up and surrounded it with bags of sawdust and with newspapers over them to show if any bullet tried to escape sideways. All the bullets were fired for the brain. All penetrated to the brain except the soft-nose .220 Swift, which disappeared in lead smoke on the surface of the horn.

The 250-grain, lead-filled .318 "solid" disintegrated into two recoverable parts, the envelope forming one and the lead core the other. Neither of these particles was capable of any further damage. But they had penetrated and passed through the brain.

All the homogeneous bullets did likewise, and although deformed and bent, they were still in one piece and capable of further damage. Their noses were bulged from .298 to .325, showing the astonishing resistance of Nature's raw materials for defense.

I very much doubt if any bullet capable of being fired from a man's shoulder would penetrate two buffalo horns from side to side. The utmost limit in our experiments was reached in traversing one buffalo horn. That there was nothing left in the bullets was shown by their locality in the sawdust trap. They were truly battered and tired out by the time they got through. They were all fired from a distance of five paces.

Just for luck we tried a solid copper homogeneous bullet of 48 grains from the .220 Swift. This one penetrated all right but deviated and was recovered three inches in the ground. It had mushroomed perfectly, although no aid to do so had been given it.

Now all these bullets would have killed a buffalo instantly had they hit where, in fact, they did. The brain is a small target and the chances are that in practice it would be missed in a large proportion of cases. What then would have happened to these bullets?

In the case of lead-filled and normally jacketed bullets, I'm afraid the answer looks as if they would fly into useless fragments. In fact, one might do better with a shot-gun loaded with steel shot. The worst aspect of the lead-filled bullet is the faster it is driven, the smaller the fragments it dissolves into. It begins to look as if a homogeneous bullet—of the very toughest materials—for these shots is a necessity. When you think what a bullet has to contend with in an elephant's head, steel itself would not be too stout a material for the job.

How many of the abortive shots at big game are caused by the break-up of the lead-filled "solid"? Then, too, there is the price and scarcity of copper, zinc, and nickel. This tends to reduce still further the thickness of that jacket. I recently got a 7mm round that was marked 18 D.M. K99 on the base; I sectioned the bullet. What a jacket! The nose was solid steel and the jacket heavy throughout its length. That was the bullet that served me so well in the past. It was the only bullet that ever traversed a top-weight bull elephant's head from side to side and could be heard whistling away and whining through the air.

While trying a magnet on this bullet, as I suspected the presence of steel in the jacket, it was curious to see it lift the round up out of the collection. Thus, another fact was disclosed. All the European bullets were attracted by the magnet while all the American ones remained unmoved by the passage of a magnet over them.

All the conventional lead-filled jacketed bullets used in these trials had wrecked themselves on the dry, hard bone that protects the brain from the shocks of sexual battle. It is this bone that forms the bony base upon which the horns themselves grow. The process of disintegration had then been completed by contact with the hard, dry walls of the skull-housing of the ball-joint end of the vertebral column. After this mauling, I doubt if they would have traveled six inches in the tough muscles of the neck. As it was, the fragments were but a few inches into the sawdust.

As for the .220, 48-grain solid copper bullet, we never recovered it. The skull, 4 feet of sawdust, and a heavy, 2-inch board had not held it, and there was too much disturbance of the brain area to try again. The brain pan on this buff was only 2¾ inches wide by 2½ inches deep. Either we are driving our bullets too fast for the envelope, or the envelope is too fragile for the job. I would say the way out is the homogeneous bullet. That one you can drive as fast as you like, with a blunt form of nose to prevent too great a penetration yet set up enough tissue destruction to accomplish clean and competent kills.

All these bullets would have killed a buffalo stone dead because they all traversed the 2¾-inch-wide brain. What would have happened had they not done so? The .313 "solid" and soft-nose bullets both would have flown to bits on any part of the skull away from the brain area. If shot high, they would have splintered to fragments on even heavier bone than that encountered in their passage through the brain. If shot to one side or low, they would have shattered on jaw bones, joints, back teeth (molar roots are close to the brain), or what not, and it is doubtful, indeed, if any of the fragments would have retained sufficient energy to have dropped the old buff before he ran you down.

The really solid homogeneous .220 would with certainty have gone on intact. If high, it would have gone through all head obstructions, entered the neck with great prospects of encountering and damaging some vital area, and if to either side or low, it would have had almost equally rosy expectations. It would reap the reward of penetration of the outer defenses. Give me a bullet that remains a bullet and does not become a scrap heap. I have tried these solid copper .220 bullets on deer, and believe me, they not only kill your buck but cook it at the same time. But don't leave your fire-making apparatus behind. I am exaggerating when I say they cook your buck; they only grill the walls of the wound channel.

The Neck Shot

Chapter 35

The red stag of Scotland weighs on an average about 210 pounds, live weight. Legally it is not a game animal, there is no closed season on it, and it belongs to the owner of land who succeeds in "reducing the animal into possession" when upon his holding.

In pursuit of "reducing the animal into possession"—an old legal phrase—sundry more or less up-to-date rifles have, in recent years, become prominent. The .22 Hi-Power cartridges, for example, have completely ousted the .275 and the .303 from several large forests. On one of these holdings nothing but double-barrel rifles that have been fitted with telescopic sights and chambered for the .22 Hi-Power cartridge is used. Apparently the load has given complete satisfaction to a variety of shooters, both experienced and inexperienced.

For many years a yearly bag of 70 to 80 stags and 50 to 60 hinds was taken from this forest. The head hunter, or stalker as he is called, told me the little 70-grain bullet was a marvelous game getter—nothing but the soft-nose bullet was used. He should know as it was his job to complete any reduction job some nervous guest might have left unfinished. I don't suppose a single seriously wounded beast ever escapes throughout the seasons.

On the other hand, when another very experienced hunter in the same forest was asked what rifle he would choose as a present for himself, he said somewhat diffidently that he would like a .250-3000.

In one of the largest forests where the average yearly bag was 120 to 135 stags and 70 to 80 hinds, the .275 Mauser is the favorite. It is a good, reliable cartridge and, of course, when properly used, is a killer. Indeed, a well-known match shooter reliably related that he had never missed a stag and had never wounded one. He had his rifle sighted in at 150 yards and would take deer up to 300 yards without changing the sight setting. Over a number of years that is a reputation to be greatly envied. But what a nerve-racking business for his attendant stalker. Everything had to be just right—the shooting stance had to be right, the animal had to stand just right, the light had to be right.

By far the commonest rifle in Scotland, and still the most popular for deer shooting, is the old .256 Mannlicher or the .256 Mannlicher-Schöenauer. With its long heavy bullet, it is hard to beat for use by impatient or inexperienced shooters. It is good for end-on or raking shots, or for broadside neck or body shots. Although the velocity of the Mannlicher is nothing to shout about in these days, what velocity it has it maintains for some distance. It has almost certainly killed more deer than all the other calibres put together.

My own personal experience with the .220 Swift, the .22 Hi-Power Savage, and the .256 Mannlicher-Schöenauer is that these calibres are all good, but—like whiskies—some are better than others. For instance, you are out in bad weather, and there is a low cloud, the light is poor, and perhaps there is rain. You spy a deer, with difficulty. You make your approach and reach a point that you judge to be between 150 to 300 yards from him, but a ravine lies between you and the animal, so the air distance is hard to guess.

Now, if you carry a .256, you dare not risk a neck shot since the trajectory of your bullet is too high—not flat enough—to cover the error your guess of the distance may contain. Therefore, you must take a body shot and spoil some meat. Maybe both shoulders will be pierced and much good meat spoiled. Your best chance in such circum-

The red stag of Scotland.

stances, and so armed, is to hold for a point halfway up the body and slightly behind the line of the foreleg.

Should you carry a .22 Hi-Power, or better still, a .220 Swift, and have confidence in your shooting, you may unhesitatingly go for the neck shot. This is by far the most satisfactory shot of all, for you do not mess up good meat. The neck of a stag begins to swell in the season of his prime, just after the deer has shed the velvet, and the neck is a much larger target than one would believe. With anything like decent shooting, there should be no danger of a broken jaw.

But the greatest advantage of all is the fact that if the neck muscles are hit anywhere by one of the small, high-velocity soft-nose bullets, the animal collapses instantly, can feel nothing, and remains motionless. It is shock to the nervous system that does it, and shock seems to be directly the result of velocity. All the nerve channels are closely grouped together in the neck, to the undoing of the animal and to the satisfaction of the hunter at a job properly and mercifully carried out.

The .220 Swift seems to be the cartridge expressly designed by Providence, acting through the agency of the Winchester Company's experts, for the humane killing of wild animals at distances hitherto considered risky or even impossible, provided that the neck is selected as the target. For body shots, it can be used only with caution; it is not so merciful. One must avoid at all cost touching heavy bone, such as that of a foreleg. The soft-nose, 48-grain bullet will simply blow up, and one is handed a nasty job and a bad conscience.

I find the Winchester bolt, with its speed lock and short striker travel, an enormous advantage. If the weight of the metal to be set in motion at trigger release could be still further reduced, it would cut down that shudder that is inseparable from the reaction of a mechanism suddenly set in motion. When you are looking through a high-power telescopic sight, there is an indubitable jump of the weapon at the instant of trigger release and a deflection from the line of sight. Small, if you like, but still there and possible of elimination. In a bolt-action, this mass of metal is of considerable weight. The Mannlicher-Schöenauer is particularly bad in this respect. It is pertinent here to notice that if a single-shot, falling-block action is put through a similar test, the jump, as shown by the scope sight, is considerably less.

But I think there is more to it than that. Consider the pressure that has to be exerted on the trigger. In a bolt-action it is not safe to have the pull much less than, say, four pounds. What happens when this pressure suddenly stops, as it does when the striker is released?

As in all strokes, whether in golf, tennis, or any other hitting game, follow-through is essential. So in rifle shooting it is essential to follow through, that is, to continue to dwell on the aim an instant or two after the bullet has left. Equally so the trigger squeeze or pressure should continue smoothly on its course. But it cannot do this; it has been suddenly cut off in mid-air, as it were, and there is a considerable disturbance before the pressure is renewed once more on the abrupt ending of the trigger travel.

I have played about with rubber stops to the trigger travel but with slight success. For one thing it is difficult to fix the rubber securely and neatly. There is not space to do it properly. If you bring the rubber into firm contact with the trigger, then you still have a break in the pressure line. It is a problem for the back-room boys, and I hope to live long enough to see a smooth trigger travel evolved. Possibly a progressively acting spring would give results.

With the 70-grain .22 Hi-Power and its lower velocity, you are slightly better equipped for body shots. In fact, I have seen a .22 Hi-Power Savage lay flat a whole herd of West African buffaloes. It happened during a more than usually acute famine in what had been a cannibal tribe. Meat is in a chronic state of shortage in those parts—hence the eating of human flesh. At the time of which I write, grain food had also failed these unfortunate people. In fact the hunter could with truth persuade himself that by killing a large quantity of meat, he would thereby save the lives of sundry young natives in and about the villages.

The finding of the game was, of course, entrusted to the chief medicine man, and he knew his stuff. Bright and early he might have been seen, loaded with his charms, preceding a man armed with a .22 Hi-Power Imp. The country would be open elephant grass, recently burned off and now newly grown to two or three feet high, and with long bands of dark forest here and there cutting the horizon.

Presently they stop and appear to be watching something moving toward them. This something resolves itself into a closely bunched herd of buffaloes, running determinedly toward their midday sanctuary—the forest. Their path led them straight toward the little group of motionless figures.

Presently fire was opened. Instead of dispersing in all directions, the buffalo herd halted its forward movement, and the buffaloes started ringing around, milling, goring, and bellowing. And the Imp continued to talk. The herd began to dissipate, apparently into thin air; the grass was just high enough to cover most of the bodies. The last one disappeared. The Imp was silent. The shooter looked at the medicine man. The medicine man looked as if he alone had done it.

There were twenty-three bodies within a ring perhaps twenty-five yards across, and they were all dead. I glanced at the shooter's cartridge belt. When full it held thirty-five rounds; it now showed three rounds. If his magazine had been full—which it was—he had fired twenty-seven shots.

Of course, what he had done was to take a tip from the old American bison hunter's technique and got them ringing and goring the wounded by using the lung shot. Only thus could that herd have been brought to bag. No doubt in the general mix-up, several of the animals had received more than one bullet each, but what a deadly little gun—just right for the job.

A noisier gun might have stampeded the herd. Neck shots might have dropped them stone dead and merely alarmed the others, without enraging them with the smell of blood and without arousing that peculiar bovine lust to kill off any of its own kind when it becomes wounded.

This case will hardly pass as one of humane killing, rather the contrary in fact. It is given as an example of how deadly these small-bore bullets are in the hands of a capable shot who appraises correctly the abilities of the cartridge he has at hand. If he had wanted one buffalo for his own camp, as normally would have been the case, he would have killed the fattest one in sight with a shot in the neck. The others would have dispersed and the affair would have ended unnoticed.

These high-precision, lightweight, fast-flying bullets are no good for end-on shots. They are no good for raking body shots where considerable penetration is required. Such shots simply wound and should be avoided at all cost, with one exception—the shot at a buck facing directly toward you and at such a distance as to ensure the clean, unobstructed entry of the bullet into the chest cavity. It is at best a risky shot; it is far better to try for the neck itself. The flatness of the trajectory should obviate any risk of shattering the lower jaw. The neck, even when the animal is facing you, is a large target.

The effect of wind on light bullets is of supreme importance, especially so in these Scottish hills where they have to encounter strong gusts from maybe two or three directions during their flight from muzzle to target. But here again experience teaches one to choose the target. Take the shot across a ravine at a stag feeding and moving slowly along. Wind may be anything from directly against to broadside for the little 48-grain pellet you propose to launch against the enemy. Speed of wind is 20 to 30 miles per hour, and distance through the air is about 200 yards. It is no use juggling with the wind gauge because the wind is swirling about, and you are just as likely to magnify as to correct the drift. Leave it alone, at zero.

Elevation with the .220 Swift will not bother you. The target presents itself as an oblong, and it constantly changes its direction. Sometimes it is pointing downward at 40 degrees as when feeding, sometimes it is horizontal as when standing, sometimes it is facing toward you, and sometimes it is facing away from you.

When in the horizontal position, it is obvious that the target will allow four or five inches deviation in either direction if one holds for the centre of the oblong. Remember that the whole of the oblong is target to a high-velocity bullet anyway. There is no other area of similar size in any part of the body about which the same may be said.

Should the stag be lying down, there is no choice in the matter: The neck is the only target that should be attempted. When in this position all the body vitals are protected by the animal's sloping shoulder blades, folded leg bones, and whatnot. But what a magnificent target the neck is.

A word of caution to the inexperienced, though. If the stag is sleeping and facing you, it will require care to place the bullet so as to avoid the point of the chin. The head is carried pretty low in slumber, and in one's anxiety to avoid touching vegetation, one is inclined to hold a little high. Note, too, that the small bullets will not tolerate any interference with their flight, even from the slightest of grass stems. They fly off at the most exasperating angles.

I have had one or two queer things happen while using the .220 Swift. A stag was standing in all the virility of his recently awakened sex-fever, broadside, at a subsequently measured distance of 205 yards. He was above me and roaring at another stag down below. As the neck was in almost constant movement and as his forelegs were braced forward, thus uncovering the heart, I selected the latter as the better target.

At the shot, the stag stood motionless for a second and then fell over sideways with its legs still stiffly outstretched. I had never seen this happen before, so, when the carcass came to larder, I made a careful examination.

The target presents itself as oblong, and it constantly changes its direction in relation to the rifleman.

The 48-grain soft-nose bullet had struck the heavy dense bone of the chest cavity wall about two inches low from the tip of the heart, which was untouched. In fact, the inner surface of the chest cavity was quite undisturbed. The bullet had set up nicely into a perfect mushroom, but, of course, had only penetrated about one-and-a-quarter inches. No vital had been touched, and yet that stag was stone dead. By that I mean that there was none of the nerve twitching that one gets after more normal body shots. Looking at that stag, one would have said it showed every sign of having been shot in the neck—in other words, total nerve paralysis.

Another queer experience occurred when I found a good stag enjoying a rest from his labors, lying in the morning sun, with his harem of hinds scattered about between the rifle and stag. The distance was on the two-hundred-yard mark, the light was good, and the stag's neck presented sideways. It was one of the few times when everything was right. There he lay with ears cocked, gazing bright-eyed at his wives lying slumbering slightly below him.

At the shot—a .220—he simply dropped his head. No other movement whatsoever. No kicking or twitching limbs—nothing. Moreover, there was not a move from the hinds beyond the raising of an outstretched neck here and there. To them their lord and master continued to sleep there on his bank. So no one moved, even to get up. Peace remained unbroken until I finally had to show myself so as to perform the gralloch, as the disemboweling is called in Scotland.

Here another question arises. Why does an animal that has been shot in the brain itself twitch and even lash about, whereas one shot in the neck completely paralyzes it and it shows no movement at all? After a brain shot, the heart may be observed to continue to beat for a considerable time.

In my elephant-hunting days I would often be actually standing on the fallen victim and would feel the *thump-thump* coming up through the soles of my shoes. In fact, if I did not feel these thumpings or see the leg twitching, I was immediately suspicious that the bullet might only had stunned by passing close to the brain, and I would instantly give him another, often down between my legs.

But with the neck shot, nothing of this appears to happen. The heart and nerves seem to cease to function simultaneously. Explain it who can. Meanwhile the neck shot remains the hunter's surest, safest, and kindest means of reducing into possession any of the deer tribe.

Small Bores Versus Big Bores

Chapter 36

I suppose there are few more hotly contested subjects than that of the calibre of rifles for use against large game, especially against that considered to be dangerous.[1] Ever since man began to walk erect—even before that, I expect—this controversy probably raged as freely as it does now, if not about rifles then about clubs, bludgeons, battle axes, and bows. It may, in fact, be stated, with fair reason, that bores of all kinds have existed in great numbers since the word go.

It will be observed that it is almost invariably the Big Bore who attacks the Small Bore. Why this should be so is at first glance not apparent. It can be stated with very fair accuracy that the Small Bore does not usually bear any ill will toward the Big Bore. I should say that, on the contrary, the Small Bore rather commiserates with his brother Bore for having to burden himself with his heavy equipment.

On the other hand, the Big Bore will take every opportunity to attack the Small Bore. He will perjure his soul by declaring the small-bore rifle to be unsporting. He will even go so far as to declare that the use of small bores should be made illegal. Why should the Big Bore get so hot under the collar about the number of the thousandths of an inch that constitutes the difference between, say, a .270 and a .375?

Is it that the Big Bore has devoted painstaking, laborious research into the effect on animals weighing several tons of this so important 105 thousandths of an inch? Has he, perchance, stumbled on some important truth hidden from less penetrating eyes? Not a bit of it. He generally knows rather less of matters

[1]From the *American Rifleman,* December 1954. This is perhaps the last article written by W. D. M. Bell before his death late in June 1954. It summarizes Bell's strong opinions on rifles for dangerous game, opinions he developed over a lifetime of adventuring. "Karamojo" Bell advocated the use of the high-velocity, small-bore rifle for big game; indeed, he is thought to be the first man to use a .275 Rigby Mauser on Africa's elephants.

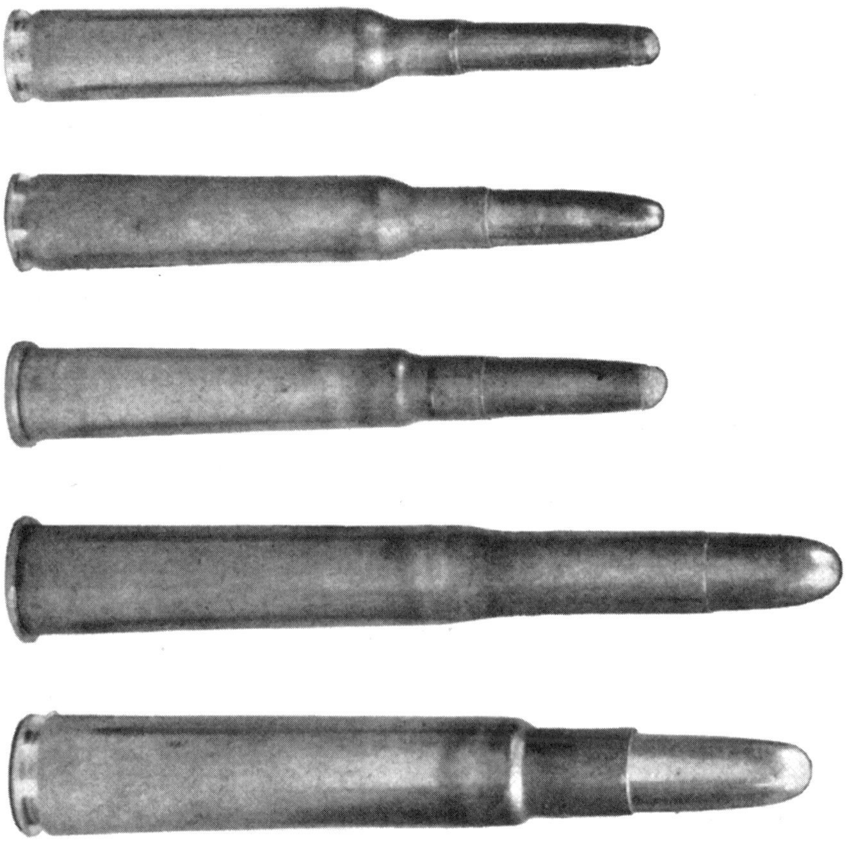

From top to bottom: .256 Mannlicher-Schöenauer; 7mm Mauser solid; .303 mark VI; .450/.400 solid; and .416 solid.

of moment to riflemen. Usually he will leave the matter of choice of weapon to his chosen gunmaker and should he be successful—as very often he is, for even a .600 calibre, 900-grain bullet in the right place will kill as dead as a 100-grain bullet—they forever swear by that particular rifle, and damn all others of smaller calibre as being unsporting. In fact, they show a heat and venom quite unknown to the small-bore addict, leaving him wondering what all the fuss can be about.

It is this curious inner rage—in some respects like the rabies of the canine world—shown for the Small Bore by the Big Bore that forms the subject of this article. Before a positive hatred of this magnitude can be generated, there must be deep-rooted forces of great intensity at work. I have known of a man who wrote a whole book of bitter attacks on small-bore practitioners. Obviously it was intended in some inscrutable way to get his own back, to re-instate himself in his own esteem.

Perhaps this case conceals a clue worth following up. He projected his jet of venom against the .220 Swift in particular. He argued that because a friend of his fired at a wounded buck at 20 paces and the .220 had failed to kill; therefore, the .220 was not a suitable rifle for the killing of deer. No word, be it noted, where the bullet struck or even if it hit the buck at all. That spotlights my allusion to the canine-rabies-nature of these attacks in no uncertain fashion.

Using a telescopic sight and shooting at the neck, I have found the .220 Swift, 48-grain bullet with a muzzle velocity of 4,150 f.p.s. beyond compare for country where a shot is clear of obstruction and where the prone position can be used. Nothing could surpass it or, I venture to say, join the same class. Anyone who denies this has either failed to zero his rifle properly—for Scottish red deer it should be on the dot at 220 yards—or he suffers from some defect and should see a specialist or something.

Similarly the same can be said when it comes to big game. The argument here is that the small calibre often wounds and loses game where the large bullet kills. This is a very attractive proposition much favoured by the Big Bore school. When they quote the striking energy in foot pounds, it becomes almost irresistible: The weight of the piece, the size of the cartridge, the noise it makes, and the cost of it all quite overcome the totally inexperienced man or those of naturally weak reasoning powers.

Of course, it must be recognized that some of the very finest of craftsmanship goes into these heavy weapons. They are things of entrancing beauty and have an attraction quite apart from their utility as killers. I myself once upon a time fell under their sway. I bought myself a double .450/.400 hammerless ejector, first-grade rifle by Daniel Fraser of Edinburgh. I knew Fraser well and often fired his heavy pieces on his regulating range. In fact, he tried to persuade me to have a monstrous double .577 in place of the .400, but I thought the latter would serve my purpose all right.

It fired 60 grains of cordite behind a 400-grain bullet in each barrel, and I thought that if I wired the two triggers together I would get the equivalent of 120 grains of cordite pushing 800 grains of bullet. This seemed near enough to the 900-grain bullet and 100 grains of cordite of the .600 or the 750-grain

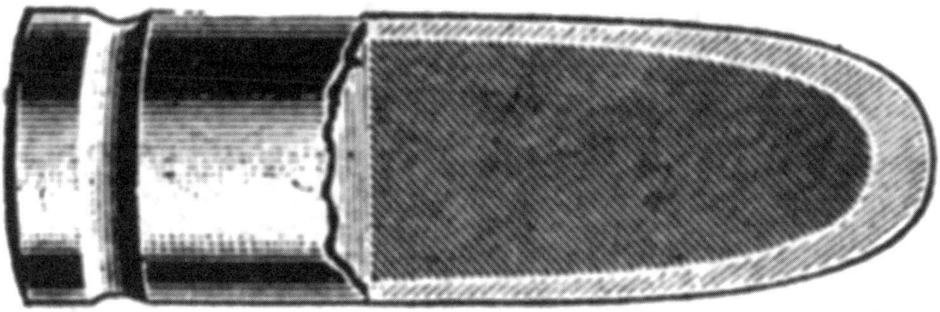

Solid, steel-covered bullet.

bullet and 80 grains of cordite of the .577 to convince me whether there was anything to this big stuff or not.

As well as the .450/.400, I acquired a Magnum Mauser .416 Rigby four-shot magazine rifle with its own design of steel-jacketed bullet drawn so that the metal in the nose end was very thick. At the same time I had my .303 ten-shot, the .275 Rigby Mauser, and the meat-providing .256 Gibbs Mannlicher. Whether the newly acquired .400 double or the .416 Mauser failed me or not, I was still adequately armed. Thus equipped, I left for the hunting grounds.

Let me say right away that they all killed dead. All rifles using proper bullets do. None kill deader than dead because they can't. But there are other considerations.

The double .400 with its gold-washed locks weighed ten pounds. It carried, or rather you carried, two barrels to do the work of one. The noise of a discharge, especially of both barrels together, was disturbing to a great extent of the country. Also, a discharge seemed to be more alarming to game, whether by waves of air pounding them or merely by cracking their sensitive ear drums, I do not know. The ammunition was nowhere obtainable away from its place of origin, and it was heavy and costly. Finally, you did not like to use such hard-to-come-by cartridges in mere practice.

Here the Double Barrel Bores always bring in their favourite argument about having a much quicker second shot than that of the magazine rifle. All I say to that is that it is possible to fire a second barrel slightly quicker than to do the same from a light bolt-action rifle, but whereas the former will be a shot into the blue, owing to the disturbance of aim of the first discharge, the latter will be a properly aimed shot—into a second victim more than likely. That is how bags are made.

A STRONG D.B.B.B.

I remember meeting up with a well-known Double Barrel Big Bore at a river crossing. His particular weakness was for double .500s. These come in between the .470 and .475s and the .577 and the .600s. It was the dry season, and all the elephants in creation seemed to be gathered in the still-green swamps. All the country away from the river had been burned off, and nothing you could do to those enormous herds would induce them to leave the shelter of the high grass, which at that time was ten to twelve feet.

The great burly D.B.B.B. seemed very discontented with things in general; in fact, he was in a slow-motion simmering fury. It appeared that his boys had struck at swimming the river—it was really an arm of the Upper Nile and full of crocs—and had actually refused to mount a raft the B.B. had had made for their transport. This filled the Big Bore with fury. But they weren't such fools, those boys. They knew perfectly well that the wood used in the raft would not float, as the B.B. found when he launched it with some of his loads on board.

I had been doing pretty well with my light rifles at this swamp hunting, just having taken fifteen head of bull elephants on two consecutive days. I was feeling pretty good, and as I had some whisky, I asked the hunter to have a drink while I told my very experienced gang to give a hand with getting my rival hunter's boys and gear across.

Over our drinks a mellowed B.B. confided with many curses that his rifles—two double-barrel .500s—knocked him tail over tip off the ant-heaps or elephant bodies every time he fired them. As he looked a burly sort of beggar, I suggested his rifles might be too light. This set him off.

"Too light," he roared, "try humping them through long grass, and you'll soon find them too bloody heavy."

"Why not try a light small bore?" I asked him.

"What do you use?" he asked.

I showed him the modest little .275.

"Hell, I wouldn't use a ruddy popgun like that," he declared.

But when he saw the proceeds of the .275 in actual ivory—30 tusks—and I told him they were the result of two days' hunting, he began to think hard.

Is That Convincing?

Was he convinced? No! You cannot penetrate the hide of a confirmed, fully adult Big Bore. Catch an immature one, and he will at least try out the small bores. But once the skin has hardened into a shell, no proof, however convincing, stands a chance of even being considered.

In this high-grass hunting, where to see at all, you must have some means of at least bringing your eyes level with the thinner tops of the grass, and that's when the recoil of your rifle becomes of vital importance. Often the only eminence sufficiently high is the carcass of a slain elephant, especially that of a brain-shot kneeling one. You run quickly up his bent-up foreleg onto the highest point of his back, often with the thumps of his still-beating heart throbbing through the soles of your light shoes. From this vantage point, great lines of heads and tops of backs will be discovered, sometimes quite near you. These great herds are making so much noise, belching and whatnot, that the report of a .256, 7mm, or .303 passes unnoticed by the majority of the herd, resulting in only partial movement.

Although the target is so presented, with the important bulls standing well above the cow elephants, care must still be exercised. Only the brain shot is feasible, generally speaking. But close inspection, especially with the binoculars, which should never be absent from the hunter's person, will show that the path of the bullet is cluttered up with the quite strong grass stalks.

As everyone knows, even one of these pests will deflect a light, high-velocity bullet, but one of the old heavy round-nose solids, traveling not faster than 2,400 f.p.s., will sedately pursue the course entrusted to it by the hunter, and a clean kill will ensue to the satisfaction of all concerned.

All rules have this in common: They are subject to the exception. I once killed an elephant with a high-velocity .280 solid with a heart shot at 600 yards. Normally the distance for this shot would be from 20 to 100 yards. The pointed abomination had lost most of its superfluous velocity. This was yet one more instance of the utter futility of supposing that the shocking power of the rifle used has anything to do with its killing power.

STRONG MAN, BIG GUN

I happened to be staying with the district officer of a very wild, backward area. There was a detachment of troops under a white officer. This man was a young, splendid-looking chap, and he had ambitions anent the elephant, in pursuit whereof he had acquired a very beautiful double .600.

The day he left, we both thought he would be successful. The man was six feet, four inches tall, and broad yet lean, and he checked the .600 about as if it had been a 12-bore shotgun. Elephant were numerous and native trackers able and keen. He left at dawn and returned next day having spent the night in the bush. He took forty rounds with him and returned with none. He swore he had put all forty into the same elephant.

The case of this particular man could not be passed off as one of inexperience, nor could his guts be queried. As stout a fellow as could be found, as his later exploits proved to the hilt, he said he fired at close range. Knowing the country, I can well believe him. He told us that at first there was plenty of blood spoor, but that this tended to diminish as time and the battle went on. How like some of the old hunters' encounters it sounds, where, if you found a suitable bull in the morning, it occupied you fully to get him down by evening by pouring into his body 4-, 8-, 10-, or 12-bore bullets driven by enormous charges of powder.

All the same and laying aside all prejudice, I am still wondering where those forty, 900-grain slugs ended up. As I have before remarked, even a .600 will kill, and we know from the presence of blood spoor that some bullets must have found a billet in the elephant. Yet that elephant simply vanished. Never was his body found. He must have been a ghost, if ghosts have blood.

With some 150 to 200 men and women depending solely on a couple of rifles for food and footwear, beer and 'baccy—for all could be bartered for meat—ruggedness of construction seemed to me to be the greatest asset. To get a repair effected would have taken at least three months by foot-runner to the coast, even if an armorer could have been found willing and able to do it. So it will be seen how vitally important it was to keep the battery in working order.

The best way to do so was to have everything of the simplest and most robust description possible. The military arms of the various nations are the most highly developed of any as they have had more thought, time, and money spent on them than would be possible on any commercial arm. I chose from the start to pin my

The rifle on top is a .256 Gibbs that weighs 7 pounds, and the one on the bottom is a .450/.400 Rigby double-barrel rifle that weighs 10¼ pounds.

On top is a .256 Mannlicher-Schöenauer that weighs 7 pounds, and on the bottom is a .275 Rigby Light Model that weighs 6¾ pounds.

The rifle on top is a .416 Rigby that weighs 10 pounds, and the one on the bottom is a .303 Lee-Metford 10-shot that weighs 7½ pounds.

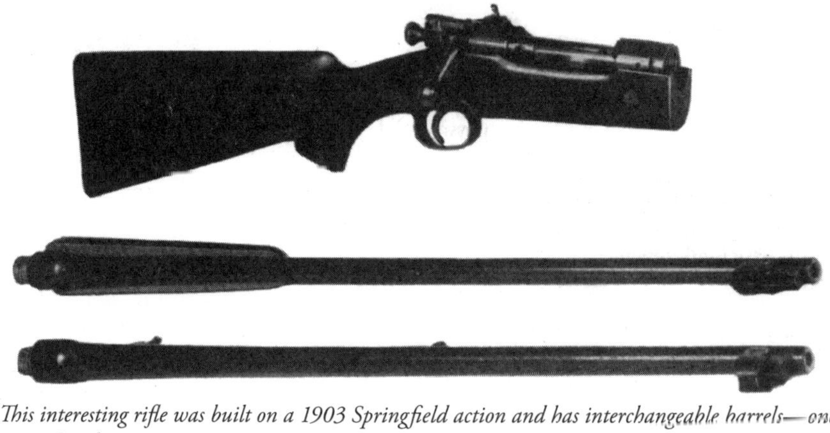

This interesting rifle was built on a 1903 Springfield action and has interchangeable barrels—one .30-06 and one .318.

faith on the .303, the 7mm Mauser, and the .256 Mannlicher. These arms formed the backbone on which all depended. Similar remarks apply to their cartridges.

In pursuit of this ideal of simplicity, I used only one plain, open-V backsight of very robust construction with plenty of metal on the .303 and 7mm Mauser. I used to file down the V so that the full ivory bead covered the group of shots at 80 yards. In this kind of hunting, it is important to always use the full bead as this is the only amount that remains constant. If you start monkeying about with just the top of the bead appearing in the bottom of the V, then in poor light your shot will go high as you will unconsciously take more of it.

Whenever I had to do any file cutting, and it was surprising how often you wanted to alter the profile or the width of the backsight, then the whole backsight was heated to a dull red and quenched in vegetable oil or ground nut. This was a quite adequate substitute for bluing and could be renewed at will.

On the .256 there were the usual iron sight leaves for 100, 200, and 300 yards. As at first I got only soft-nose bullets, this rifle was used exclusively for providing meat. Without experiencing it, no one would credit the amount of buck meat a hundred boys could consume—in addition to having all the elephant meat they could carry off.

Buck game was quite unmolested and in parts was still in countless numbers. It was nothing out of the way for the .256 to slay 15 or 20 bucks handy to camp for their meat and for rawhide saddles for the donkey ivory-packers.

It must not be thought that I had any facilities for experimenting with different loads for my rifles. We just had to be content with the military load worked out by the various armies concerned. It was just pure good luck that the bullets with their considerable weight, their round noses, and their moderate velocities proved in practice to be so well suited to the job.

The .303 wirh its 215-grain bullet (with a muzzle velocity of about 2,100 f.p.s.); the 173-grain, 7mm bullet (muzzle velocity 2,300 f.p.s.); and the .256 Mannlicher with its 154-grain bullet (muzzle velocity 2,200 f.p.s.), were just about perfect for the job.

When it came to testing the larger bores against these small, handy, light, and deadly rifles with which I had already been so successful, it was almost certain that their imperfections would stand out vividly. First of all their weight, to a man who habitually carried his rifle, seemed excessive and unnecessary.

The .416 Rigby was certainly a grand killer and showed great penetration and true course-holding ability. It was handy, too, and well balanced, and did not seem its weight.

In fact, it was only when you had been toting it through the bush for eight hours or so that you began to say, "Why the hell am I carrying this heavy brute around when it kills no deader than the .303 or .275?" That would be when you had reached the stage where you carried the thing on your shoulder, hand grasping the barrel near the muzzle, the hot steel cutting you in two.

> Weight: 9½ pounds. Too heavy.
> Muzzle velocity: 2,300 f.p.s. Bolt travel too long.

But I can well imagine what confidence those four great cartridges with their steel-coated jackets would inspire in a beginner in high grass or dense bush. It was only that I had begun with the small bores—and had been convinced of their deadliness—that I looked on the larger calibres with such a critical eye. Perchance had I started with such weapons I might now find myself among the Big Bores or even among the elite, the Double Barrel Big Bores. A lot depends on what rifle you begin with and whether you are successful with it or not.

The double .450/.400 suffered from soft-jacketed bullets. Although completely metal covered, they often collapsed. The jacket did not break up, but the lead squeezed out at the base. I think it undoubtedly became melted by the heat generated when passing through skin, muscle, and tissue. I think, also, that the solid base of the soft-nose bullet explains its astonishing penetration. As it seems quite impossible to devise a totally enclosed lead filling for a bullet, it would seem that the next step would be to use a homogeneous brass or Monel metal bullet.

With both triggers of the double-barrel .400 wired together, the result on the animal was just the same as from a 173-grain slug from the 7mm., although the firer was left in a sort of shock-drunk state. You were firing 120 grains of cordite behind 800 grains of bullet from a 10-pound rifle. For a second or two you were off balance and in no condition to select another target and to fire an aimed shot in spite of having braced yourself for the coming explosion.

In case anyone is crazy enough to wish to repeat this experiment, I would like to warn him that it is no easy matter to get the two barrels to go off together. As a result of the construction of these mighty pieces, the recoil is partly reduced by the bend in the stock. This tends to throw the muzzles up. It will be readily understood that the merest fraction of time difference in the fall of the strikers results in the second shot going much higher than the first. Altogether an abomination, these doubles.

Then coming down the scale we reach the .318 with its 250-grain bullet. This is a killer. It holds its course through almost anything and is superior in this respect to all other bullets I have tried. For oblique shots into large animals, it is quite the best (muzzle velocity 2,400 f.p.s.). Cartridge about the same length as .30-06. Could be shorter with advantage. Also requires more shoulder on cartridge case. I have a .318 weighing seven pounds, ten ounces exactly when empty. The deadliest weapon of the push-bolt type known to me. It is quite sufficiently pleasant to fire in the standing position, and is heavy enough to keep the arm muscles in trim for standing shooting when carried all day.

Next is a .303 British Mark VI, round-nose, 215-grain solid. The rifle has many advantages. It is light—can be 6¾ pounds. Stock is bolted to action through grip and can hardly be broken, although it may work loose and requires a very long turn screw to tighten it. By continuous working of the bolt smeared with very fine emery powder, the bolt can be brought to a fine polished performance. With its 10-shot magazine, it is a very useful, hard-working, and efficient rifle. Can hardly be stopped from functioning by mud or sand.

I also have a seven-pound (empty) .275 (7mm) Rigby Mauser rifle: muzzle velocity 2,300 f.p.s., 173-grain bullet. The scientist's rifle par excellence. Weight can be 6¾ pounds. A delightful companion with its German D.W.M.–made bullet, it killed over 800 head of large bull elephants. Its diameter to length of bullet and its rather pointed round-nose bullet gave it extraordinary penetration. Its true course-holding quality very good except in extreme conditions as when firing for the brain in an elephant from behind—an extremely severe test. Out-performed by the .250-grain, .318 in this case alone. Bullet may be required to enter at an angle of 20 degrees from the body's axis. The least deflection cannot be tolerated as the brain is presented in least favorable aspect. Bullet has thinnish hide, heavy muscle, thinnish bone to contend with, but all at a 20-degree angle. Failure to connect with the brain was one in three. Human error says 50 percent. Misses due to deflection, say one in four. Similar figures for .318, say one in 3½. I never saw a mangled or bent 7mm bullet, possibly because most of them had passed on whistling as they went. An inspiring little rifle, requiring knowledge of anatomy and exact pointing.

Finally, there is the .256 Mannlicher and .256 Mannlicher-Schöenauer. Here we are approaching the limit of safety, in diameter to length, for long traverses in heavy game. These long, narrow-for-diameter bullets bend into the most extraordinary hook-like shapes and this oddity of theirs inevitably brings under suspicion their true course-holding properties. I must say I only once failed to kill the animal I fired at with the .256 and that was due to a misfire because of a faulty round.

I once had a carbine Mannlicher-Schöenauer 20-inch barrel down to 5½ pounds with a hollowed-out walnut stock that was simply lightning for the brain shot on elephant. I believe a homogeneous Monel bullet might overcome the bending propensities of the lead-filled bullet even in .256 calibre. It would certainly be stiffer. Once that is overcome, the thing is perfect as far as bullet goes.

The bolt action could be improved. The delay between striker release and firing of the cartridge is much too long for good off-the-shoulder work from wobbly or insecure stances.

GOOD WORD FOR THE .30-06

The .30-06, I regret to say, never came my way, so I cannot speak of it from experience on African game. But coming as it does between the .275 and .318, it might well prove to be the ideal calibre, large enough in diameter to resist bending, heavy enough to hold a true course, and with sufficient density to give good penetration. The new short version, the .308, with a suitable bullet may yet prove to be the answer to the hunter's prayer. Its sufficient diameter with enough penetration and no bending is a specification that would answer others than the hunter's dream.

There is a simple test for bullets suitable for killing large game. The bullet should never be less than four times its diameter in length and should have a short, round-nose point and long parallel sides. Its jacket should be of steel of a thickness that will keep it together through any going, however tough. Or it should be of homogeneous metal. Granted these conditions, let the Big Bores choose their own calibre.

It would be interesting to speculate on what sort of punch such cartridges would give. Take a .475. I suppose its bullet would measure maybe 1½ or 2 diameters in length, weighing 500 grains. A bullet to measure four diameters would, therefore, weigh somewhere about 1,000 grains. Although it would be an adequate killer, the Big Bore school can have it—it would kill at both ends.

Yet another bone to pick with the cannon-worshippers. They often say that small bores wound when they do not kill and that the animal goes off to die a lingering death—a favourite phrase this—whereas a large-calibre bullet causes such a wide area of destruction that the animal is more likely to die.

But it must not be overlooked that the small bore, while making a smaller wound channel, also makes a longer one. It is much more likely to be a well-directed shot also, and, anyhow, with heavy game where the vitals are so large, there is no excuse for wounding to enter into the question. Any long-range stuff is out of place on these animals.

We now come to what I would take to Africa if I had to go through the whole thing again under the same set of conditions. I would base my battery on a Winchester .308 Model 70 that burns a cartridge loaded with a homogeneous bronze or Monel metal bullet of the form as worked out by Kohlbacher. At the same time, I would have a .318 barrel and action to fit the same stock, and I would have a supply of 250-grain conventional, lead-filled, steel-jacketed solid bullets, just in case any unforeseen snags arose from the use of homogeneous bullets in the .308.

My reasons for choosing the .308 are that it most nearly meets the elephant hunter's dream—sufficient penetration with no bending. My reason for preferring the .308 case is that it is shorter than the .30-06. My only really close calls in hunting African game have come from the too-long-bolt travel of bolt-action rifles and from firing at very close range into elephants with a body shot in very thick stuff when they were facing me. They launch themselves straight ahead when hit in the heart, and they are as likely as not to tangle you up in their legs.

THE GREATEST MENACE

The too-long bolt is, I think, the greatest menace a man has to face in African hunting. My own experiences happened with rhinos in long grass. With sighting ranges of three yards or so, the backward-bolt travel is liable to be cut prematurely. The empty case is not ejected but reinserted in the barrel, and you have a misfire at contact range.

A thing I miss very much in the modernized copies of the Mauser bolt-action is the cut-out thumb slot on the left side of the action body. This thumb recess was probably intended to help the thumb press down a clip load of cartridges into the magazine. In the field I found it suited me for the loading of single cartridges: the left hand holding the light rifle, the thumb pressing the single cartridge down into the magazine, and the right hand extracting a round from the belt. This could be done while the eye remained on the game.

I have tried out these homogeneous bullets in brass on Scottish red deer and on African buffaloes, and from its performance, I feel sure it would probably knock all ordinary bullets right out of the field.

Instead of going back with the old Four Bores and Eight Bores of the last century, I would go forward and form a new school of bores—the Homogeneous or All-Metal Bores.

On Killing Elephants

Chapter 37

In these days of camera hunting, it may be well to begin my chapter[1] on "killing" with a short quotation from the *Annual Report of the Uganda Game Warden,* 1929:

"The presence of numerous elephant herds in the heart of settled Toro calls for more drastic action than mere scaring away. In many cases a thinning-out is now essential; in others, the herds have either to be moved or exterminated."

There is a tendency among camera enthusiasts to treat somewhat contemptuously the shooting of elephants with "modern rifles," implying that the "modern" rifle, if merely shown an elephant, will straightway lay it low. This is not the case. It is as necessary to direct firmly the "modern" rifle at a vital spot as it ever was with the older weapons.

If anyone has the notion that there is no danger in the killing of African elephants, let him fire a rifle at close range into a herd accustomed to firearms when denned up in one of their bush strongholds. Such a furious resistance and devastating uproar as then arises will surely convince the boldest. The killing of an African elephant is unlike any other shooting. It takes place at close range, the animal is enormous, but the vital spots are comparatively so small that it is not nearly so easy as one would imagine.

It is the object of this chapter to endeavour to help the inexperienced shot to bring about, firstly, the speedy and painless death of the elephant, and secondly, to avoid a lengthy and possibly dangerous experience for the hunter.

Without hesitation I say there is no shot like the brain shot. It is painless and silent; there is no groaning or bellowing as with the body shot. The game is located; it cannot wander off into the thick stuff and require tracking up. The tail may be cut off immediately, others may be followed up, and it has no alarming effect on the rest of the herd. It has neatness, finality, lack of mess and

[1]From Bell's chapter in *Game Animals of the Sudan* by Capt. H. C. Brocklehurst, London, 1931.

blood, and an altogether satisfying effect on the hunter. Finally, if the brain is missed no harm is done—only a bullet is lost in that spongy cranium.

Against it is its difficulty. It is not often that an elephant's head is still. If listening or slumbering it is, but if he is feeding, it is decidedly not. Then the brain is desperately small when compared with the size of the head. It is placed well away inside an intricate mass of jaw bones, teeth, and tusk sockets. Its position is in no way indicated externally.

Luckily there are "leading marks": the eyes and the ear holes. The former are unmistakable but the latter are minute, situated on an edge and very liable to be overlooked for the much larger and shadow-black fold immediately behind it. But, just as in man, there is a little lump or rudimentary flap guarding the orifice itself, and it is this that indicates the spot. With these "leading marks" in mind, perhaps the accompanying sketches may help the inexperienced shot to bring off a satisfying kill.

It cannot be too deeply impressed on the mind of the hunter always to look beyond the surface presented toward him. Try to imagine the position of the far ear hole when calculating where to enter the bullet in the case of a shot at a more or less right angle. Try to imagine the position of the far eye when a shot from behind the "beam" is attempted.

It will be seen that for every shot where the head is approximately at a right angle to the beholder, a line drawn toward the far ear hole will intersect the brain. That is the line the bullet should take. It is rare that the far-off ear will not be seen over the top of the head and the position of the ear hole indicated by the "hinge" of any movement made by it. Always try to imagine the exact position of the far-off ear hole and shoot for it, using the visible eye and ear hole of the side presented to you as guides to level only. Slightly above a line intersecting the eye and ear hole would indicate nearly enough the level of the brain at thirty to forty yards on flat ground.

A successful shot from the front is another affair altogether. Now we have only the eyes as marks. Generally speaking, a bullet placed three or four inches above the line of the eyes will penetrate the brain. Of course if his head is up higher than it usually is held, the aim must be lower, and *vice versa.* If it is lower or you are standing higher, the aim must be higher. But even when standing face to face with an elephant, the position of the ears will help greatly to keep the level correct. It is useless to be below the line of the eyes, for then the bullet

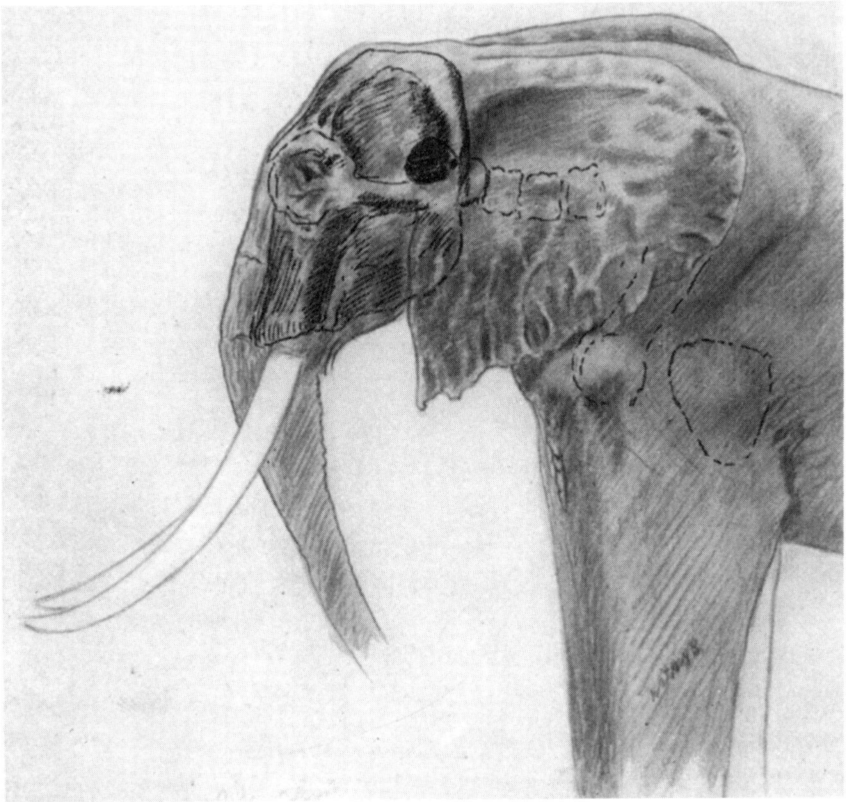

Elephant—body shot.

encounters the dense mass holding the tusks and will be straightaway held up however "modern" it may be.

It is a thrilling moment, not unmixed with relief, when that awesome, brooding mass kneels suddenly to the shot, for I do not believe that any man can stare into the eyes of a twelve-foot African elephant in his native wilds at a few paces range with any great detachment.

The heart shot is easier than the brain shot, but even here it is essential to be careful. Anywhere "behind the shoulder" will not do in the case of an elephant. The heart and lungs and the great arteries altogether form a large target, but the waste areas where a bullet will do no good are vast also. Just as with the brain shot, it is most essential to grasp the angle at which the animal presents itself to the beholder. The reason for this is that an elephant's organs lie far from the surface,

Frontal brain shot on an elephant.

and so a shot intended for the lungs may easily penetrate one only if the angle has not been properly taken into account. In that case, away goes the elephant for miles and miles with the hunter toiling and cursing behind him. In spite of bright red lung blood showing everywhere, he may go twenty or thirty miles.

When not obstructed by high grass, a glance at the far-off leg will surely indicate the angle at which he stands. If it is upright, his weight will be on it and it will give a wonderful lead. Very often it will not be visible at all, and if only his back is showing above the grass or bush, great care is necessary to avoid shooting too high. There is a large area of waste up about the shoulder blade where a bullet will only be effective should it sever the spinal column or fracture the shoulder. It is rare that it does either. In the case of grass-screened elephant, I always used to take the brain shot.

To kill an elephant with the body shot, it is not at all necessary to hit the heart itself. In fact, far more elephants are killed with the shot above the heart. Lying rather low down in a bony cavity, its immediate surroundings offer no prospect of a kill in the case of a miscalculated shot, whereas a little higher up it is almost certain that an artery will be cut or the lungs penetrated if the shot is a little behind. If low, the heart itself will be got. If too far forward, the leg bone may be broken or so weakened that it breaks when his weight is brought on to it. Should this occur, he is practically anchored. An elephant can just move along by under-propping himself with his tusks in place of the useless leg, but only just.

When his head is up, as when tree-browsing, he may be killed by a bullet carefully entered where the throat emerges from the body. A shot on either side will encounter enormously resistant bone and be held up or deflected. A body shot from behind should not be attempted. To do any good, the bullet would have to penetrate several yards of intestine and the grass-filled stomach. An upward shot from close range may damage the spinal column it is true, but the chances are that the only result will be instant flight either to, or away from the hunter.

When a stern chase has become unendurably long, as they often are, the only counsel I can give, and it is very often that of despair, is to wait for a glancing shot at the brain from behind and through the neck. If you happen to have a keen and fast native runner with you and if you can induce him to do so, he may, by making an arduous detour, at great speed, get in front of your quarry and turn him for an instant with a shout. You, of course, must be awaiting the fleeting chance from a close-up position.

I had a native, Pyjalé by name, who was a perfect marvel at this game. Needless to say he was a wonderful runner, had enormous endurance, and was full of courage. With heavy buffalo sandals to protect his feet from the terrible thorns, he would dart away at the speed of 10 seconds to the 100 yards. He would run at a right angle to our course, through the most appalling thorn scrub, and holding nothing but a pair of spears. Presently the elephant I was following would check, throw up his head and trunk, facing right or left as the case may be, and I would get a chance at his brain. Sometimes the elephant or elephants would charge straight at Pyjalé. He would then discharge one of his spears and dodge leisurely about, driving the game quite distracted with rage and fear. Together we have taken as many as seven fleeing elephants in this way, and no one would have given a shilling for our chance when the chase began.

THROUGH THE SUDD OF THE GELO RIVER

The hunting of elephants in this swamp region was of the severest description. That is the reason for their congregating there in such numbers, I think. The ground was too rotten for ponies or mules, even should they survive the myriad flies and mosquitoes. The grass was mostly the twelve-foot stuff, and with razor-like edges and countless, almost invisible spines, this grass sticks into any exposed limb. Locomotion was only possible for humans when following elephant tracks.

When within even a few paces of the animals, it was generally impossible to see them. I used to mount on a boy's shoulders and fire from there, but the stance was so wobbly and the view so obstructed by grass tops as to make it most unsatisfactory. So I next tried mounting a tiny board on a stout tripod originally intended for a large telescope. I found this new perch most satisfactory, although the jump from the rifle, slight as it was, knocked me off once or twice.

On this safari, the health of everyone was excellent, considering the hard work and poor food. We whites were troubled somewhat with indigestion that was caused, I think, by eating native-grain flour that had got wet and then fermented a bit. There was practically no fever, and my tough old Swahilis came through without turning a hair. The Arabs, however, lost condition.